SANCTUM SANCTORUM;

OR,

PROOF-SHEETS FROM AN EDITOR'S TABLE.

BY

THEODORE TILTON,

EDITOR OF THE INDEPENDENT.

"NOT THAT, IN MY ANXIOUS DETAIL OF THE MANY COMMODITIES INCIDENTAL TO THE LIFE OF A PUBLIC OFFICE, I WOULD BE THOUGHT BLIND TO CERTAIN FLAWS WHICH A CUNNING CARPER MIGHT BE ABLE TO PICK IN THIS JOSEPH'S VEST."—CHARLES LAMB.

NEW YORK:
SHELDON & COMPANY.
1870.

CONTENTS.

PREFACE.

In gathering these papers from *The Independent*, I first tried to link a chain of editorial opinions on the chief public questions of the last seven years. But an editorial article is like a June lily; it blooms for a day, then fades. I found that almost every essay had been so moulded to the vanishing image of the flying hour—so tempered to the changeful pulse of the popular heart—as to need in re-publication a troublesome fringe of explanatory notes. So the whole quiver of arrows had to be condemned, seeing how time had rusted their chief points.

Instead of a chronological commentary on slavery, civil war, emancipation, and suffrage, the present series is a mosaic of biography, art, politics, and criticism. Nevertheless, as I should be ashamed of my pen if in its lighter tasks it could forget its serious aims, these pages bear an incidental testimony against enslaving negroes, against hanging criminals, against murdering Indians, against oppressing Chinamen, and against disfranchising women.

The articles were written with no ambition for their permanent sepulture in this ostentatious tomb. Some of them I had entirely forgotten, until, in searching the file, I came upon them unexpectedly. Others I might never have read a second time, had I not been asked to revise them for this volume. Only one among them holds a high place in my affection: I mean the opening sketch, which, slight as it is, and altogether a trifle, nevertheless had the happy fortune of first making me known as a writer. I vividly remember how I kissed the page on which I first saw it in print. Neither the Merchant of Venice, nor the Mask of Comus, nor the Vicar of Wakefield ever pleased me half so much as my first perusal of the published narrative of "A Visit to Washington Irving." I was the last stranger who saw him alive. Kind old man! He took my hand in his, as if he had been my grandfather, and said at parting, "I hope you will win a name among your countrymen." The ink was hardly dry on the printed sheet when all the city's flags sank to half-mast at his sudden death. Instantly the sketch caught a dignity not its own—stole, I may say, a plume from his hearse. It was simultaneously copied into not less than five hundred journals, as if it had been a president's message—only (I trust) not quite so bad. Thus it unexpectedly fulfilled the good wishes of its subject by lifting the unknown name of its writer out of the shadow into the sun. My critics are welcome to ply a birch switch on all the rest of my bantlings, but I pray them to be gentle to my first-born. In my own eyes, the opening leaves of this book wear even yet their spring-time glory; and for the sake of these unfaded few, I can bear to be told that the others are already summer-wilted, or even winter-killed.

I will add that this medley of miscellanies would stand inscribed to my friend Frederick Douglass, except that his worth merits a worthier book.

A VISIT TO WASHINGTON IRVING.

I HAD half an hour one day last week at Sunnyside—the home of Washington Irving. Such a visit ought to have been one of the pleasantest in one's life; and so it was. The pleasure began before taking the old man's hand—in the thousand associations of the place. A ramble at Sunnyside is equal to a pilgrimage to Abbottsford.

The quaint, grotesque dwelling, with its old-fashioned gables, stood as solemn and sleepy among the trees as if it had been built to personate Rip Van Winkle at his nap.

The morning had been rainy, and the afternoon brought only a few momentary openings of clear sky; so I saw Sunnyside without the sun. But under the heavy clouds lay a stately landscape of sombre autumnal hills, of sere and yellow woods, and of Hendrik Hudson's historic river loitering forever at the ancient Palisades.

The mansion of Sunnyside has been standing for twenty-three years. When first its sharp-angled roof wedged its way up among the branches of the primeval forest, the region was almost a solitude; our busy author secluded himself from everybody but one near neighbor. He has since gathered around him a community of New York merchants, whose country seats, opening into each other by intertwining roads, form what looks like one vast estate, which is fitly called by the honorary name of Irvington. But even within the growing circle of his many neighbors, the genial old Knickerbocker lives in true retirement, and takes his afternoon nap within echo-distance of Sleepy Hollow. He withdrew a year ago from all literary labor, and is spending the close of his life in well-earned and long-needed repose—without thought, and almost without knowledge, how the great world

"Is praising him far off,"

Mr. Irving is not so old-looking as one would expect who knew his age. I fancied him in the winter of life; I found him in its Indian summer. He came down stairs and walked through the hall into the back parlor with a firm and lively step, that seemed to bid a cheerful defiance to his seventy-seventh year. He was suffering from asthma, and was muffled against the damp air with a Scotch shawl, wrapped like a loose scarf around his neck; but as he took his seat in an antique arm-chair, and, despite his hoarseness and troubled chest, began an unexpectedly vivacious conversation, he made me half forget that I was the guest of a patriarch long past his "three-score years and ten."

But what should one talk about who had only half an hour with Washington Irving?

I ventured the question,

"Now that you have laid aside your pen, which of your books do you look back upon with most pleasure?"

He immediately replied, "I scarcely look with full satisfaction upon any; for they do not seem what they might have been; I often wish that I could live twenty years more, to take them down from the shelf, one by one, and write them over."

He spoke of his daily habits of writing, before he had made the resolution to write no more. His usual hours for literary work were from morning till noon. But though he generally found his mind most vigorous in the early part of the day, he had always been subject to moods and caprices, and could never tell, when he took up the pen, how many hours would pass before he would lay it down.

"But," said he, "these capricious periods of the heat and glow of composition have been the happiest hours of my life. I have never found, in anything outside of the four walls of my study, any enjoyment equal to sitting at my writing-desk, with a clean page, a new theme, and a mind awake."

His literary employments, he confessed, had always been more like entertainments than tasks.

"Some writers," said he, "appear to have been independent of moods. Sir Walter Scott, for instance, had great power of writing, and could work almost at any time; so could Crabbe; but with this difference—Scott always, and Crabbe seldom, wrote well. I remember," said he, "taking breakfast one morning with Rogers, Moore, and Crabbe; the conversation turned on Lord Byron's poetic moods; Crabbe insisted that, however it might be with Lord Byron, as for himself he could write as well at one time as at another. But," said Irving, with a twinkle of humor at recalling the incident, "Crabbe has written a great deal that no mortal man can read."

He mentioned that while living in Paris, he went a long period without being able to write. "I sat down repeatedly," said he, "with pen and ink, but could invent nothing worth putting on paper. At length I told my friend Tom Moore, who dropped in one morning, that now, after long waiting, I had the mood, and would hold it, and work it out as long as it would last, until I had wrung my brain dry. So I began to write shortly after breakfast, and continued without noticing how the time was passing, until Moore came in again at four in the afternoon—when I had completely covered the table with freshly-written sheets. I kept the mood almost without interruption for six weeks."

I asked which of his books was the result of this frenzy? and he replied, "Bracebridge Hall."

"None of your works," I remarked, "are more charming than the 'Biography of Goldsmith.'"

"And that was written," said he, "even more rapidly than the other."

He then added:

"When I have been engaged on a continuous work, I have often been obliged to rise in the middle of the night, light my lamp, and write an hour or two, to relieve my mind; and now that I write no more, I am sometimes compelled to get up in the same way to read."

Sometimes also, as the last Idlewild letter mentions, he gets up to shave.

"When I was in Spain," he remarked, "searching the old chronicles, and engaged on the 'Life of Columbus,' I often wrote fourteen or fifteen hours out of the twenty-four."

He declared that whenever he had forced his mind unwillingly to work, the product was worthless; he invariably threw it away, and began again; "for," as he observed, "an essay or chapter that has been only *hammered out*, is seldom good for anything; an author's right time to work is when his mind is aglow; when his imagination is kindled;—these are his precious moments; let him wait until they come; but when they come, let him make the most of them."

I referred to his last and chief work, the "Life of Washington," and asked if he felt, on finishing it, any such sensation as Gibbon enjoyed over the last sheet of the "Decline and Fall." He said the work had engrossed his mind to such a degree that, before he was aware, he had written himself into feeble health; that in the midst of his labor he feared he would break down before the end; that when at last the final pages were written, he gave the manuscript to his nephew to conduct it through the press, and threw himself back on his red-cushioned lounge with an indescribable feeling of relief. He explained that the chief fatigue of mind had resulted from the care required in the construction and arrangement of materials, and not in the literary composition of the successive chapters.

But what pains-taking volumes! What a success foı an old man to have achieved! What a fitting close to the labors of a long life! They unite on one page, and will perpetuate in one memory, not only a great name, but its great namesake—the Father of the American Republic, and the Father of the American Republic of Letters.

On the parlor wall hung the engraving of Faed's picture of "Scott and his Contemporaries;" and I alluded to it as presenting a group of his former friends.

"Yes," said he, "I knew every man of them but three; and now they are all gone!"

"Are the portraits good?"

"Scott's head," he replied, "is well drawn, though the expression lacks something of Scott's force; Campbell's is tolerable; Lockhart's is the worst. Lockhart," said he, "was a man of very delicate organization, but he had a more manly look than in the picture."

"You should write one more book," I hinted.

"What is that?"

"Your reminiscences of those literary friends."

"Ah," he exclaimed, "it is too late now! I shall never take the pen again. I have so entirely given up writing that even my best friends' letters lie unanswered. I must have rest. No more books now!"

He referred to a visit, a week before, by Mr. Willis, whose letter he had just been reading in *The Home Journal*.

"I am most glad," said he, "that Mr. Willis remembered my nieces; they are my housekeepers and nurses; they take such good care of me that really I am the most fortunate bachelor in the world. Yes," he repeated, with a merry emphasis, "the most fortunate old bachelor in all the world!"

It was delightful to witness the animation of his manner as he continued to relate how these ladies supplied all his wants—gave him his medicines at the right time without troubling him to look at the clock for himself—called him down to breakfast—cloaked him for his morning rides—brought him his hat for his fine-weather walks—and in every possible way humored him in every possible whim.

"I call them sometimes my nieces," he said, "but oftener my daughters."

As I rose to go he brought from a corner of the room a photograph of a little girl, exhibiting it with great enthusiasm. It was a gift from the child herself; she had made him a visit every day during his sickness. The picture was accompanied with a note printed in large letters with a lead-pencil, by the petite correspondent who said she was too young to write. He spoke with great vivacity of his juvenile visitor. "Children," said the childless man, "are great pets; I am very fond of the wee creatures."

The author's study, into which I peeped before leaving, is a small room, almost entirely filled by the great writing-table and the lounge behind it. The walls are laden with books and pictures, which evidently are re-arranged every day by some delicate hand, for none of the books were tumbled into a corner, and none of the papers were lying loose upon the table. The pen was laid precisely parallel to the edge of the inkstand—a nicety which only a womanly housekeeper would persevere to maintain. Besides, there was not a speck of dust on carpet or cushion.

I stood reverently in the little room—as if it were a sacred place. Its associations were as sweet as a garden of flowers. On leaving, I carried the picture of the spot vividly in my mind, and still carry it—the quiet, sequestered, bewitching haunt in which a great author wrote his greatest works.

As I came away, the old gentleman bundled his shawl about him and stood a few moments on the steps. A momentary burst of sunshine fell on him through the breaking clouds. In that golden light he looked still less like an old man than in the dark parlor by the shaded window. His form was slightly bent, but the quiet humor of the early portraits still lingered in his face. He was the same genial, generous, merry-eyed man at seventy-seven, as Jarvis had painted him nearly fifty years before. I wish always to remember him as I saw him at that last moment.

November 24, 1859.

A WORD FOR THE GOVERNOR'S EARS.

WILL His Excellency, Governor Morgan, of the State of New York, have the goodness to listen while we drop a word into his ears? There is a story which needs telling, and which we hope, when told, will make them tingle.

The Police Gazette—a journal never charged with too much humanity toward criminals—contained recently an article understood to have been written by Mr. Matsell (Chief of Police for many years in New York), in which he describes the punishments inflicted on convicts at Sing Sing in terms fitted to make the reader shudder. The key-note of the testimony of this old policeman is in these startling words:

"*The tortures of Sing Sing exceed by far the punishments of the prisons of Naples, or of any other country in the world.*"

He then gives a long and painful description of these cruelties, from which only a few passages will be quoted here:

"We were present," he says, "while the shower-bath was inflicted on four of the prisoners. The first who was stripped and fastened in the box was a pale, consumptive-looking creature. After being fixed on the stool, the water was allowed to drop on his naked person for a few minutes, which chilled him all over, and the knees shook and trembled, the teeth chattered together, and the eyeballs protruded from their sockets with a painful, despairing glare. Down came the water in volumes upon the head, over the face and the body, filling the box till it reached the nostrils, and in vain was the head shaken from side to side to get air without water; for no sooner was the mouth opened than the throat filled, and only when the victim was evidently suffocating, the bath was stopped. Three or four minutes were given him to spit up the water imbibed, and recover, when down came the shower again, and the same scene was re-enacted for a quarter of an hour, which to him must have been an eternity, in which he bore the sufferings of a hundred strangulations. The others were similarly punished, and when lifted out of the bath were partly insensible, unable to stand, and as soon as full recollection returned burst into a flood of tears.

"And what were they punished for? Aye, that is the question; and it was hard work to find it out; everybody's tongue was tied. The answer was, 'insolence.' Further than that none would speak. But the men under the shower-bath let the secret out; they were sick; they were poor; which is an offence all the world over. They applied to the physician for relief for a pain in the chest; they were denied a ticket of sickness; they could not complete their work; and dying men were punished with the shower because they could not accomplish impossibilities."

The writer continues:

"Then came Tom Kelly. His was no ordinary case. Half a dozen keepers surrounded his cell when he came out of it, and followed him to the shower-bath. Half a dozen men, armed to the teeth, conducted him to the scene of his sufferings, where were waiting half a dozen more to conquer him should he make the slightest demonstration of resistance.

"Kelly came into the room pale and livid. The lips were compressed, the eyes sunken and half closed, and the cheek-bones projected more prominently than in ordinary cases, from the compression of his jaws.

"'Take off your clothes, sir?' said the keeper.

"The mandate was obeyed without a reply, and the victim stripped himself naked and entered the bath. A convict, who stood by, fixed Tom's feet in the stocks, his hands in the armlets, and his head under the bath. As soon as he was placed under it, while no one was looking, he shook his head, as much as to say, 'I've got to suffer.' The water was allowed to trickle down his face and warm body for a few minutes before the bath fell on his head. At length it fell. Tom bore it well—not a shiver of the legs, not a muscular movement of the hands or fingers, not a single cry of distress, although he was actually being drowned for about five minutes.

"'You bear it well, Tom,' said one of the keepers, after the first five minutes had elapsed, and time had been given him to recuperate.

"'It's awful,' was Tom's reply; 'but I can't ask for mercy.'

"Down came the water again, and for five minutes longer the gurgling sounds of a strangulated man were audible; and when he was exhausted, the cord was let up, and the water stopped. A few minutes of release were granted, and down came the water again; and the scene was more terrible than the worst execution we had ever witnessed. At length, congestion of the brain was threatened, * * * and a 'hiss' from the physician brought the third scene to a close. Several minutes were allowed the unfortunate man to recover; but the punishment was too terrible to witness to the end, and we left.

He had been fifteen minutes under the shower, but had twenty-five minutes more of the same suffering to endure when we left; and for the next forty days the same sort of punishment will be meted out to him, unless he dies under the hands of the keeper.

"It was an awful spectacle to witness this man under the bath. Every muscle contracted, and became corded; sometimes the hands would become convulsed, and every nerve strained; when there would follow a relaxation. Then the water would cease to pour, and then would appear the sufferings of the culprit; the retching, the vomiting, and * * * Hanging is nothing to the torture of the shower-bath. The man subjected to the bath for half an hour suffers ten times the amount of pain caused by strangulation, for the simple reason that just as consciousness is about leaving, and when he would be happy to die, he is brought back to a full realization of his sufferings."

We will quote no further.

Now, we respectfully remind the Governor of New York that the Spanish Inquisition is commonly supposed to have passed away, and that the cruelties of the rack, the pincers, the thumb-screw, and the vice, are commonly supposed to have passed away with it. To what Christian purpose is the horrible system revived in this State Prison, and intensified by new tortures unknown of old?

This same punishment, inflicted on a negro in the Auburn Prison, *put him to death.* The fall of water on the bare skull—as is well known not only to those who suffer it, but to those who inflict it—stuns the brain, quenches the nervous energy, destroys the power of the will over the muscles, produces emasculation, fever, and an inevitable tendency to wildness of mind, resulting often in partial and sometimes complete insanity. It is a greater barbarity than the scalping-knife among Indians. It reduces a man to within one gasp of death, and only brings him back to life after he has wished and tried to die. The Juggernaut itself is more humane, because, though designed to torture, it does not refuse to slay. The cat-o'-nine was long since abolished from our Navy (and from some of our State Prisons), in obedience to a public sentiment which decried it as brutal. But here, substituted in its place, hid in a small dark closet, is an instrument which, at the pull of a string, will more nearly kill a man in three minutes than to flog him at a whipping-post for an hour. Forty days under this stunning rain—in which every drop falls like a millstone—in which the flood of water, rising above the lips and nostrils, strangulates the victim with continuous drownings from which he is only rescued to be drowned again—in which the passing minutes seem lengthened into a lifetime—in which the mortal agony of the sufferer is beyond the power of words to describe:—if any device of cruelty were ever needed for racking and ruining the body and mind of a strong man without shedding his blood, what more could be asked for than this?

We know of a stout, muscular, hardy man—a State prisoner—confined, we will not say in what prison—who went into the shower-bath carrying with him in his great frame the strength of a giant, yet who, after his prostration by the shower, was carried exhausted to his bed, where paralysis crept into his limbs, and he has never walked a step since!

Peter Titelmann, the Inquisitor of the Netherlands—whose name hushed children at their play—whose cruelty has gone unchronicled for lack of a fit word to paint it—

whose bones have been rotting for three Christian centuries since William the Silent—has suddenly been raised from the dead, and now, armed with a new scourge hitherto unknown, has become again, worse than before, the arch-tormentor of human bodies and souls.

In the case of Tom Kelly, what was the provocation to the punishers, and what their justification for the punishment? Was not Tom Kelly a bad man? Yes! But men, however bad, are not to be treated worse than brutes. Did he not merit unusual chastisement? Grant that he did. His offence was grave; he was the leader of a revolt; he broke away from the prison with a small company of followers, boarded a sloop, fought fearfully with the captain and a keeper, and wounded them both with a knife-blade before the revolt could be quelled. He committed no ordinary offence, and merited no ordinary punishment. But was there any warrant for a vengeance unnamed even in Torquemada's list of cruelties to heretics? Were there none of Philip II.'s penalties that could have been substituted for a water-shower, which is worse than them all? Nay, in the name of mercy, were there no commoner but sufficient instruments for vexing human flesh, known and used from time immemorial in the prison at Sing Sing, and tested many a time and full well by many a poor fellow's tears and groans?

We do not enter here a single step into the wide question as to what principles should underlie a true system of prison government; whether humiliating and degrading punishments should be admitted or excluded; whether confinement and privation should be the limit of discipline, or whether there should be inflictions of bodily pain. We may leave out of sight entirely the claims of a milder method, and still say that the advocates of a severe administration—even such as vindicate sharp tortures of flesh and nerve, and who exclaim: "The rascals deserve the Russian knout;"—even these sternest of disciplinarians may banish the water-shower, and have still remaining all the needed apparatus for a moderate Inquisition, sufficient for the dungeons of Naples, and sufficient for the prison at Sing Sing.

Look, good reader! What instruments had the keepers which, instead of this drowning bath, they might have used on Tom Kelly? There was the chain-and-ball —a harness for the ankles, easily set tight enough to excite shooting pains of inflammation. There was the crucifix, ready to stretch out a man's arms and hold them apart till he must faint from exhaustion. There was the iron crown—heavier than Charlemagne's—loading the neck and head with fifteen pounds of solid weight in iron, to be worn day and night, at the work-bench and on the pillow. There was the rope and pulley, for tying a man under the arms and hoisting him into the air, where he hangs until conquered. There was the dark cell, from which every ray of light is excluded, that the victim may crouch in a corner and surrender himself to despair. There was the device of bucking, which consists in binding a man's ankles and knees, handcuffing his wrists under his knees, and then placing between the wrists and between the knees a pole, each end of which is supported at the height of a barrel from the ground, and on which the man hangs, struggles, and swings, head downward, until the keeper is satisfied. There was also the biting agony of starvation, by which the worst of men may at any time be punished horribly enough, God knows! through the pangs of hunger and thirst.

All these whips and stings were ready at hand, to execute any moderate or immoderate vengeance on Tom Kelly. Why did the keepers forget all these, and remember only that they had a scourge more barbarous still?

It is high time that people outside of prison walls should know something of what exists inside. Tom Kelly's case ought to thrill the public, not merely for Tom Kelly's sake, but for humanity's. Criminals are human creatures notwithstanding their crimes. God's image may be stamped very obscurely on a bad man's heart, but it is still there. In the darkest nature, buried under the guiltiest passion, under the deadliest malice, under the rottenest vice, there still remains some part of the man's immortal manhood—some vestige of a better self—which may be hidden but cannot be annihilated, which may never be seen of men but is never forgotten of God. And because every man's nature contains some element of God's, it is sacrilege to treat the worst of men as worse than men. A prisoner, however bad, cannot be worse than the worst; and many a poor fellow who wears the striped jacket is guiltless of the crime for which he wears it.

> "If he is guilty, you must mend him,
> If he is innocent, defend him."
>
> —*Dean Swift.*

The State has a right to mete out to offenders a just penalty, but has no right to inflict a cruel torture. Barbarity to men, to beasts, or to insects, is despicable. If you slay an ox for food, he has a right to his death by a single blow; and should you prolong his miseries, the law would interfere. If you lift your hand against the fly that stings your cheek, you are to kill the little assassin at a single stroke; and should you pluck off its wings and let it go alive, you are to be pointed at for cruelty, and nicknamed a Nero. A majority of men assent to hanging criminals for capital crimes; executing quick punishment with a sheriff's rope; but the moral sentiment of all mankind revolts at the process of killing men by inches.

If Tom Kelly, before his imprisonment, had not only stabbed but killed the captain of a sloop—and not in an unexpected fray, but in cold blood—he might have been arrested, tried, found guilty, and sentenced to be hung; but no jury or judge would have dared to go so far as to decree that a prolonged, unparalleled, and inhuman torture should be inflicted either on Tom Kelly or on any other criminal under the sun. An assassin, a pirate, a highwayman, may be decently executed; that is all. Even the old vengeance on the dead body—drawing and quartering—has been done away. Nay, in this late and Christian century of the world, a criminal may stand on the edge of the scaffold—with the cowl ready to be drawn over his head, and the trap ready to be dropped under his feet—and yet his executioners dare not superadd so small a cruelty as to scratch his flesh with a pin.

The immediate agony and the permanent injury, falling to the lot of Tom Kelly during this Forty Days' Flood, were greater than if he had lost day by day a joint from a finger or toe, or suffered a gradual clipping of half-inch pieces from his lips or ears. Men taken from the closet of this shower are not unfrequently so nearly dead that they need the most violent stimulus—like men rescued from drowning—to restore them to consciousness. Nor is this all. The most disastrous of the effects of this punishment are of such a character that a proper delicacy forbids their mention in print. But leaving the worst untold, what shall be said of tolerating in a public institution a torture which, in less time than it takes to tell the story, chills the naked body into an apparent corpse, beats the brain into senselessness, clenches the muscles into whip-cords, starts the eyes from their sockets, chokes the throat with the strangulations of drowning, and, by successive shock and shudder through the frame, drives the soul well-nigh to its final struggle of parting from the flesh!

We therefore take the liberty of dropping a word into the Governor's ears. That word is this: Let his Excellency remind the Legislature in his next message that as the cat-o'-nine was years ago thought bad enough to be driven by law beyond every prison-wall in the Empire State, so now a nine-fold greater abomination is waiting for a similar banishment by a similar law. In the meantime, before the Legislature shall be able to put a stop to it finally and for ever, let His Excellency seek ten minutes' conversation with the State Prison Inspectors, and then let the next mail bring down from Albany a joint order to the following purport:

"*To the Keeper of Sing Sing Prison: Lock up your little Chamber of Inquisition—throw the key to the bottom of the Hudson River—and let the door be never opened again. By order of the Inspectors.*"

This is an earnest word for the Governor's ears. Is it worth his heeding or forgetting? We know that many words are spoken for the Governor to hear; words which pass in at one ear and pass out at the other; words of complainants stating their grievances; words of criminals petitioning for pardons; words of politicians soliciting appointments; words of lobby-men pushing their schemes; words of enemies coining their slanders; words of friends making their generous acclamations and renominations;

words so various that he can neither hear all, nor answer half. But among so many words, some must be entitled to a hearing. What will he do with the word which we have dropped into his ears to-day?*

* Governor Morgan promptly responded to the appeal; the subject was laid before the Legislature; an investigation was energetically prosecuted; and punishment by the "Water Shower" was interdicted in Sing Sing Prison for several years; but (to the shame of civilization) it has been recently revived in that ever-heathenish institution.

SEPTEMBER 27, 1860.

ELIZABETH BARRETT BROWNING.

"Died in Florence, Italy, on Saturday morning, June 29, 1861, half an hour after daybreak, Elizabeth Barrett Browning, aged fifty-two years, wife of Robert Browning."—*European Dispatches.*

LIFE of suffering thus ended in peace. A frail body, bearing the burden of too great a brain, broke at last under the weight. After six days' illness, the shadows of the night fell on her eyes for the last time, and half an hour after daybreak she beheld the Eternal vision. Like the Pilgrim in the dream, she saw the Heavenly glory before passing through the gate. "It is beautiful," she exclaimed, and died:—sealing these last words on her lips as the fittest inscription that can be written on her life, her genius, and her memory. In the English burial-ground at Florence lie her ashes. What she wrote of Cowper's grave now stands written of her own:

> "It is a place where poets crowned may feel the heart's decaying;
> It is a place where happy saints may weep amid their praying;
> Yet let the grief and humbleness, as low as silence, languish;
> Earth surely now may give her calm to whom she gave her anguish."

On both sides of the ocean, this death was nowhere lightly written, nor lightly read. Famous names every year are added to the dead, and without tears. But Mrs. Browning's death was mourned in every household where her books had entered. When her friend Cavour dropped down in the midst of his work, and good men stood with serious face asking, Who but he could finish it? there was regret; but at this other loss there was more; there was grief. In many households there was weeping; this too by strangers who never saw her face; and this too although she herself had forbidden it.

> "And friends, dear friends,—when it shall be
> That this low breath is gone from me,
> And round my bier ye come to weep,
> Let one, most loving of you all,
> Say, *Not a tear must o'er her fall*—
> He giveth His beloved sleep."

What shall we now say of her? Death looses all tongues to speak the praise of the dead. Let us say, then: not a finer genius ever came into the world, or went out of it; not a nobler heart ever beat in a human bosom; not a more Christian life was ever lived; not a more beautiful memory ever followed the name of man or woman after death.

Is this overpraise? Not for one whose life and genius were each above praise. Of course not every one will award such meed; and many, hearing it awarded, will ask, "For what?" But there was a circle of loving yet unknown friends of Mrs. Browning, who, when first they heard of her death, were startled at a sudden sundering of something that had bound their hearts closer to hers than the mere ordinary tie between author and reader, even of such authors as have loving readers. So the shadow that fell at Florence crept hitherward across many a threshold.

It is easy to account for this unusual sense of loss. Persons who had read Mrs. Browning at all, had read her over and over again. They never closed the books without meaning to open them many times more. Her pages, once truly known, are never afterward slighted. A friend of ours reads "The Eve of St. Agnes" once a year to his family, but on the lips of the same reader

"Bertha in the Lane" counts all the months between. Of reading "Aurora Leigh" when can there be an end? One need never be athirst for a book while that is at hand. So to lose Mrs. Browning—to those who knew their loss—meant something more than to lose any one else.

Beside, in the hearts of a few who knew not only her genius, but something of her personal life—especially the sad story of those sufferings which found their compensation in the ripening of her character into a loveliness as perfect as it seems possible for human nature to attain—there always existed an indescribable reverence for this noble woman, which her death has hallowed into a saintly memory. But that story, inasmuch as her own lips never told it, and her own heart wished it might never be told, shall find no chronicle here. It is enough to say that she bore patiently, sweetly, and with perpetual forgiveness, a grievous and unnatural wrong, which pierced her like a thorn for years. Daughters turning cold-hearted to a kind father have made one tragedy; and the reverse of such a tale might make another equally pathetic. But let it remain unwritten; for the dead have gone to meet the dead; and who knows what reconcilements there may be in the shadowy land?

The record of her outward life is brief. A few dates and common facts comprise it all. Born in London in 1809, she became a writer in 1819, and a publisher in 1826. Her first volume, an "Essay on Mind"—written in the verse of Pope's "Essay on Man"—was afterward withdrawn from print, and cannot now be found in any bookseller's garret. She decreed a like fate to her next book, published in 1833, "Prometheus Bound," translated from Æschylus—excluding it from a subsequent volume of collected works, and giving this reason in the preface:

"One early failure," she says, "a translation of the Prometheus of Æschylus, which, though happily free of the current of publication, may be remembered against me by a few of my personal friends, I have replaced by an entirely new version, made for them and my conscience, in expiation of a sin of my youth, with the sincerest application of my mature mind."

So her first ventures in authorship were triumphant failures.

We will leave the reader to guess how much of personal autobiography is written in the ensuing lines:

"I apprehended this,—
In England, no one lives by verse that lives;
And, apprehending, I resolved by prose
To make a space to sphere my living verse.
I wrote for cyclopedias, magazines,
And weekly papers, holding up my name
To keep it from the mud. I learnt the use
Of the editorial 'we' in a review,
As courtly ladies the fine trick of trains,
And swept it grandly through the open doors,
As if one could not pass through doors at all
Save so encumbered. I wrote tales beside,
Carved many an article on cherry stones
To suit light readers,—something in the lines
Revealing, it was said, the mallet-hand,
But that, I'll never vouch for."

Three years after her atoning preface of Prometheus, she began an acquaintance with Mary Russell Mitford, who has left a very pleasing sketch of her friend; yet the sketch must have been written half at random, for it is full of misconceptions and misstatements; but it painted this life-like picture of the poet at twenty-seven:

"A slight, delicate figure, with a shower of dark curls falling on either side of a most expressive face—large, tender eyes, fringed with dark lashes—and a smile like a sunbeam."

This description of twenty-five years ago is true, every word, of a photograph now lying on our table, copied from Macaire's original, made at Havre in 1856, and which Robert Browning esteems a faithful likeness of his wife. The three-quarter length shows (what photographs sometimes fail to show) the comparative stature of the figure —which here is so delicate and diminutive that we can easily imagine how the story came to be told (although not true) that her husband drew this same portrait in "The Flight of the Duchess" when he sketched

—"the smallest lady alive."

The one striking feature of the picture is the intellectual and spiritual expression of the face and head; for here, borne up by pillars of curls on either side, is just such an arch as she saw in the "Vision of Poets":

"A forehead royal with the truth."

A photograph, taken in Rome only a month before she died, wears a not greatly changed expression, except in an added pallor to cheeks always pale; foretokening the near coming of the shadow of death.

In 1837 she had the misfortune to burst a blood-vessel in the lungs, and shortly afterward to be brought trembling to the edge of the grave by a shock experienced from the accidental drowning of a brother, upset in a yacht. She was standing on a balcony and saw him sink. The haunting memory of this tragedy kept her in such continual prostration that not until several months afterward were her friends willing to risk removing her, even by short daily journeys, from the sea-side where the disaster happened, to her father's house in London. Here for a few years she was an exile from society, shut in a dim chamber, her chief companions (beyond a few chosen friends) being a Hebrew Bible, a shelf full of large-print Greek books, and no small range of polyglot reading. Here the Attic bee brought its honey to her lips. Here she thought and studied, and ripened her genius until it grew worthy of the fame which was to crown it. Here she gathered from many tongues what she afterward embalmed in one. A patient prisoner behind drawn curtains in Wimpole-street, she was twin sister, in genius and suffering, to Charlotte Brontë in the shadowy room at Haworth. Yet the question which she asked of Mrs. Hemans:

> "Would she have lost the poet's fire, for anguish of the burning?"

she answered of herself; for one of her favorite ideas was Shelley's, that poets

> "learn in suffering
> what they teach in song."

She confessed in her own words:

> "If heads
> That hold a rythmic thought must ache perforce,
> For my part, I choose headaches."

Suddenly, one day, as the product of one day's work, she astonished her friends with the rhapsody of "Lady Geraldine's Courtship"—which straightway led to the rhapsody of her own. This poem had the faultiness which one might expect of a hundred and three stanzas forced by green-house heat into full bloom in twelve hours; this too by a weak invalid lying on a sofa; but must we spoil the pretty story that the sweet ballad had the merit of winning for its writer the hand of Robert Browning? Yet the story is only a fiction of the gossip-mongers. Nor is it true that the poet with whom she was to mate was then known to her only by his little book of "Bells and Pomegranates." She had more than a stranger's reasons for making the wooer of Lady Geraldine speak in this wise:

"There, obedient to her praying, did I read aloud the poems
Made to Tuscan flutes, or instruments more various of our own;
Read the pastoral parts of Spenser—or the subtle interflowings
Found in Petrarch's sonnets—here's the book—the leaf is folded down!—
Or at times a modern volume—Wordsworth's solemn-thoughted idyl,
Howitt's ballad-verse, or Tennyson's enchanted reverie—
Or from Browning some 'Pomegranate,' which, if cut deep down the middle,
Showed a heart within, blood-tinctured, of a veined humanity!"

Mr. Hillard of Boston mentions in the "New American Cyclopedia" a story of this happy allusion, which we will repeat in his own words:

"The story," he says, "has been told to us—we will not vouch for its truth, as 'imaginations as one would' are apt to be interpolated into such incidents—that the grateful poet called to express in person his acknowledgments, and that he was admitted into the invalid's presence by the happy mistake of a new servant. At any rate, he did see her, and had permission to renew his visit. The mutual attachment grew more and more powerful, and the convergence more and more rapid; the acquaintance became the friend, and the friend was transformed into the lover. Kind physicians and tender nurses had long watched over the couch of sickness; but love, the magician, brought restorative influences before unknown; and her health was so far improved that she did not hesitate to accept the hand that was offered to her. She became the wife of Robert Browning in the autumn of 1846."

This incident in the sick-room is charming; fit to happen to two poets. But it must have been taken from a novel; it did not occur in reality. Indeed, nearly all the public stories of their private life have been only guesses or idle pleasantries; for no one who has written on the subject has known anything about it. Nothing authentic has been told. Yet as for the several myths afloat, they are fancies that do no great harm. It may be mentioned that before the marriage, so strong and so lasting was the impression still remaining on her mind concerning her brother's death, that she exacted a promise from Mr. Browning never to refer to the subject. This promise he kept for years.

So much of the courtship as the world has a right to know, she herself has confessed in the "Sonnets from the Portuguese," which she might have named with an English name, Sonnets from her own heart. At the wedding the bride rose from a sick-bed to receive the wedding-ring on her finger. It is said that some of her kinsfolk disapproved the match. This is probably true, for the marriage proved a happy one. But her father never added his blessing.

Part of the wooing is told in these words, and what can be more exquisite?—

"First time he kissed me, he but only kissed
The fingers of this hand wherewith I write,
And, ever since, it grew more clean and white,
Slow to world greetings . . quick with its 'Oh, list,'
When the angels speak. A ring of amethyst
I could not wear here, plainer to my sight
Than that first kiss. The second passed in height
The first, and sought the forehead, and half-missed,
Half falling on the hair. O beyond meed!
That was the chrism of love, which love's own crown,
With sanctifying sweetness, did precede.
The third upon my lips was folded down
In perfect purple state; since when, indeed,
I have been proud and said, My love, my own!
* * * * * *
How do I love thee? Let me count the ways.

I love thee to the depth and breadth and height
My soul can reach, when feeling out of sight
For the ends of Being and ideal Grace.
I love thee to the level of every day's
Most quiet need, by sun and candle light.
I love thee freely, as men strive for right;
I love thee purely, as they turn from praise.
I love thee with the passion put to use
In my old griefs, and with my childhood's faith.
I love thee with a love I seemed to lose
With my lost saints—I love thee with the breath,
Smiles, tears of all my life!—and, if God choose,
I shall but love thee better after death."

After the nuptials he led her immediately to Italy, whither she followed willingly; to the land of song, of art, of romance, and of the dead past. But the dead past was already turning in its grave for resurrection into life and a future. The sympathies of the Brownings for Italy were as deep-hearted as Garibaldi's. Robert Browning was one of the few great Englishmen who, after Milton, loved Italy. His wife, loving him, loved what he loved. That love had a fruition which proved itself not wasted; for the Italy she found, and the Italy she left, were not the same. When that wedding-tour ended at Pisa, she saw a shadow resting on the sunniest land in Europe. Night was on the nation. But the poet was the prophet. In her new home she sat and watched for the day-dawn through "Casa Guidi Windows." It waited long, but dawned at last, and she saw it—then died! Is there not more than a sick-bed meaning in the brief story of the telegraph that she expired "half an hour *after day-break?*" For the dream of her life—a free and united Italy—was finally fulfilled in Napoleon's formal recognition of Italian freedom and unity, in the very week she died. The full day-dawn of Italy was to shine from France; and she saw it and died—just after the day-break.

It is fitting to ask here the question, Had she not some

warrant in being a Napoleonist? Who that had disagreed with her for five years had not a half-wish that she might have lived a year longer, if only to enjoy that triumph? In a letter to the writer of this memorial, she said: "A great nation is called up from the graves." But almost at the next moment, she was called down into hers. Even *The Athenæum* must have felt a generous regret at this. That little volume of Napoleonic poems, shaded by the frowns of many critics, turned out to be more prophetic than men could believe, who then read and shook their heads. She mentioned these doubters in a letter written just after the poems appeared: "My book," said she, "has had a very angry reception in my native country, as you probably observe; but I shall be forgiven one day; and meanwhile, forgiven or unforgiven, it is satisfactory to one's own soul to have spoken the truth as one apprehends the truth." The day of her forgiveness came soon—outstripping the day of her death:—a speedier reward than often falls to prophets who prophesy against the united voices of their own times.

But after all what was her Napoleonism? In a letter alluding to the American feeling against the Emperor, she said: "Mr. F—— hints that your people are not very Napoleonist. Neither am I, in any partisan sense;" and then pointed to her "Summing Up," a poem sent to *The Independent*—in which she thus wrote of the Imperial object of her so-called homage:

"Napoleon—as strong as ten armies,
  Corrupt as seven devils—a fact,
You accede to, then seek where the harm is
  Drained off from the man to his act.
And find . . . *a free nation!* Suppose
  Some hell-brood in Eden's sweet greenery
Convoked for creating . . . . . *a rose!*
—Would it suit the infernal machinery?"

This in prose is:—if the Devil's workman be doing God's work, who ought to hinder? Such was Mrs. Browning's Napoleonism. How far was it from right? If she erred, she erred with a man as wise as Cavour; and if Cavour was not the greatest statesman of his day, who was greater? We have no overstock of praises to waste on the third Napoleon. But fair play gives even the devil his due.

Of Pope Pius IX., she once wrote a good opinion; for that bishop had once the wit and luck to persuade most of the world, the poets with the rest, that he had no wish for Italy save benediction. Whether his heart lost its goodness, or only his face lost its mask, is a question. But the poet blotted out her early praise, as the pontiff blotted out his early pledge.

Some of her English opinions were more high-minded and noble, more generous and Christian, than many of her countrymen wished an Englishwoman to entertain. For instance, she was called visionary and impracticable for such words as these:

"I confess that I dream of the day when an English statesman shall arise with a heart too large for England, having courage, in the face of his countrymen, to assert of some suggested policy—'This is good for your trade; this is necessary for your domination; but it will vex a people hard by; it will hurt a people further off; it will profit nothing to the general humanity; therefore, away with it! It is not for you or me.' When a British minister dares to speak so, and when a British public applauds him speaking, then shall the nation be so glorious that her praise, instead of exploding from within, from loud civic mouths, shall come to her from without, as all worthy praise must, from the alliances she has fostered, and from the populations she has saved."

Mrs. Browning lived in one house in Florence for fourteen years, and went out of it to her grave.

"From Casa Guidi's windows I looked out."

For those who wish to look in at these same windows, we draw the curtain by another's hand. A letter from Florence in *The Atlantic Monthly*, written shortly after her death, said:

"Casa Guidi, which has been immortalized by Mrs. Browning's genius, will be as dear to the Anglo-Saxon traveller as Milton's Florentine residence has been heretofore.

"Those who have known Casa Guidi as it was, can never forget the square ante-room, with its great picture, and piano-forte at which the boy Browning passed many an hour,—the little dining-room, covered with tapestry, and where hung medallions of Tennyson, Carlyle, and Robert Browning,—the long room, filled with plaster casts and studies, which was Mr. Browning's retreat,—and dearest of all, the large drawing-room, where *she* always sat. It opens upon a balcony filled with plants, and looks out upon the old iron-gray church of Santa Felice. There was something about this room that seemed to make it a proper and especial haunt for poets. The dark shadows and subdued light gave it a dreamy look, which was enhanced by the tapestry-covered walls and the old pictures of saints, that looked out sadly from their carved frames of black wood. Large book-cases, constructed of specimens of Florentine carving, selected by Mr. Browning, were brimming over with wise-looking books. Tables were covered with more gayly-bound volumes, the gifts of brother authors. Dante's grave profile, a cast of Keats' face and brow, taken after death, a pen-and-ink sketch of Tennyson, the genial face of John Kenyon (Mrs. Browning's good friend and relative), little paintings of the boy Browning—all attracted the eye in turn, and gave rise to a thousand musings. A quaint mirror, easy chairs and sofas, and a hundred nothings that always add an indescribable charm, were all massed in this room. But the glory of all, and that which sanctified all, was seated in a low arm-chair, near the door. A small table, strewn with writing materials, books, and newspapers, was always by her side."

Thus far the letter; but we have this scene still more vividly drawn in a photograph of the favorite room in which she oftenest sat, taken after she had quitted it for ever. If the reader could look over our shoulder, he would be welcome to see the picture; but there is hardly need to add more by mere words to those already given.

While the quoted letter still lies open we copy a passage on another topic, as having a fit place here:

"Mrs. Browning's conversation was most interesting. It was not characterized by sallies of wit or brilliant repartee, nor was it of that nature which is most welcome in society. It was frequently intermingled with trenchant, quaint remarks, leavened with a quiet, graceful humor of her own; but it was eminently calculated for a *tête-a-tête*. Mrs. Browning never made an insignificant remark. All that she said was always worth hearing; a greater compliment could not be paid her. She was a most conscientious listener, giving you her mind and heart, as well as her magnetic eyes. Though the latter spoke an eager language of their own, she conversed slowly, with a conciseness and point which, added to a matchless earnestness that was the predominant trait of her conversation as it was of her character, made her a most delightful companion. *Persons* were never her theme, unless public characters were under discussion, or friends who were to be praised, which kind office she frequently took upon herself. One never dreamed of frivolities in Mrs. Browning's presence, and gossip felt itself out of place. *Your*self not *her*self, was always a pleasant subject to her, calling out all her best sympathies in joy, and yet more in sorrow. Books and humanity, great deeds, and, above all, politics, which include all the grand questions of the day, were foremost in her thoughts, and therefore oftenest on her lips. I speak not of religion, for with her everything was religion."

Mr. Hillard, who visited the Brownings at Florence in 1847, says in his "Six Months in Italy:"

"A happier home and a more perfect union than theirs it is not easy to imagine; and this completeness arises not only from the rare qualities which each possesses, but from their perfect adaptation to each other. . . As he is full of manly power, so she is a type of the most sensitive and delicate womanhood. . . I have never seen a human frame which seemed so nearly a transparent veil for a celestial and immortal spirit. She is a soul of fire enclosed in a shell of pearl. . . Nor is she more remarkable for genius and learning, than for sweetness of temper, tenderness of heart, depth of feeling, and purity of spirit. It is a privilege to know such beings singly and separately; but to see their powers quickened, and their happiness rounded, by the sacred tie of marriage, is a cause for peculiar and lasting gratitude. A union so complete as theirs—in which the mind has nothing to crave, nor the heart to sigh for—is cordial to behold and soothing to remember."

Robert Browning's address to his wife in "One Word More" has these lines:

* * * * *
"God be thanked, the meanest of his creatures
Boasts two soul-sides, one to face the world with,
One to show a woman when he loves her.
* * * * *
This to you—yourself my moon of poets!
Ah, but that's the world's side—there's the wonder—
Thus they see you, praise you, think they know you.
There, in turn I stand with them and praise you,
Out of my own self I dare to phrase it.
But the best is when I glide from out them,
Cross a step or two of dubious twilight,
Come out on the other side, the novel
Silent silver lights and darks undreamed of,
Where I hush and bless myself with silence."

Mrs. Browning's mind matured early; her pen at once became prolific; her genius grew apace; every succeeding book showed an increase of power; every new performance gave better promise for the next. Turn over her pages, and mark the grand beginning and grander progress to the end.

How wide is her range of subjects! She hardly ever goes back to the same strain twice. Her husband's sweet-singing English thrush, that sang each song twice over,

"Lest you should think he never could recapture
The first fine careless rapture,"

is like many poets who are born, with the birds, to a few strains, and sing them all their lives. Of these were Pope, Young, Montgomery, Scott, and almost Words worth. But Mrs. Browning had an unequalled variety of subjects. She wrote in as many different veins as Coleridge or Hood. Even her husband is less free of range; less given to roaming at wild will. "Prometheus Bound" opens the door of the Greek Mythology. The drama of "The Seraphim" depicts the thoughts of the angels of heaven on witnessing Christ's crucifixion. "The Drama of Exile" follows Milton into the Garden of Eden, and out of it. "A Vision of Poets" calls up the long train of the famous bards of all times and tongues. "The Poet's Vow" is the sad story of Rosalind's heart, wounded by pride and broken by love. "Isobel's Child" reveals the struggles of a mother's soul, wrestling with God for life and blessing for her babe. "The Brown Rosary" is a story of a maiden's temptations, her falsehood to an absent lover, and the strife of an evil spirit to get possession of her soul. "The Rhyme of the Dutchess May" is a romance of chivalry, ending with a thrilling scene of a horse and two riders, bride and bridegroom, leaping from a castle-wall a hundred feet down to death. "Lady Geraldine's Courtship" is a delicious story of a lady who gave a splendid party at her country-seat, and fell in love with a poet among the guests. "The Cry of the Children" is a twin-poem with Hood's "Song of the Shirt." "The Four-fold Aspect" shows four ways of looking at death—carelessly, awfully, mournfully, hopefully. "Earth and her Praisers" sets forth how differently the world appears to a child, to a lover, to a scholar, to a mourner, to a poet, to a Christian. "A Child Asleep" is a poem of a mother's fancyings at the cradle-side. "Crowned and Wedded" is the story of Victoria's wedding day. "Crowned and Buried," its counterpiece, celebrates the death of the first Napoleon. "To Flush, my Dog," is a head-patting tribute which, we fancy, must often be read for sympathy's sake by the author of "Rab and his Friends." "My Doves" is a plaintiff song of her pet-birds taken from the country to the city. "The Lost Bower" is a reminiscence of an invalid who recalls, while shut in a sick chamber, her sunshiny out-of-door wanderings in fields and woods. "Loved Once" celebrates the eternity of love:

> "those *never* loved
> Who dream that they loved *once*."

"The Runaway Slave at Pilgrim's Point" is the unreasonable complaint of a slave-mother who knew so little the duty of a bond-woman as to sigh at the selling of her husband and child out of her sight for ever. The "Sonnets from the Portuguese" are forty-four love-letters, the most exquisite that ever were written. "Casa Guidi Windows" is a poetical essay on Italian politics in the struggle of 1848. "Aurora Leigh" is a modern novel in blank verse, discussing many of the social questions of England, and revealing the writer's maturest experiences of life. "Poems before Congress" (called in this country "Napoleon III. in Italy") gave utterance to her French opinions. The "Last Poems," edited by the writer of this sketch, are in every key from love to grief. Such was the wide range of her verse!

Mrs. Browning had an established reputation in this country before she became widely known in England. Even now she has more readers here than there, just as Longfellow has more readers there than here. But it often happens that poets, like prophets, get their best honors not in their own country.

The qualities of her style are many and various, including great merits and greater faults. She abounds in figures, strong and striking; sometimes strange and startling; sometimes grotesque and weird; often, one may say, unallowable; but always having a piercing point of meaning that gives warrant for their singularity. Swords have not keener edges, nor flash brighter lights, than sudden similes drawn by this poet's hand. She illustrates at will from nature, art, mythology, history, literature, scripture, common life. She plucks metaphors wherever they grow; and to those who have eyes to see, they grow everywhere. Occasionally, taking for granted a too great knowledge on the part of her readers, even of such as are cultured, her figures are covered with the dust of old books, and their meaning veiled in a vexing obscurity. But, on the other hand, her sentences often are clear as ice, and have a lustre of prismatic fires. Innumerable are her happy conceits, successful expressions, exquisite turns of remark, strokes of the brush known as word-paintings, sayings quaint as any in Quarles. Some of these, of different sorts, we gather here for show—plucked from her pages without search, and almost at random.

What daintier words could be dropped on a lady's head than these?—

"No one parts
Her hair with such a silver line as you;
One moonbeam from the forehead to the crown."

Here is a more muscular stroke:

"'Tis true that when the dust of death has choked
A great man's voice, the common words he said
Turn oracles,—*the common thoughts he yoked
Like horses, draw like griffins*,—this is true."

The opening stanza of "The Lady's Yes" has the fittest possible figure for the thought:

"'Yes,' I answered you last night;
'No,' this morning, sir, I say;
*Colors seen by candle-light
Will not look the same by day.*"

Aurora, doubting whether from her early rhyming she is to grow into a poet, says:

"Alas! . . . near all the birds
Will sing at dawn—and yet we do not take
The chaffering swallow for the holy lark."

After speaking of the Alps, she turns to the English rolling country thus :

"View the ground's most gentle dimplement,
As if God's finger touched, but did not press,
In making England."

In the picture of Isobel with her child in her lap, both asleep, the mother is drawn as in motionless repose,—

"Only she wore
The deepening smile I named before ;
And *that* a deepening love expressed :
And who at once can love and rest?"

Mary looking on the Child Jesus exclaims:

"Art thou a king, then? Come, his universe,
Come, crown me Him a King!
Pluck rays from all such stars as never fling
Their light where fell a curse,
And make a crowning for this Kingly brow!"

Lady Waldemar's parting is a favorite passage with Henry Ward Beecher, himself a prose poet :

"Whereat she touched my hand, and bent her head,
And floated from me like a silent cloud
That leaves a sense of thunder."

In the "Vision of Poets," are these grand lines of an angel :

"His eyes were dreadful, for you saw
That *they* saw God."

Here is a touch to the quick :

"Full desertness
In souls, as countries, lieth silent bare
Under the blanching, vertical eye-glare
Of the absolute heavens."

Of Savonarola she says:

"Who, having tried the tank
Of old church waters used for baptistry
Ere Luther came to spill them, swore they stank!"

Now and then she misses a point of history, as for instance :

"Calvin, for the rest,
Made bold to burn Servetus:"

though certainly Calvin did not burn Servetus.

Buckle has thrown out the idea that southern countries, having earthquakes to arouse the imagination, are the natural homes of painters and poets, but Mrs. Browning thought differently:

"Mountains of the south
When, drunk and mad with elemental wines,
They rend the seamless mist, and stand up bare,
Make fewer singers, haply. No one sings
Descending Sinai."

The following are examples of fine, terse expression:

"Austrian Metternich
Can fix no yoke unless the neck agree."

* * * * *

"What is holy church unless she awes
The times down from their sins?"

* * * * *

"God, in cursing, gives us better gifts
Than men in benediction."

* * * * *

"The mountains live in holy families."

* * * * *

"Earth's fanatics make
Too frequently Heaven's saints."

* * * * *

"A holiday of miserable men
Is sadder than a burial-day of kings."

Her power of satire was severe, having a wholesome bitterness in it; most intense, sometimes, when most unintentional; oftenest used in vindication of her sex:

"I perceive!
The headache is too noble for my sex.
You think the heartache would sound decenter,
Since that's the woman's special proper ache,
And altogether tolerable . . except
To a woman."

She puts into men's mouths a biting welcome to woman's authorship:

"Oh, excellent!
What grace! what facile turns! what fluent sweeps!
What delicate discernment . . almost thought!
The book does honor to the sex, we hold.
Among our female authors we make room
For this fair writer, and congratulate
The country that produces in these times
Such women competent to . . spell."

But she does not spare even her own sex; thus at the wedding at St. Giles':

"A woman screamed back, I'm a tender soul,
I never banged a child at two years old
And drew blood from him, but I sobbed for it
Next moment,—and I've had a plague of seven!
I'm tender!"

Aurora has this jesting with herself:

"I wonder if the manuscript
Of my long poem, if 'twere sold outright,
Would fetch enough to buy me shoes, to go
A-foot (thrown in, the necessary patch
For the other side of the Alp)? It cannot be."

Her qualification for a bishop is:

"He must not
Love truth too dangerously, but prefer
The interests of the church."

Sometimes she wedges into a single line a whole bar of gold:

"She thanked God and sighed:
(*Some people always sigh in thanking God.*)"

Her descriptions of persons show a fine knack at portraiture. With a few strokes, she gives a face with a whole character in it. No one needs to go to the parlor-wall to see Aurora's aunt in oil-colors, after reading these few lines — as nearly pre-Raphaelite as if Millais had drawn them:

"She stood straight and calm;
Her somewhat narrow forehead braided tight
As if for taming accidental thoughts
From possible pulses; brown hair pricked with gray

By frigid use of life. (she was not old,
Although my father's elder by a year);
A nose drawn sharply, yet in delicate lines;
A close, mild mouth, a little soured about
The ends, through speaking unrequited loves,
Or peradventure niggardly half truths."

Her descriptions of such scenes as in art would be called figure-pieces have always a striking and graphic brevity:

"He ended. There was silence in the church;
We heard a baby sucking in its sleep
At the furthest ends of the aisle."

What more was needed to complete that description?

She is skilful in putting into words the experiences of the inner life; a rare translator of latent thoughts. She writes what the reader has often felt, but has never found written before; one is surprised at beholding one's secrets lying bare upon her page. She is the elect historian of all joys and sorrows. Her verse throbs with all human hopes and fears. All hearts may here find their personal story told. All aspirations, all struggles, all defeats, all victories have their fit memoirs in these books. This poet keeps the sybil's record of life and death.

Mrs. Gaskell, in setting a text for her life of Charlotte Brontë, took these words of Aurora Leigh's:

"My Father!—Thou hast knowledge, only Thou,
How dreary 'tis for women to sit still
On winter nights by solitary fires,
And hear the nations praising them far off."

The same fine strain is continued in these words, which we quote for the sake of their author's personal confessions therein:

"To sit alone,
And think for comfort, how that very night,
Affianced lovers, leaning face to face
With sweet half listenings for each other's breath,
Are reading haply from some page of ours,

> To pause with a thrill, as if their cheeks had touched,
> When such a stanza, level to their mood,
> Seems floating their own thoughts out—'So I feel
> For thee;'—'And I, for thee;—this poet knows
> What everlasting love is!'
> * * * To have our books
> Appraised by love, associated with love
> While we sit loveless! is it hard, you think?
> At least, 'tis mournful. Fame indeed, 'twas said,
> Means simply love. It was a man said that."

This revealer of the inward life is no less an out-of-door painter. Never were landscapes on canvas more charming than her's on the page. Look! Is not this a picture by Gifford?

> "On your left the sheep are cropping
> The slant grass and daisies pale,
> And five apple-trees stand dropping
> Separate shadows toward the vale,
> Over which in choral silence the bells peal you their all-hail!
>
> Far out, kindled by each other,
> Shining hills on hills arise,
> Close as brother leans to brother,
> When they press beneath the eyes
> Of some father praying blessings from the gifts of paradise."

Here are two lines that contain many pictures:

> "And brooks that glass in different strengths
> All colors in disorder."

Resemblances to other poets, both in style and thought—imitations, accidental and unconscious—are not infrequent in her writings. Her "Lament for Adonis," from Bion, opens with nearly the same words as Shelley's "Monody on the death of Keats." Her's begins:

> "I mourn for Adonis—Adonis is dead."

His begins:

> "I weep for Adonais—he is dead."

The poem of "The Virgin Mary and Child Jesus," quoting its motto from Milton's "Hymn of the Nativity," has manifestly followed Milton's style.

Her story of the dead Rosalind resembles Tennyson's of the dead Elaine.

A line in "Lady Geraldine"—

> "With a rushing stir, uncertain, in the air, the purple curtain . . ."

is like a line in Poe's "Raven"—

> "And the silken sad uncertain rustling of each purple curtain . . ."

At the close of "Aurora Leigh," Romney is made almost the identical Rochester of "Jane Eyre"—not merely in the fact that both are smitten blind by falling timbers in a burning building, nor in the similarity of their marriages, but in the essential likeness of the two characters, particularly after each has become softened by suffering and love.

A general resemblance to her husband is pointed out. If the faces of man and wife are said to grow alike, are not their thoughts quite as apt to take fashion of each other? Why, then, if husband and wife be authors, should not their styles grow akin? But the resemblances between the Brownings, although many exist, are often more fancied than real.

They did not revise each other's writings. Neither knew what the other had been doing, until it was done. "Aurora Leigh" was two-thirds written before her husband saw a word of it. Nor did he know of "The Sonnets from the Portuguese" till after the marriage, when she showed them to him for the first time, and he in his delight persuaded her to put them in print. Otherwise they might never have been published; for, with her characteristic modesty she at first thought them unworthy even of *his* reading, to say nothing of the whole world's. She felt so doubtful, too, of the merit of "Aurora

Leigh" that at one time she laid even that aside, with the idea never to publish it.

Her method of writing was to seize the moment when the mood was on her, and to fix her thought hurriedly on the nearest slip of paper. She was sensitive to interruption while composing, but was too shy to permit even her friends to see her engaged at her work. When the servant announced a visitor, the busy poet suddenly hid her paper and pen, and received her guest as if in perfect leisure for the visit. Giving her mornings to the instruction of her little son, and holding herself ready after twelve o'clock to give welcome to any comer, it was a wonder to many how she could find the needed time to study or write.

She made many and marked changes in her poems in successive editions. These show her fastidious taste. She was never satisfied to let a stanza remain as it was. Most of these amendments are for the better, but some for the worse—as orators who correct their printed speeches sometimes spoil the best parts. In many cases, she substituted not only new rhymes but new thoughts, turning the verses far out of their old channels; in others, she struck out whole lines and passages as superfluous; in others, she made fitter choice of single words, so adding vividness to the expression. As illustrations, we take some passages as they stood in the edition of 1845, and the same passages in the changed dress she gave them ten years after—the Roman type in the extracts showing the originals, and the Italic the revisions:

"Hark! the Eden trees are stirring,
Slow and solemn to your hearing!"
Soft *in*
"Plane and cedar palm and fir,
Oak *linden*
Tamarisk and juniper." [*Drama of Exile.*

"And the calm stars . . . far and fair."
spare
[*A Vision of Poets.*

"Through the solstice and the frost,"
sunshine [*The Lost Bower.*

"Our blood splashes upwards, O our tyrants,"
O gold-heaper
"And your purple shows your path;
But the child's sob curseth deeper in the silence,"
in the silence curseth deeper
"Than the strong man in his wrath!"
[*The Cry of the Children.*

"——the first fruit wisdom reaches"
wisest word man
Hath the hue of childly cheek."
Is the humblest he can speak.
[*Lessons from the Gorse.*

"She has halls and she has castles, and the resonant steam-eagles
among the woodlands, and has castles by the breakers;
Follow far on the directing of her floating dove-like hand—
She has farms and she has manors, she can threaten and command,
With a thunderous vapor trailing, underneath the starry vigils,
And the palpitating engines snort in steam across her acres,
So to mark upon the blasted heaven the measure of her land."
As they the
[*Lady Geraldine's Courtship.*

"You may speak, he does not hear; and besides, he writes no satire,—
And that antique sting of poetry is all we need to mind.
All the serpents kept by charmers leave the natural sting behind
[*Ibid.*

Howitt's ballad-dew or Tennyson's God-vocal reverie,—
-verse enchanted
[*Ibid.*

"Enter a broad hall thereby,
Build a spacious
Walled with cloudy whiteness.
Boldly, never fearing,
'Tis a blue place of the sky,
Use the
Wind-worked into brightness;
Which the wind is clearing.

Whence such corridors sublime
Branched with
  Stretch with winding stairs—
  Flecked
Praying children wish to climb
Such as
  After their own prayers.
  Following

"In the mutest of the house
  I will have my chamber;
Round its door I keep for use
Silence at the door shall use
  Northern lights of amber.
  Evening's light
Silence gave that rose and bee
Solemnizing every word
  For the lock, in meteness;
  Softening in degree
And the turning of the key
Turning sadness into good
  Goes in humming sweetness"
  As I turn the key.
[*The House of Clouds.*

She knew the true art of choosing words. The rule to take Saxon instead of Latin is easy to give but hard to follow. Words are instruments of music; an ignorant man uses them for jargon, but when a master touches them they have unexpected life and soul. Some words sound out like drums; some breathe memories sweet as flutes; some call like a clarinet; some shout a charge like trumpets; some are sweet as children's talk, and others rich as a mother's answering back. The words which have universal power are those that have been keyed and chorded in the great orchestral chamber of the human heart. Some words touch as many notes at a stroke as when an organist strikes ten fingers upon a keyboard. There are single words which contain life-histories, and to hear them spoken is like the ringing of chimes. He who knows how to touch and handle skilfully the home-words of his mother-tongue, need ask nothing of style. No finer instance of this skill is found in the whole realm of good English, out of Shakespeare, than in the writings of Mrs. Browning,* particularly in those which pay homage to the affections.

Mrs. Browning was a keen lover of art. Her talk of artists is more discriminating than Hawthorne's; for the author of "The Marble Faun" told chiefly what he had been told. But *she* was able to speak of what she had learned with her eyes, as well as with her ears. Both the Brownings were gifted with the genuine artistic insight. Both always caught eagerly at everything that indicated the progress of art. When William Page, lying sick of a fever in Rome and tossing on his pillow, made his singular and beautiful discovery of the true measurement of the human figure, the first person to whom he communicated it was Robert Browning, who, long before Mr. Page published his diagram and explanation, hinted it in these two purposely mysterious lines in "Cleon:"

"I know the true proportions of a man,
And woman also, not observed before;"

---

* George P. Marsh, in his "Lectures on the English Language," notices the following proportions of Saxon words in three of her poems and in one of her husband's:

"Mrs. Browning, Cry of the Children, - ninety-two per cent.
" " Crowned and Buried, - eighty-three "
" " Lost Bower, - - - - seventy-seven "
"Robert Browning, Blougram's Apology, eighty-four "

Mr. Marsh notices, however, in several of Mrs. Browning's minor poems, a large number of *Romance* words, but used almost wholly as *rhymed-endings*. Thus, of the Cry of the Children, he says:

"The proportion of Romance words in the *whole* poem is but eight per cent.; but of the eighty double-rhymed terminals, twenty-four or thirty per cent. are Romance. . . . . In the Dead Pan, there are about one hundred double-rhymed endings, less than one-half of which are Anglo-Saxon; and in the Lost Bower, out of about one hundred and fifty double-rhymes, more than one-third are Romance.

"I have made this examination of Mrs. Browning's works, not as a criticism upon the diction of one of the very first English poets of this age, the first female poet of any age, but to show that even in the style of a great artist, of one who, by preference, *employs native words wherever it is possible*, a conformity to the rules of a continental versification inevitably involves the introduction of an undue proportion of Romance words."

and Mrs. Browning set it in "Aurora Leigh," in the passage beginning:

"——I write so
Of the only truth-tellers now left to God—
*   *   *   *   *
The only teachers who instruct mankind,
From just a shadow on a charnel wall
To find man's veritable stature out,
Erect, sublime—the measure of a man,
And that's the measure of an angel, says
The apostle."

Mrs. Browning's imagination threw a glow over her whole nature. This strange faculty acts not only by itself, but upon all the other faculties of the mind: upon the Affections—setting apart the objects of them as sacred from the common world, and clothing them with white raiment like the saints: upon the Reason—giving dignity and grandeur to the intellectual convictions: upon the higher Moral Nature—inspiring faith and worship to a greater grasp of the spiritual and invisible, and leading the soul upward to that Mount of Vision whence there is fore-looking into the other world. Mrs. Browning's imagination struck a stimulating power into all her faculties. It kindled her affectional nature until out of this grew her glowing ideal of womanly love and devotion: —a conception of womanhood which hallows the mind into a half-awe on receiving it from her pages, and which made Mr. Ruskin pronounce her Eve in "The Drama of Exile" superior to Milton's, and her Dutchess May the finest female character brought into literature since Shakespeare's day. It quickened her logical faculties; giving them clearness of insight into all the great ranges of social problems and political questions; creating within her a noble intellectual sympathy for the age in which she lived as the grandest of the ages. It gave illumination to her moral and religious nature; unveiling before her that spiritual realm which to others is wrapped with impenetrable clouds; leading her up to a clear vision of such glories as Milton saw in his blindness; giving her the power to incite other souls to yearnings like her own, to fill them with vague unrests and aspirations for a higher life, and to quicken them to a nobler faith in the one living and true God.

Her sympathy with the weak and oppressed breaks out in many tender passages throughout her works. She could not look upon the Greek Slave in marble without saying:

> "* * * Appeal, fair stone,
> From God's pure height of beauty against man's wrong.
> Catch up in thy divine fall not alone,
> East griefs but west—and shake and shame the strong,
> By thunders of white silence overthrown!"

Her interest in the American anti-slavery movement was deep and earnest. She was a watcher of its progress, and afar off mingled her soul with its struggles. She corresponded with its leaders, and entered into the fellowship of their thoughts. Had her life been passed in this country she would have been one of that small circle (round whom a larger is now widening, until it shall compass the land) who gave an early but unheeded testimony against the great crime which the nation is now blotting out with blood. She would have stood with those whom God made worthy to stand as a few in the right against the many in the wrong. She had a kindred faith and courage with Mrs. Mott, Mrs. Child, Mrs. Chapman, and Mrs. Stowe. Her songs would have been as full of America as now they are of Italy. But the nightingale's breast would have been set against a thorn. She could not have escaped the same obloquy which fell upon other brave women. She would have earned the honorable slanders of a corrupt press; she would have received cold criticisms from white-gloved ladies and gentlemen in fashionable drawing-rooms; she would have seen proud lips turning scornfully upon her in the streets; and had her windows of Casa Guidi looked out upon Boston Common, she would more than once have been startled with the spectacle of a man in chains, and a mob following: all which she never saw in Italy. She was never forgiven for writing "A Curse for a Nation." Some condemned it without reading. Among these, strange to say, were literary Englishmen who thought it meant England, and who recently made a clamor against it as if it had been recently written. True, its English references were in no flattering strain; but it was written for "The Liberty Bell," a little book of the Abolitionists of New England, published in Boston as long ago as 1848. Every word in the poem, whether of England or America, stands yet

"Very salt, and bitter, and good."

Let those who rebuked her for it, go rebuked themselves!

"Because ye have broken your own chain,
With the strain
Of brave men climbing a Nation's height,
Yet thence bear down with brand and thong
On souls of others—for this wrong
This is the curse. Write.

Because yourselves are standing straight,
In the state
Of Freedom's foremost acolyte,
Yet keep calm footing all the time
On writhing bond-slaves,—for this crime
This is the curse. Write.

Because ye prosper in God's name,
With a claim
To honor in the old world's sight,
Yet do the fiend's work perfectly,
In strangling martyrs,—for this lie
This is the curse. Write.

True poets are lovers of the poor; they are knight-errants of the down-trodden. They catch their fire from the Apostle: "Who is offended, and I burn not?" Nor are they respecters of persons. They cannot narrow themselves to classes. They cross palms with the brotherhood of mankind. Mrs. Browning could not withhold her sympathy from the lowliest slave. When she saw that Freedom had a sacred cause in this land, although she never set her foot upon our soil, she never took her heart out of our struggle. The hope of a day of ransom glowed in her soul with a constant enthusiasm. What she gave to the cause was much; what she gained from it was more. The love of a great cause makes a great soul greater.

As a religious poet, Mrs. Browning is more devout than George Herbert, more fervid than Charles Wesley. The religious element was predominant in her mind. A full body of divinity, a whole system of theology, might be made out of her writings. She is the Sir Thomas Browne of women; or shall we say rather the Blaise Pascal? Her books are half-prayer-books. Hannah More's "Private Devotions" are not so devotional; Hervey's "Meditations" are not so meditative. Her favorite themes were always the heavenly glory; the angelic state; the soul after death. She saw visions and dreamed dreams. She had wrestlings with angels, like the sleeper on the pillow of stone. Yet her faith was neither dreamy nor visionary, neither transient nor moody; it was strong and vital, full of comfort and inspiration; such a faith as of itself can make a great character. She was truly led of the Heavenly Father. A light from heaven shone perpetually within her soul. She had the divine illumination. God's daily benediction was upon her. She held to the great creed, little believed, of simple love to God and Man. She belonged to that Holy Catholic Church of which the Pope is not vicar. She communed unceasingly with the One Head of the One Church. "I know that my Redeemer liveth:" this was her text. It may be almost said that out of Christ's own hand she ate the bread and drank the water of life. This was one secret of the unexampled love which many strangers bore to her: for no writer could draw so near to the world's heart without first drawing near to God's.

A sacred familiarity with the Divine Mind is the best inspiration for literature. Many an author, dead and forgotten, might have been alive in the world's memory to-day, only for lack of that quickening into greatness which comes of God's breath upon the soul. The world's teachers must first be God's learners. Wisdom does not dwell in books which students pore over blindly in dim closets. The cloister must open outward to the world and upward to the heavens. The chief knowledge is God's divinity and man's humanity. Who knows this, knows most of all; after this, what remains to be learned is little. God first; man next; the rest are trifles.

Great writing, therefore, is more than a mental—it is a moral product. The intellectual faculties need spiritual light. Human reason needs divine fire. If rhetoric be (as Plato calls it) the art of ruling men's minds, the prime maxim of rhetoric should be, first to wrestle with God and be overcome, so as next to wrestle with men and conquer. It was the crown of this victory that gilded the brow of the Christian woman of Florence.

Dr. Johnson, in his sketch of Dryden, quotes some stray letters of the poet, "in order," as he says, "that no scrap of Dryden be lost." In order that no scrap of Mrs. Browning be lost, the writer drops into this place a few further extracts from her latest letters. Here on the table lie the unmistakable manuscripts. No other handwriting is like hers. It is strong, legible, singularly un-English (that is, not a slanted or running hand), and more like a man's than a woman's; such a penmanship as Poe would have read a character from.

In one of these letters she says—though we cannot agree to it: "When did Mazzini's finger ever touch Italy *without a blot showing where?*" Yet this is only a new expression of an old opinion—long ago rhymed and printed. Of President Lincoln's Inaugural * she said: "With the exception of certain expressions (which *did* strike me as a superfluity of the official form), I admired and liked the Address. It seemed to me direct and resolute, simple and intense." The "superfluity" which she mentions, was Mr. Lincoln's voluntary and unnecessary offer to return fugitive slaves—an offer which, we think, he never will renew.† In reply to a request to prepare a prose work for publication in this country, she said: "In regard to prose-writing, *my voice is spoiled for speaking, perhaps, by singing.*" But her prose was magnificent, notwithstanding her distrust of it. She heaped up glowing sentences like fagots on a fire. Her letters make Cowper's poor. Wendell Phillips calls them above

* His first inaugural.

† Three years afterward, he wrote in another message these words: "If the people should, by whatever mode or means, make it an executive duty to re-enslave such persons, another, and not I, must be the instrument to perform it."

praise. In a hurried note, whose hurry is evident in the handwriting, she drops the following incidental but brilliant words—just as if the jewels in her rings, jarred by her rapid fingers, had been suddenly unset and fallen out on the paper: "What affected me most," said she, alluding to a speech which she had read in an American paper, "was not the eloquence . . no . . but the rare union of largeness and tolerance with fidelity to special truth. In our age, faith and charity are found, but they are found apart. We tolerate everybody, because we doubt everything; or else we tolerate nobody, because we believe something." Such a sentiment Carlyle would not have allowed to run to waste in a private letter, but would have saved for printing.

In a note of thanks to a friend who had sent to her from London some little English books of Henry Ward Beecher's writings, she said: "In opening the volumes I already fall upon fine and thrilling things. They will help me to live, I dare say—and perhaps they will help me to suffer."

Writing to a lady in Brooklyn, whose daughter had suddenly died, she gave expression to her own Christian faith for the hour of sorrow, and dropped a hint of her theological creed in the closing sentences: "I receive your letter, read it, hold it in my hands, with a sympathy deeply moved. No, we had not heard of your loss. . . Hearing of such things makes us silent before God. What must it be to experience them? I have suffered myself very heavy afflictions, but the affliction of the mother I have not suffered, and I shut my eyes to the image of it. Only, where Christ brings his cross he brings his presence, and where he is, none are desolate, and there is no room for despair. At the darkest, you have felt a hand through the dark, closer perhaps and tenderer than any touch dreamt of at noon. As he knows his own, so he knows how to comfort them—using sometimes the very grief itself, and straining it to the sweetness of a faith unattainable to those ignorant of any grief. . . Also, it seems to me that a nearer insight into the spiritual world has been granted to this generation, so that (by whatever process we have got our conviction) we no longer deal with vague abstractions, half closed, half shadowy, in thinking of departed souls. There is now something warm and still familiar in those beloveds of ours, to whom we yearn out past the grave—not cold and ghostly as they seemed once—but human, sympathetic, with well-known faces. They are not lost utterly to us even on earth; a little further off, and that is all; further off, too, in a very low sense. . . Quite apart from all foolish 'spiritual' (so-called) literature, we find these impressions very generally diffused among theological thinkers of the most calmly reasoning order. The unconscious influence of Swedenborg is certainly to be taken into account. Perhaps something else."

Mrs. Browning has more readers than her husband, but both deserve more than either has. One reason why the poems of Robert Browning fail to ingratiate themselves with some persons arises from a certain fastidious reserve of the author which lends itself to his style. His poems carry their meaning and sympathy shut within the lines, as a gentleman carries his thoughts and feelings hidden within his mind. This is partially true also of his wife's writings. Hence, while many who hear these poems read are caught at once with their fascination, many who set about reading them fail of the charm. It is better therefore that they should be read to a beginner than that he should run the risk of not liking them by reading them to himself. In a winter evening sitting before the fire, or in a summer day lying under some apple-tree, let a patient listener receive these poems from the lips of some reader who, having taken them into his heart, can supply with his voice the sympathy which they have, but hide; and then, whoso hears will like the Brownings.

In introducing a stranger to Robert Browning, take first "The Flight of the Duchess," afterward the "Good News from Ghent," "The Pied Piper," or "The Italian in England;" after which, no man will willingly forget their author. In beginning with Mrs. Browning, take "The Lay of the Brown Rosary," "The Duchess May," "The Lost Bower," or for a shorter piece "L. E. L.'s Last Question;" and though many say at first, "she is hard to be understood," yet after a little mastery in the reading, the listener will not fail to catch the meaning, enjoy the poem, and love the writer.

A special remark to be made of Mrs. Browning is, the proof which her genius gives of the possible equality of woman's mind with man's. This, of late years, has been a point of no small discussion. But, after all, what is any brain? Only a casket to hold awhile such of God's gifts as He chooses to lend; and in giving, as in withholding, He is no respecter of persons. In this woman's case, how stands the divine partiality? Does she not rank with men, and with the first of men? Before she died, there lived three great poets for England. Of the two Brownings and Tennyson, we will not dispute who is greatest, nor seek to disturb the green leaf upon the head of the laureate. But had Robert Browning lived in England instead of Italy, it is far from unlikely that he might have taken for himself

"The laurel greener from the brows
Of him who uttered nothing base."

Nor is the suggestion of such a possible reversal of ranks invidious; for there cannot be small rivalry between great souls. Tennyson is faultless—almost, like Maud, "*faultily* faultless"—while both the Brownings are full of faults. Robert Browning has few poems which the reader would not wish to change here and there in word or rhythm. His wife dropped blots on every page; every reader has exclaimed, "If only she had carried her pen a little more carefully here!" But notwithstanding the blemishes, the obscurities, the infelicities, the provoking hide-and-go-seek meanings, the fact still stands that no finer English poetry has been written since Shakespeare and Milton than is bound into books under the gilt labels of the Brownings.

No one can predict how much of present fame will escape eclipse in the future, or what unknown claimants, better titled than the rest, may rise out of darkness into perpetual light. But it is safe to say that if the age which follows ours be not far more rude than these rough times, it will pass judgment that the writings of Elizabeth Barrett Browning be not "willingly let die."

There will be a rare and special help to this fame:—another like it is married to it. Never again in the history of literature may there be another instance of two poets, the chiefest of their time, standing, like these, with clasped hands and wedded hearts. Many a husband is known to the world, whose wife's name has hardly crept from the threshold of her chamber; or a wife (like Mrs. Norton) wins a more than national reputation, while an ungenerous husband grasps avariciously at the profit of it. But with the Brownings, fame's common divorce of husband and wife failed of an example. Such a wife never had such a husband; such a husband never had such a wife. Their son—a pet of twelve years—will by-and-by, if he live to manhood, point back to the most illustrious lineage in literature.

The mother was as proud of her son as the son will be of his mother. It is a pleasant story told of the street-beggars who walk through Via Maggio under the windows of Casa Guidi that they always spoke of the English woman who lived in that house, not by her well-known English name, nor by any softer Italian word, but simply and touchingly as "the mother of the beautiful child." This was pleasanter to her ears than to

"hear the nations praising her far off."

Indeed, her greatest greatness was in being the Christian wife and mother. First out of Sorrow, and then out of Love—those two unfathomable wells!—she drew the fullness and richness of her life. This fullness and richness, rising above her own heart's power to contain it, overflowed in song, and so entered into the great heart of the world. Our chief thought of such a woman is not of her revered genius, but of her hallowed life. After all, compared with this, what is all else? This makes the sweetest fragrance of her fame. For the sake of this, that month of June that lent its sunlight to her grave shall never leave it, but must evermore add summer greenness to her memory, and render it perennial. So as she said of Mrs. Hemans:

"Albeit softly in our ears her silver song was ringing,
The footfall of her parting soul was softer than her singing!"

JULY 25, 1861.

THE SECOND SON OF SOUTH CAROLINA.

THE man whom John C. Calhoun styled the greatest of living Americans has just gone down into his grave without leaving behind him—in any record that we have been able to consult—the date of his birth. Among the newspapers of the church to which the Rev. Dr. James H. Thornwell belonged, neither *The Observer*, nor *The Presbyterian*, nor *The Journal of Commerce*, has succeeded in finding it. His age is mentioned as "about fifty years." Not even his name has place in the "Men of the Time." A late report states that he died of typhoid pneumonia in Charlotte, N. C., August 1, 1862. As this statement comes from "rebel sources," and as a similar rumor concerning Dr. Hoge (who is still living) not long ago gained currency, some acquaintances of Dr. Thornwell in New York express a belief that he is not yet dead. But, as the journals just named have given him their usual obituary record, we add our own. If he be alive and shall see these notices, he will not be the first man who has read his own epitaph.

By common fame Dr. Thornwell was the most eloquent minister in the Old-School Presbyterian Church, and the most brilliant debater in its General Assembly. This reputation he early gained and never lost. When present at the annual convocations, he was always the first person pointed out to a stranger, just as visitors to the House of Representatives used to ask, "Which is John Randolph of Roanoke?" In not a few traits, both physical and mental, the two men bore each other a resemblance.

A grave-looking, elderly clergyman, with a boy's stature—pale and cadaverous face—hair black as a raven, and floating about his neck like a woman's—shoulders round, and crowding his chest forward—a frail frame, plainly carrying the burden of an over-active brain:—this was the exterior of the little, great man who, after the death of Calhoun, was esteemed the first citizen of South Carolina.

The most singular point in his history is the earliest—his origin. Strange as it may seem, the chiefest of South Carolinians sprang, not from the "first families," nor from the blood of the Cavaliers, but from the lowest stock in the social order of the South—from a level even beneath the black man's—known in the social strata as the fundamental White Trash. He was born not in a house, but in a cabin; not under a ceiling, but under a thatch. Not that this is any discredit to him;—not at all! Only, when he afterward turned against those of his fellow-creatures whom God likewise had set in lowly stations, he ought to have remembered the "rock whence he was hewn," and "the hole of the pit whence he was digged."

A happy accident early brought good fortune to this young piece of friendless White Trash. South Carolina having no common schools where a poor lad might open a gate to a career, he was caught up by a rich planter in the neighborhood, who, enamored of his fine eyes and fair forehead, sent him as a charity scholar to South Carolina College at Columbia—chiefly because of his handsome looks. Here he began immediately to make a young man's fame; devouring books with passionate appetite;

out-stripping his mates in all studies; conquering in all debates; running through his course with such distinction, that the student left the College to return as professor, and to remain as president.

This presidential chair—the chief literary post in tho whole range of Southern institutions—he kept until a few years ago, when he resigned it for the Professorship of Theology in the Old-School Presbyterian Seminary, which stood as neighbor to the College in the same town. This change his friends always regarded as unfortunate; for, after having exerted an unbounded influence on each succeeding company of students—so that even yet they imitate the tones of his voice—he found, on entering a second-class seminary, his sphere of activity abridged. Nor did the students of the College quietly submit to the vote which transferred him to the Seminary. When were South Carolinians ever in the habit of submitting quietly to adverse votes? To intimidate his successor from taking the vacant chair, the young men rose in rebellion, armed themselves with pistols, pointed a cannon at the college-walls, and undoubtedly would have begun a bombardment, had not Dr. Thornwell suddenly appeared, and by his fascinating arts charmed the chivalry into peace. But on the breaking out of a rebellion against the American Republic, Dr. Thornwell ranked himself with the rioters, and invoked on his country a tempest of fire.

The theological professorship was twinned with the pulpit of the First Presbyterian Church: a double office, in which he served till his death. It was on Sunday mornings that his abilities had their best display. His voice, though hardly well-modulated, was as mellow as a flute; his gestures, though consisting of little else than throwing out his arms and drawing them back, were never ungraceful; his eyes, which he never took off his audience to rummage through a manuscript, or seldom to glance at a note, had a strange power of riveting attention; his whole manner of speech, while rarely exciting the speaker to any apparent enthusiasm, always kindled the assemblage into a glowing fervor of feeling.

He took the palm for conversation. He was the talking centre of every circle where he entered. His confident manner, his facility of expression, his ability to seize an idea and make the most of it on the spot, compensated largely for a natural barrenness of humor. He was master of a peculiar sarcasm which, like Shelley's, was sharp on occasion, yet which, to cut clean, needed an edge of finer wit. But in describing something which he had seen, he was a rare narrator. For instance: in telling some friends in New York of Blondin's feats on the tight-rope at Niagara, which he had just witnessed, he made everybody in the parlor shudder.

Of his publications, the best known are his "Discourses on Truth," consisting of a series of sermons on Christian ethics; beside which, he wrote with vigor against Popery; and from time to time, during the last twenty-five years, he printed sermons, pamphlets, tracts, political essays, and reviews; his latest production being a vindication of the new "Old School" Church of the South, of which he laid the corner-stone, as Dr. Ross laid it for the new "New School." His style is vigorous, direct, unimaginative, devoid of illustration or ornament, carefully weeded of unnecessary words, never needing a second reading to make the meaning clear; on the whole, resembling Brownson's, though less rigidly Saxon than the fine, brave English which puts such spirit and fire into *The Quarterly Review*.

Speaking of Dr. Thornwell's habits of mind, a writer in *The Presbyterian* says:

"Dr. Thornwell's favorite studies (outside of theology) were in the departments of metaphysics, logic, and moral science. An unfortunate remark, smacking somewhat of a boast, that he possessed the best private library on the subject of logic in the country, brought upon him the laugh of many, but we doubt not that it was true, as his fondness for this study was remarkable. The writer chanced to go at one time into a room which he had occupied for two days, at some distance from his home, and, seeing scraps of paper lying upon the carpet, picked some of them up. To his astonishment, they were covered with logical symbols, the work, evidently, of a few leisure moments, and of a character which showed the writer to be perfectly at home in the most difficult parts of the science."

This extract furnishes the key-note to Dr. Thornwell's intellectual character. His chief power of mind—a power which he was constantly strengthening, like a gymnast, by exercise in these studies—was logical deduction. He constructed an argument with rare skill, and presented it with winning grace. This was his forte. Beyond this, we do not see that he possessed any quality of greatness. Certainly he was not, in any broad sense, an original thinker. In all that he said, he said nothing new: at least, in all that he published, we have seen nothing new. Taking away from the "Discourses on Truth" their fine precision of statement, their carefulness in covering the whole ground, and their pure English, the remainder—that is, the actual substance of the book—is not the author's own, but is to be found (where *he* found it) in other writers. In Moral Philosophy, he corrects Paley; in Mental, he corrects Locke; but everybody nowadays corrects both Paley and Locke, without evincing profound originality of thought. It seems to us that Dr. Thornwell's failure to discover any new truths, or to lead any new ideas into the world, was on account of his deficient possession of that quick camera of the mind which, for lack of a better name, we call the intuitive faculty. So, with all his fine parts, he was not a man of genius.

In the General Assembly, he usually made more speeches, and gained less votes, than any other man on the floor. The reason for this was two-fold; first, because he was always bringing forward some narrow, technical side-issue, to which less acute but more practical minds attached no importance; and next, because—unlike all other South Carolinians since the world began—he had neither taste nor ability for ecclesiastical strategy. If he had a measure to introduce, he consulted no committee beforehand; he arranged no programme of tactics. He always expected to carry his point unaided, except by his own speech. Often in a debate he confessed himself so sanguine of the success of his measures, that when the final vote left him in a lonesome minority, his surprise was ludicrous to the audience. Thus, two years ago, in the Assembly at Rochester, when he sought by a grand assault to demolish the organized Boards of the Old School Church, and to substitute committees in their place—arraying Dr. Hodge in battle against him—he made a long, brilliant, and absurd speech, at the close of which he remarked: "I think I have made the subject so clear, that I shall have an overwhelming majority." "You will get," said a friend who congratulated him on his speech, "about 50 votes out of 325." On the count, he had 47! Many South Carolinians believe that, had he not been a clergyman, he would have followed Calhoun into the Senate. But he had one virtue too great for a politician—he despised caucusing! We say it to his honor.

But Dr. Thornwell chose to cast a shadow upon what might have been a shining name. Born to no inheritance but poverty, to no station but obscurity; shaking from his small-clothes the dust of Dirt-Eaters before he could step into decent society; belonging to a low class who looked up with envy at the negro above them; he afterward rose to the height of the oligarchy only to look down with unmanly arrogance on the dusky multitudes who once were his superiors in caste.

While South Carolina was organizing the Great Outbreak, such was Dr. Thornwell's influence among the masses of the people, such was the prestige of his name, such was his power of appeal, that during the few critical days before the ordinance of Secession, it is hardly an exaggeration to say that he held in his own hands the decision of peace or war for the whole land. For if South Carolina had not rebelled, no other State would have followed: and one man might have saved South Carolina. But when the Legislature met to pass the treasonable ordinance, *who* was the hot gospeller that rose in the capitol to inaugurate the revolution with public prayer? It was Dr. Thornwell.

What shall be his just fame? A man to whom God gave brilliant gifts—to whom a broad culture added rare facility in their use—to whom the ears of the multitude were always open—to whom some golden opportunity for usefulness was always at hand; shall such a man, after lending his whole life and strength to a national crime, now at last, on going down to his grave, leaving his mischiefs at work behind him, bequeath a memory green and fragrant to the world? After devoting for thirty years the best energies of his mind to finding reasons for an institution that violates the most sacred rights of human nature—turning manhood into merchandise—making bargain and sale of the chastity of woman—orphaning children before the eyes of their parents—himself a buyer and seller of souls for whom Christ died!—can a church that is charged to keep itself unspotted of the world afford to claim for such a man a place in its remembrance as a faithful minister of the Gospel of good will? Bringing discredit upon religion; casting dishonor upon the church; binding heavy burdens grievous to be borne; shutting his ears to the cries of the oppressed; hurrying the nation into civil war:—this is his true record, which no man can say is overdrawn. In loyalty to justice, we give his name its true place in the history of the times. Beyond this, not man but God is the Judge.

SEPTEMBER 1, 1862.

AN EDITOR'S VISIT TO AN EDITOR'S FARM.

SHUT within the city for three months past, not a green field had I set eyes on, all this summer, till Mr. Greeley said a week ago, "Come up and spend a Saturday on the farm."

Mr. Greeley's farm is at Chapequa, a station which in spite of being on the Harlem Railroad is not a great way from New York. Every Friday night, our venerable friend, weary with the week, leaves Printing-House square, and goes up to smell his own grass, to nod to his own cattle, and to drink water at his own rock-spring. All this freshens away his venerable look, and turns him into a young man in twenty-four hours. This farm supplies vegetables to the market and good reading to *The Tribune*—just as a certain farm at Peekskill grows apples for New York and preaching for Brooklyn. What other acres in the country yield better crops?

Drawing near the station, I overheard a passenger say to his companion:

"We are coming upon Horace Greeley's country-seat."

"I suppose," said the other, "he lives in fine style."

"No, he lives like a laboring man," was the reply.

How could I help turning round and remarking,

"Well, he *is* a laboring man!"

Living in the woods, in a romantic haunt, barricaded against the world by palisades of forest trees—this busy man, taking his rest in hard work, drops his pen to shoulder his axe, and for twelve years has been chopping hemlock, birches, chestnuts, maples, oaks—yet his woods still stand. He can cut a tree or split a rail as well as Abraham Lincoln, and could write as good a proclamation.

"I am proudest of my oaks," said he, as we walked in the shade of aged boughs that once shook their leaves to the same wind that filled Hendrik Hudson's sails. Older than these, some others were coeval with Columbus and the New World. An army of venerable veterans, they encamp on this farmer's hillsides—soldiers of many battles against tempest and thunderbolt—still flaunting their banners to every breeze—standing where they will stand long after we who walked under them shall have faded like a leaf. A man looks at a flower, saying, "How short-lived!" But what say the trees when they look down at men? Or what say the rocks when they look up at the trees? Nay, what says the globe itself to all these, except to bear a faint witness of Him to whom a thousand years are as one day, passing like a tale that is told!

"Do you employ slave labor?" I inquired.

"We will walk round the farm," he replied, "and perhaps you will meet some contrabands."

I found—O marvel of the times!—that the best blood of South Carolina was tilling Horace Greeley's fields!

Never were seventy acres more diversified than on this farm—crowding together meadow, garden, orchard, ravine, precipice, cascade, and forest primeval. Part of it is level as a prairie, and part too steep for a goat to climb. It is nature in her wildness and her tameness; a little Switzerland.

There were three of us—the third being our friend Morton, at whom the geese hissed because he makes the famous gold pens.

"Let us go down into the ravine and dip our cups into the well in the rock," said our host, who has a known fondness for cold water. After drinking our fill with a relish better than of wine, we sat on the rocks at the foot of the waterfall, and stripping our arms bare, plunged them into the rapids till the blood grew cool, and we rose like giants refreshed. Sometimes in a freshet this stream plays tricks, and like the wolf in the fable has once destroyed a dam. But like a pert maid, it makes up in fair looks what it lacks in fine manners. The fishes in the fish-pond would have come to our hands for a few crumbs, only we forgot to carry the crumbs. Mr. Greeley talks to them sometimes; but they, just as when St. Anthony preached to their shallow pates for the first time, still turn their tails and swim away. Climbing up to higher ground in the woods, *whirr-r-r* went the partridges from under our feet, a very picture of unnecessary "skedaddling"—for not a gun is ever fired among these trees, and all sensible birds know it. The squirrels were taking their comfort, whistling as contentedly as if they owned the place. The locusts were as loud as a brass band. They have a sound of Sunday in their voices. The bees, though having the whole garden to themselves, envied us the few flowers that we carried in our hands, for they settled on our roses and pinks and heart's-ease, as if they were custom-house officers come to search for contraband goods. Knee-deep we walked in clover, the grasshoppers flying out before us like rebels before General Grant. A grasshopper eats like a hungry man, yet even while he devours your substance, you bear no grudge against him, because of the wiseness of his face. When he happens to leap awry and loses his hold of the clover-stalk, his yellow belly turns up so like to a frog's as to delight a

Frenchman. Besides, this creature speaks the dead languages, and "chirps on in Greek still." But the acrobats will soon stop their ground and lofty tumblings, for yonder come the turkeys with sheriff's warrant for every one of them. Grasshoppers are for gobblers to gobble; turkeys must grow fat for Thanksgiving.

Walking in the apple-orchard, we were morally rebuked by the trees—they were such fruit-bearers; living such profitable lives; making so much of their opportunities; yielding such a flavor of good character. "By their fruits ye shall know them," is a judgment that falls less lightly on trees than on men. Look at those russets, with boughs bending down like banyans, and touching the earth with an over-weight of ripening fruit!

"How do you make your apple-trees so thrifty?" I asked.

"An apple-tree," he replied, "is like a cow tied to a stake; you must carry food to it, or it will starve."

Mr. Greeley's apple-trees live as well as if they drank from Eden's streams, which once nourished the most tempting of all fruit.

Every field on this farm made us think of Douglas Jerrold's account of Australia, "where, if you tickle the earth with a hoe, she laughs with a harvest."

The pinnacles of Mr. Greeley's grounds lift one up into the presence of half a dozen magnificent prospects—on one side a rolling country, sculptured "as if God's finger touched but did not press" in the making it—on another, hill-ranges running off northward toward Mount Kisco—on another, great and precipitous depths yawning at one's feet, and tempting one to cast himself down.

After a long walk, during which we debated the best spot for building the new house, yet concluding that the new house would never be built, we lay down on the grass and mutually agreed that God made the country and man made the town. Should we take a nap in the shade? The most famous man in our party of three has a famous knack at sleeping either under a sermon or a tree! But the day was breezy, and there was danger of taking cold —even at a time when a city-full of people were broiling in the sun like fowls on a gridiron. But to lie flat on one's back and look into the sky was a delight that a certain school-boy used to take, and he took it once again. How one's head swims in the blue ocean, and how the clouds pass over him like waves! Getting dizzy, and looking back at the earth again, how everything goes gallopading round in a circle—trees, rocks, and hills, all dancing as if mad! A little drunkenness may not only lose an army but turn the earth upside down.

What majesty in all the world is like unto clouds! They are the investiture of the Invisible Throne. They are the fading, yet never fading, frescoes on the roof of God's temple. Castles in the air, battlements in mid-heaven, tumbled ruins of great cities, upheaved rocks and mountains, illimitable coast-lines, profiles of human faces—all these, and a thousand more pictured glories, one sees in the clouds! What shadows they cast on shining fields! Then, as clouds and shadows pass away together, and the grass is gilded again of the sun, one is left to think of a shadow on the land that passes not yet—the shadow of war and death. On such a day of peace, could there be war in the world? Yet why was I thinking, just then, of Robert Shaw meeting death and fame at Fort Wagner, and of Bayard Wilkeson falling a hero and martyr at Gettysburg? Summer days are not bright enough to cover the shadows on human hearts. What shall herald the final consummation? "Coming in clouds and great glory!"

is the prophecy. May the overhanging cloud of battle-smoke be the sign that the coming of the Son of Man is at hand, and that the day of our redemption draweth nigh!

Does any one ask, How does Mr. Greeley find time to manage his farm? I reply, The farmer's wife is a good farmer. That is how he manages—and how, being a good man, he is managed! Garden and hot-house, with flower-pots innumerable, containing not only the "dear common flowers," but curious plants from all countries, are her special care. A farm without a flower-garden is like a shirt without a collar, good for use but not for show. And as, somehow, flowers grow better for a woman than for a man, a farm without a farmer's wife remains an ill-graced bachelor.

It was a perfect day. Our visit was like a jewel without a flaw. Now and then comes some rare and special day, set in the round year like a diamond in a ring. This was such a day; not possible to a man living in the country, but possible only to one who had not seen God's grass since last summer. It was cool water to long-thirsty lips. As a captive loosed from prison goes home to look with ravishment on the faces of his children, so one escaping from the bedlam of hot streets in midsummer finds his first look at the sky and fields a delight unspeakable. It belongs to him and to no one else. It was the exclusive inheritance of one member of this party of three. It was to him the whole summer crowded into a day.

Of course, the truer life is the one which is lived in the constant presence of these same wondrous scenes. Often, however, they who look at nature most discern it least. But men ought to be daily readers of what good old Sir Thomas Browne calls "the liberal manuscript of nature."

All eyes ought habitually to see the sun in his rising and setting: the spectacle is needed both for body and soul. "Day unto day uttereth speech, and night unto night showeth knowledge." But when we are shut out from this speech, we go ignorant of this knowledge. How long a journey the Queen of Sheba made to see Solomon! Yet, his glory was outrivalled by the lilies of the field. And since the Lord spake of His lilies once, the lilies evermore speak of their Lord. What a magnificent song of Nature is the Psalmist's! "Praise the Lord, . . fire and hail; snow and vapor; stormy wind fulfilling his word; mountains and all hills; fruitful trees and all cedars; creeping things and flying fowl . . . . His glory is above the heavens and earth. . . Praise ye the Lord."

By-and-by, looking at our watches, it was time for the train. We carried off with us the best part of the farm—its master. A plain man, plainer than his neighbors, with a face as kindly as a child's and a heart as simple, he trudged with stick in hand away from his happy fields, not to see them again for six days. When a man owns a paradise, it is a self-denial to live in it only one day in a week. But there is hard work to be done in the world, and this is one of the men who must do it. What if all men did theirs as faithfully! And for his work's sake, he will be remembered long after his two summer-day companions shall be under the grass and forgotten.

August 27, 1863.

THE PICTURE OF THE PROCLAMATION.

MEASURING about fifteen feet by nine, Mr. Carpenter's ample canvas contains eight life-size figures—namely, President Lincoln, and Secretaries Chase, Stanton, Seward, Welles, Smith, Blair, and Bates—assembled in the chamber in which, since Jackson's day, the Cabinet-meetings have always been held. Here is the old green-papered wall; the hard-featured walnut table; the leg-worn and thread-bare cusihoned chairs; the cheaply-carpeted floor, strewn with portfolios, maps, and books; and the old-fashioned chandelier, half-hiding the portrait of Old Hickory's thin, courageous face. At the head of the table (for "where Macgregor sits is head of the table"), is President Lincoln, the central figure of the group; at his right hand, Chase and Stanton; at his left, the other ministers; some sitting, others standing. The time is July, 1862, when Mr. Lincoln first announced to his counsellors his intention to proclaim Emancipation. He has just read aloud the original draft that lies before him, and is listening to a suggestion from the Secretary of State—who appears better in a picture than in some other capacities as a cabinet minister. After this meeting (as we hardly need say) came the Proclamations of September 22, 1862, and January 1, 1863.

As a fundamental canon of criticism, we hold that a work of art should be judged, not only for its skill, but its motive—not only for technical excellence, but suggestive meaning. The fine arts are so intrinsically noble that they should never be squandered on unworthy subjects. The old masters devoted their art almost wholly to churchly uses. They were nearly all animated with religious enthusiasm. Some of them never painted except in a devout frame of mind. Out of such moral quickenings naturally sprang fine works of the imagination; for the imagination and the moral nature are so intimately co-related that they act upon each other with great suddenness and power; what fires the one, kindles the other; and when both join their individual moods into a common heat, they produce in a gifted mind a noble fervor of constructive activity—an intense tendency toward picturesque and dramatic expression. It is during this conjunction of faculties that the highest themes of literature and art are caught and fixed for ever by pen or brush. And as the highest works of literature and art spring out of these mental states in the author or artist, so the highest function of literature and art is to awaken similar mental states in the reader or spectator. The man who is himself inwardly awakened by these mysterious chords striking their solemn music through his mind, and who, at the same time, has the cunning craft to awaken like ecstacies in other men, is the great artist, the great poet, the great orator. It is easy, therefore, to set up a true standard for the relative ranking of what claim to be great works of art. Such works are truly great only according to the degree in which, like ancient questioners at the oracles, they evoke these highest responses from the human soul. This was the secret of the mediæval masters. They disdained any meaner mission for their art. The object of Corregio, and of Raphael, and of Fra Angelico, was not to win a sweet breath blown from courtly connoisseurs, but to elicit the noblest emotions possible to the human heart. Of course, the desire of fame had its full and legitimate share in rousing the artist to his utmost of genius; but this very desire of fame, in the truest and highest uses for which God has set it in the soul, is a high and heavenward passion, and not the base and selfish greed into which it too often is degraded. What Longfellow wrote of one of these ancient worthies, is true of nearly all the rest.

> "Here, *where art was still religion, and in simple reverent heart,*
> Lived and labored Albrect Durer."

It is touching to read, in the lives of these men, how they refused pay even for their master-pieces—accepting only a bare equivalent for their canvas and pigments, giving the labor of their cunning hands, and the zeal of their fiery souls, as free offerings to God and the church. What wonder, therefore, that the glory of such artists has become in history greater than the glory of kings!

Our American art, on the contrary, with some signal exceptions, lacks this inspiration, and is mercenary, frivolous, subservient to fashion, unleavened with moral meaning, poor, dry, and barren, and therefore eclipsed by the past and unpromising for the future. Some of our artists (pitifully too few!) have worthily applied their genius to higher and holier themes than the trifles which now pass current among us as works of art. But protracted observation has led us to the conviction that American artists, while far from being men of merely ordinary gifts, and while not a few are of undisputed genius, nevertheless as a class fall short of their best possible powers simply through lack of that spiritual quickening which alone can fully arouse the intellectual faculties. "No man is great," said Cicero, "without the divine afflatus." No artist can climb to the top of his art except he be lifted by God's hand. No worker works to his full ability, unless in his work he is brooded by the Illumining Spirit—as St. Gregory is pictured in the act of dictating his homilies under the wing of the Holy Dove.

Unlike the great masters, who were thoroughly imbued with the spirit of their day and generation, our own painters are especially remiss and oblivious concerning the great issues of the present age—forgetting that this is the only age to which, for the most part, their works will ever appeal. It was fully a year after the outbreak of our civil war—a war which was the outgrowth of a great moral controversy—before our artists (as a class) showed by any hint in their works that they felt the patriotic spirit of the times. When, two winters ago, Gray put the negro on canvas, exhibiting him as a human being to a fashionable audience in Fifth Avenue; and when Ward, at the same time, modelled a chain-breaking slave in an attitude of heroic manhood; not only were there connoisseurs who curled their lips, but many artists themselves joined the contemners—proving how little worthy they were of that true knight-errantry of art whose high duty it is to champion justice against tyranny—to inspire men with generosity and nobleness—to sweeten and purify the faith of mankind.

As in the Madonna of Ingres the kneeling king offers his crown and sceptre as reverent gifts to the Holy Virgin whom he serves, so art fulfils its highest mission in offering itself to the service of whatever is good, noble, true, and pure—disdaining to circumscribe itself within any sphere less comprehensive, or to content itself with any service less illustrious.

We have turned our pen into this strain because we

welcome with great joy any new work of art that seeks to lay its foundations upon these fundamental principles. Mr. Carpenter's work is so grounded. For this reason we take pleasure in mentioning him to our countrymen as an artist who approximates a true conception of the great end of art, showing it to be something more than the commonplaceness of intent which we ordinarily see in picture-galleries. He is an artist who is zealously ambitious, not only to do worthily what he does at all, but to do something worthy of being done; who labors humbly and reverently, looking to the Heavens for help; who believes in the inspiration of the Holy Ghost; who knows that any quickening less than this is unworthy of that art which, in its historic prime, was devoted to better than mere vain, fashionable, and worldly ends—that art whose departed glories will never again be achieved unless striven for in a like spirit of faith and prayer. It is the high praise of this picture that it sprang out of such a mood of mind. Since it is the work of a young man who means to try his hand again (and, we trust, many times), it is not necessary to his deserved encomium that his first memorable canvas should be in all points, either of drawing or coloring, a marvel of skill. The fact that we have among our artists this man, and a few others of like temper, who paint their pictures in religious earnest—as Straduarius wrought his sweet-sounding violins—is the victory we wish to chronicle and crown. Twenty men who, to fine natural genius, should add such a religious spirit—intensifying, developing, and multiplying the force of their intellectual faculties—would by-and-bye carry up American art into a worthiness of comparison with the elder and golden days.

So far as we know, Mr. Carpenter is the only artist

who as yet has been moved to commemorate the greatest American event of the present age—proving thereby, perhaps, that no man is more worthy of the subject than he who first had eyes to discover it; yet he has set forth his lofty theme with such a modesty of treatment that if he had chosen, instead, a far humbler subject he could hardly have chosen a much simpler style. The design is graceful and natural, without the dramatic quality which an artist with a more intense constructive faculty would have sought. The various likenesses, both in face and figure, are so true to life that one feels like saluting them by name—particularly the likeness of Mr. Lincoln, which is more nearly the man himself than any other portrait of him we have yet seen—conveying that indescribable sadness in his eyes which is the chief indication of greatness in his countenance.

Here, therefore, is a work of art which is to be judged, as all great works ought to be judged, not only by the measure of technical skill which it displays, but by the evidence it affords of the artist's consecration to that high end for which God has lent the artistic faculty to the human mind. Here is a devout young man giving his first great canvas to no less an end than the Liberty of his Country—an example worthy to be heeded by many older practitioners in a profession which is now busying itself too much with pretty trifles to the neglect of grander things.

OUR CANDIDATE FOR THE NEXT PRESIDENCY.

WE have an early word to say concerning the next Presidency. A few newspapers are protesting that something else, just now, is more important to be thought of than politics. Unmake the rebellion first, say they, and make the presidency afterward. But the appointed time to remake the presidency will come before we have unmade the rebellion. To be preparing now for the next presidential issue is one thing; to be caucusing with candidates is quite another. It is too early, we agree, to be insisting upon men, but not too early to be establishing principles. The candidate is the mere ball upon the fountain; the principle is the perennial stream that tosses him up or tumbles him down.

The presidency of George Washington was not, and of Abraham Lincoln is not, of equal importance with that of the next four years. Washington entered upon his office just after a great storm had ended; Lincoln, just before a greater storm had burst; the next president will go to his office while the tempest rages over his head. Or are we, as some predict, to have peace before next summer? No: we may not have war, but we shall not have peace. For, though military hostilities may cease (which we doubt), yet, when the war of bayonets has ended, the war of diplomacy will begin. The collision of armies will give place to the collision of parties. On the next morning after peace, a strife of cunning questions will open.

The enemy, throwing away his worst weapon, the sword, will resume his best, the tongue. So that, even if the battle-smoke shall be blown away by the breath of the next June roses, danger will still remain.

"A nation tired of war," said De Tocqueville, "will submit to be duped for the sake of peace." This nation, now confronting such a peril, seeks in advance to mould a government able to ward off the cheat. To settle a civil war is usually a harder task than to wage it. It is, in fact, the most difficult duty that can devolve upon a government, one almost never well done—the proof of which is, that almost every civil war in history has ended in a compromise. Shall ours? God forbid! But how avert it? "To be forewarned is to be forearmed." Let us be wise in time, that we may not be "duped for the sake of peace."

The next administration, if it shall open with an unexpected peace, will have its hands more full of various labors than under a continued war. Government has a cohesive power during war greater than during peace. A national emergency, such as the American Revolution, or the present Rebellion, consolidates all loyal interests—fusing all men's minds into a single purpose, and compacting the government into a terrible strength. But peace, with its diversity of interests, dividing and scattering popular sympathy, uncentralizes the governing power. It will be a harder task to unite parties under the next administration than it has proved under this. It will require a finer statesmanship to conduct the next administration than it has had for this. Great statesmen are few in any country—like great poets. But, few as they are, we must find one for the next presidency.

What a complication of problems the next four years

will bring! The establishment of Human Liberty; the reconstruction of a broken Republic; the readjustment of the rights of the States, and of the Federal Government; the status of the negro, and his conversion into a voter; the punishment of treason; the re-ownership of Southern lands; the Mexican question; the Monroe doctrine; the national finances; the re-absorption of a disbanded soldiery into citizenship; the establishment of a standing army large enough to defend liberty, and not large enough to menace it;—these and many other problems, foreseen and unforeseen, are the unparalleled difficulties which the next administration must meet and master.

That administration, facing in advance such an uncounted multitude of duties, must be equal to the emergency. The country cannot afford to risk any second-rate committee to be its President and Cabinet. It needs first-class men—every one a pure diamond! If Cromwell and Milton themselves could step from their graves to serve us with their own genius, they could bring no superfluous ability for the occasion. When one stops to think how the immediate future of this country shuts fast in its bud the whole world's hope—how by our victory or defeat the happiness of all mankind is to be hindered or helped—so solemn and serious becomes the question of the national leadership that sober men may well ask, "Who is sufficient for these things?"

The man who comes bearing credentials for the next presidency must demonstrate, as his first token of fitness, his allegiance to God, Liberty, and Human Rights—possessing a reverent mind, heightened to the noblest conception of the function of Government, the grandeur of Justice, and the nobility of Man. The chief object of government stops short of nothing less than the uplifting of humanity; and Coleridge ought to be once more alive to teach statesmen their forgotten functions. A government like ours, in which the general principles of equality, liberty, and charity give spirit to the laws, needs, as its true administrators, men of profound moral convictions—men upon whose hearts are graven the two tables of the law, love to God and love to Man. A friend of ours lately came back from Washington saying, "The great lack there, is of faith in God!" What fitness have men, lacking such a faith, to administer what ought to be a Christian government? No man is fit to stand at the head of men who does not sit at the feet of God. The only human ruler who rules sublimely is he whose soul is touched of the Holy Ghost, and who thus borrows greatness from Heaven. And a nation in a life-and-death struggle for liberty needs for its leader a man with whom liberty is not only a political idea, but a religious faith; who carries it in his breast as an unquenchable enthusiasm—as a holy and purifying fire! In the time of our trial—of our baptism of blood, not yet ended—let all devout hearts pray that God may grant us the gift of such a man!

As another requisite, let the nation, in electing a man to preside, take one born to command. The capacity to govern is native with its possessor; it cannot be loaned to him because he happens to be president. Genius for administration is made of superior sense, quickness, courage, and will,—sense enough to make a man his own best counsellor, though he have a cabinet of ministers beside; quickness enough to make *one* timely blow tell better than two tardy ones; courage enough to assume every responsibility except that of doing wrong; will enough to break through common men's impossibilities as through egg-shells. "The will," as Emerson says, "*that* is the man." It is a man with a Will that we mean to hunt for next July, and to vote for next November.

Also, let us take a man of clean hands—unvexed with an itch for gain, uncorrupted by bargain and sale, ungreedy for a paid price. It is impossible to make any government thoroughly honest. A great Frenchman says, "Government will always be as rascally as the people permit." Bailie Peyton used to say that the city of Washington was so corrupt that the man in the moon held his nose in passing over it! The present administration, though not perfect in all the virtues, is, in respect to honesty, so great an improvement on the preceding as to create a desire that the forthcoming may be an equal improvement on this. A man of incorruptible integrity is in himself a treasury to a nation. "The king's *name* is a tower of strength."

We hope our countrymen will give heed to these suggestions. If the time is ever to come in this country when, in choosing a President, we ought to take the wisest, strongest, bravest, best man, and no other, we believe *that* time now draws nigh. And what shall hinder us from such a choice? Such is the comparatively unpartisan state of the old parties, such the general unanimity of purpose among all loyal and patriotic citizens, that the nation is likely to be freer in making its nomination for the next canvass than for any previous presidential struggle for many years. With no old political favorites to be necessarily rewarded—no old debts to be settled with former placemen and continuous office-seekers—no unavoidable bargains to be made with balance-holding factions—no needful consultations with ancient and dry-rotted lobbymen at Albany and Washington — no enemy, domestic or foreign, respectable enough to be compromised with—no other object to be promoted than the welfare of the country—why should there be a committal to any other candidate than to the best man for the high place?

Nor, this time, can the common plea of "availability" be set up as an apology for putting aside such a man for some one more accidentally usable, because more politically influential. We believe the loyal party will be strong enough at the next election to carry its candidate, whoever he may be. The true presidential campaign will be waged before and during the convention, rather than after the nomination. It will not be so hard to *elect* the best candidate as to *nominate* him. This is a reason which not only justifies but urges an early survey of the entire field. Let loyal men unite, speedily and heartily, upon the one and only object of choosing THE BEST MAN.

Who, then, is he? We repeat, it is not time to be rashly nominating; but it is time to be prudently considering. The nation, just now, is busy with something besides candidating—having a toilsome task upon its hands, having a bloody sweat upon its brow. But while the blacksmith is hammering he can be thinking. It is idle to say that because the rebellion is on our hands, therefore we are to banish all thoughts of an approaching change of administration—a change that may either be the safety or the ruin of the country. Besides, if the country is expected to be able, next summer, to carry on a presidential and a military campaign, both at once, it is just as able, this spring, to be not only conquering the rebellion, but at the same time taking a wise forethought of the future, first of principles and afterward of men.

The ship of state tosses on a rough sea; the bells will

soon ring a change of watch; who shall take the next turn at the helm? Let it be the safest man to steer in a storm, the surest man to find the way into port and safe anchorage. Give us the wisest head, the stoutest arm, the bravest heart. And may God keep the ship!

February 18, 1864.

A WEEK IN A JURY BOX.

IT is provoking, when your business is at the thickest, when your engagements are most pressing, when your office imperatively needs your daily presence, to find yourself suddenly imprisoned, shut out from your clamorous duties, kept from your desk from the beginning of Monday to the end of Saturday, all on account of a bit of meddlesome paper with this inscription:

To Mr. ———:

You are hereby summoned to attend a term of the Circuit Court, and Court of Oyer and Terminer, at the Court-Room, City Hall, in the city of Brooklyn, as a Petit Juror, said term commencing on the 20th day of January, at ten o'clock in the forenoon. Fine for non-attendance twenty-five dollars each day.

Signed, ———

Commissioner of Jurors.

What will you do? Get excused? Not while such a man sits on the bench as the judge who ordered that summons. He excuses nobody on the plea of other engagements. He believes that a man who has important business of his own is just the juror to sit on important business of others. He is right.

The other day, when one of the busiest men in Brooklyn, on being summoned by a like notice, made the common excuse of urgent business, he was denied. He then offered to pay the twenty-five dollars, but the judge said, "I can make it a hundred." "And I," responded the merchant, "can pay it." "But," interposed the judge, "I can make it five hundred." "I can pay that," retorted the gentleman, a little excited. "But," added the judge, with dignity, "I can imprison you if you refuse." "Then," said the rich man, resigning himself and smiling, "I will do my duty and serve."

The duty of competent men to serve on juries, without besieging the court with excuses, needs to be urged in these cities; for lawyers and judges have complained, for years past, that trustworthy men are too ready to beg off on unworthy pleas, leaving their places to be filled by the hangers-on of court-rooms, who are in constant waiting for a chance to get a dollar a day.

The jury is the most valuable part of the court; the part which public justice could least afford to abolish; the part which the people would be least willing to surrender.

Though judges decide questions of law, and juries questions of fact, yet the majority of cases in court involve both law and fact, and need both judge and jury. But the bulk of these cases could be more safely left to a jury alone, than to a judge alone. The Turkish cadi, without appeal, makes dangerous decisions; twelve beggars of the street would be safer. We believe that, in general, the decisions of juries give greater satisfaction than the decisions of judges. Of course, after every trial, either plaintiff or defendant must have the sour lip. But the fact is noticeable that the loser usually goes out of court with less grumbling after a verdict than after a judgment. A jury-trial yields an equitable decision based on common sense, rather than a technical judgment based on a written statute. It is, moreover, an appeal to the people; a *vox populi* of twelve voices; an epitome of public opinion; an indication of what the mass of men would say of the case if the mass of men could know the facts.

One of the happy peculiarities of the jury-trial is seen in the accidental groupings of the jury-box. For instance, the jury called by the subpœna above quoted, consisted of twelve men drawn from ten different occupations in life; —two merchants, a fisherman, two carpenters, a jeweler, a house-painter, a chandler, two builders, a gardener, and an editor;—persons in different ranks of fortune, a few rich, and one or two very poor; some educated, and others illiterate; some Catholics, one Jew, the rest Protestants; all sitting together in the jury-room, taking part in a common discussion, having an equal voice in the debate, and each holding a veto over the other eleven. Such an institution not only promotes justice, but levels all ranks, makes common ground for all classes, and equalizes all citizens. It teaches the money-broker that the law counts him no better than the mortar-carrier. It lifts the poor man into peerage with the aristocracy. The street-omnibus in which every man may ride, the public meeting which every man may attend, the ballot-box at which every man may vote, all teach to the different classes of society the democratic lesson of their common equality; but the lesson has nowhere a more impressive example than in the discussions of the jury-room when the panel happens to comprise the extremes of poverty and wealth, of rudeness and culture, of humbleness and station. Where can be seen a more significant illustration of the free spirit of our institutions than in the spectacle, sometimes witnessed in court, of the vast interests of a millionaire, or of a great company or corporation, hanging for verdict upon the consenting voice of one obscure, humble mechanic, who has left his jack-plane or his trowel at a summons to sit on a jury in order to decide, with a poor man's sense, a conflict of rich men's claims? It shows that while in some respects in this country, or in some parts of it, we degrade Man, denying him his dignity and stripping him of his rights, yet in other instances the law invests him, regardless of rank or station, with a power and responsibility that fully show the high value which our free institutions set upon the humblest citizen.

The jury we have mentioned lacked one element of justice: it had among its members no women; and yet the chief case we considered during that busy week was one involving the property and honor of a woman. A jury of men, however much they may be disposed to redress a woman's wrongs, so far as they can estimate them, nevertheless cannot in human nature so accurately feel or guage a woman's sense of outrage and suffering as women can for their own sex. There are subtle injuries to women (particularly to mothers of young children) which courts can never justly adjudicate until woman's ear shall listen on the jury, and woman's voice shall speak in the verdict. On the other hand, under the specious complaint of an artful woman, a man sometimes suffers unduly in court because a jury of his own chivalrous sex are apt to show a preposterous partiality toward a fair-faced accuser, and an amazing tenderness toward a well-acted woe. In such cases, if a few of the jurors were sensible women, the woman, and not the man, would be made to feel the whip of justice. The day will come when both sexes will unite in saying that women shall consult on the jury, shall plead at the bar, and shall adjudge from the bench.

A jury is a great educator to the twelve men who compose it. This education is of a kind important for all citizens to learn; yielding not only a wider knowledge of the law, but inspiring men with a greater respect for justice; aiding the cause of good government by teaching men to be mindful of each other's rights. The protection of individual rights is the chief end of government; but this end is attained only in proportion as the people are educated into a thorough loyalty to righteous law. A man who serves on a jury is a more careful citizen afterward. A man who never serves loses something himself, and the commonwealth loses something through his loss. A juryman's reward is not a mere silver dollar a day, but an increased reverence for equity, a clearer sagacity in business, and an instructive insight into human nature.

A rough fellow, addicted to street scuffles, happened to be summoned on a jury in Brooklyn, and sat through the trials of half a dozen fellows like himself, for disorderly conduct on the highway. After the verdict was rendered, he said to a spectator, on leaving the court-room, "The jury-box has taught me a lesson which I mean to heed. The law of the land insists that all men shall keep the peace. The law is right, and I have been wrong. I mean after this to mend my behavior." In view of such influence, it is no disadvantage to the community that rude men—boisterous, refractory, and irreverent to the law—sometimes find themselves upon juries; for, thus placed, they receive from bar and bench and jury-room many a salutary lesson.

It is, therefore, with questionable propriety that the large class of men composing the Fire Department in these cities, men of bluff and hardy manners, men of a commendable but sometimes over-excited enthusiasm, men who too often are tempted into infractions of the law, are exempted from jury duty. The great mass of that impetuous throng who lead or follow rattling engines over stony streets at midnight, are just such persons as need the knowledge, the example, and the influence which other men get in the paneled jury, and which cannot be got so surely anywhere else. Nor is it wise in the municipal government of this city, or in the legislative government of this state, to set forth jury service as a burden from which the citizen, whether a fireman or not, may purchase exemption by other forms of duty. Even clergymen, who likewise are a class privileged to decline the commissioner's subpœna, would find no small instruction by sitting for a few days in the year under the influences and responsibilities of jury trials and verdicts.

Therefore, good reader, good citizen, when next you get a summons to sit with eleven of your peers—mayhap your betters—do not vex yourself into impatience, or carry an excuse on your lips, but count yourself honored by the call, and do your duty. It is a reasonable service, not to be neglected, not to be evaded, not to be shirked, but to be performed. It is such a service rendered to your neighbor as you may need your neighbor to render to you. It is part and parcel of that law of laws, "Whatsoever ye would that men should do unto you, do ye even so unto them."

THE ONE BLOOD OF ALL NATIONS.

ARRYING as a figure-head the new and strange word Miscegenation, a little pamphlet was lately launched into a sudden tempest of criticism. Remaining a while on our table unread, our attention was specially called to it by noticing how savagely certain newspapers were abusing it. A book publicly sentenced to death always breaks jail and runs at large. This brochure—which for treatment is clever, unelaborate, and ill-considered, and for style is not quite good or bad—has had a many-voiced condemnation into fame.

The most reprehensible word in the English tongue—the one harder to pronounce than all others, and more shocking than a profane oath—is Amalgamation. Miscegenation is a substitute for this; coined from the Latin *Miscere*, to mix, and *Genus*, race; the mixing of races; used in this pamphlet, both in a general sense as signifying the interchange of blood between all the world's races, and in a special sense as signifying the union of blacks and whites in this country.

On such a topic, if John Milton himself were to write an essay, he would be speared, knived, and tomahawked with all the cutlery of criticism. The authorship of the pamphlet is a well-kept secret; at least, it is unknown to us. Nor, after a somewhat careful reading, are we convinced that the writer is in earnest. Our first impression was, and remains, that the work was meant as a piece of pleasantry—a burlesque on what are popularly called the fanatical notions of the radical men named therein. Certainly the essay is not such a one as any of these thinkers would have written on the subject, though some of their speeches are conspicuously quoted in it.

The author's endeavor is to demonstrate an equality between whites and blacks, physiologically, intellectually, and spiritually; that a mingling of well-developed races produces a race superior to either of its component parts; that such a union of whites and blacks in this country is essential to the highest American progress. This general course of discussion deviates into various side issues; the author writing sometimes soberly, sometimes extravagantly, sometimes absurdly, always readably. If written in earnest, the work is not thorough enough to be satisfactory; if in jest, we prefer Sidney Smith—or McClellan's Report. Still, to be frank, we agree with a large portion of these pages, but disagree heartily with another portion.

In the epitome of conclusions, we find the following statement:

"As the rebellion has been caused not so much by slavery as the base prejudice resulting from a distinction of color, perfect peace cannot be restored to our country until that distinction shall measurably cease, by a general absorption of the black race by the white."

Certainly there is very little truth in this statement, or in its deduction. The Rebellion was caused, not by Prejudice against Color, but by Slavery—the proof of which is, that no such prejudice exists at the South; it exists only at the North. Moreover, the author is inconsistent with himself—speaking here (p. 65) of "a general absorption of the black race by the white," whereas he has previously said just the opposite (p. 17), that "in the course of time the dark races must absorb the white." Nor do we agree that we are to wait for perfect peace in this country until that far-distant future (never to come at all) when all the various bloods that make up our nation—Yankee, German, Irish, English, African—shall be indistinguishably merged in one general current—untraceable outwardly by any individuality of feature or temperament. Has there never yet been peace in the world? But has there ever been any such requisite obliteration of all differences of race? Such a universal evenness is not possible. Why should such a pre-arranged and enforced unity be supposed necessary to the peace of this country? The Germans and the Irish on our soil, even before mingling their blood with ours, do not necessarily war against our peace. An Irishman is not a July rioter by nature; he is made so by Democracy and grog. And the Negro is naturally more peaceable than either Saxon or Celt. It is not half so necessary to American stability that we should absorb the Negro—so losing him by doubly gaining him—as that we should melt down and remould his master according to a better model of man. We are not colonizationists, or expatriationists; but as between getting rid of the negro or of his master, we prefer to let the worse man go, and the better stay. Is Jefferson Davis as loyal a citizen as his escaped coachman? Does Governor Pickens weigh an ounce to the pound with Robert Small?

We make another quotation:

"It is the duty of anti-slavery men everywhere to advocate miscegenation or the mingling of all the races on this continent."

Not at all; nor will it ever be; not even till the Day

of Judgment. It is no part of the duty of anti-slavery men—or of other sensible men—to direct people as to whom they should marry, or not marry. It is, on the contrary, the duty of all men to allow all others who wish to be married, to marry whom they wish. Marriage is an affair between the bride and the bridegroom—with perhaps a mother-in-law's advice thrown in. But beyond this, the interference of outside parties is impertinent. While however we do not advise the intermarriage of blacks and whites, any more than of whites and whites, we hold that, if they choose to intermarry, it is nobody's business but their own. Further than this, we hold that before a white slave-master becomes the father of a black woman's child, he ought to be her lawful, wedded husband. As a mere question of ethics, we would like to know *The Journal of Commerce's* opinion on this point. Will it favor us?

We quote once more:

"In the millennial future, the most perfect and highest type of manhood will not be white or black, but brown, or colored, and whoever helps to unite the various races of men, helps to make the human family the sooner realize its great destiny."

It takes a far-seeing man to know what is to happen in the "millennial future." We are living in a very unmillennial present, whose dust and smoke becloud our eyes into a blindness against to-morrow. But the idea of a scientific enterprise to intermingle existing populations according to a predetermined plan for reconstructing the human race—for flattening out its present varieties into one final unvarious dead-level of humanity—is so absurd that we are more than ever convinced such a statement was not written in earnest. Here also the writer once more contradicts himself; for, after having insisted, in an earlier chapter, that color comes solely of climate—that is, that a different sun and sky make in time a different human face—he here holds that the whole human family will finally be one-colored. But in that day will there be only one climate in the world?

Dismissing the pamphlet, what is the truth concerning the intermingling of races? To settle the question justly, one must judge by broad intervals of time; for races are plants of slow growth and require centuries for their development. On a chosen spot, a race plants itself, builds institutions, founds an empire, all as if for permanence. But Time, the patient destroyer of all things, unbuilds the empire, rots the institutions, disintegrates the nation itself—recomposing its elements until its former identity is lost, and a new stock takes the place of the old. Human races are evanescent: only the Human Race remains. Looking at the present dominant clans of the world, what are their constituent parts? They are the remains of former races. Every great nation was married into its greatness by a union of many stocks. The present English nation is built upon the fragments of many former nationalities, just as the English language is a polyglot of other languages mingling to make one. The French nation is a rope of many strands—as witness the history which Cæsar left of its early beginnings; or which other historians give of its later re-beginnings—the Carlovingian and Merovingian dynasties. Like a coat of many colors, every great nation is a patch-work of the shreds and remnants of former tribes. The American people are in like manner a stock of many grafts. An amalgamation of races is going on here to an extent almost without a parallel in history. Every country under the sun is making some gift of its blood to our American veins. Immigration from foreign lands was never so multitudinous as now. Leaving out of view our native-born Americans of English descent, there are enough other stocks on this soil to make three other nations—namely, the Irish, the Germans, and the Negroes. Even the Negroes number one million more than did the whole population of the United States at the adoption of the Constitution. These three stocks have come hither not to establish themselves as distinct peoples, but each to join itself to each, till all together shall be built up into the monumental nation of the earth! Such interminglings of course are of slow growth, and not to be hastened. Thrifty nations are not grown like hot-house plants, by forcing. Nature, like God, is patient. Natural affinity between individuals is the one and only law by which races intermingle. Such affinities ripen tardily—not only between persons of different nationalities, but of different opinions and social position in the same nationality. There was a time in England when the Red Rose would not marry the White; a time in New England when a church-member would not marry a non-church-member. Twenty years ago, an American who married a foreigner was thought to have overstepped propriety; a narrowness of prejudice with which sensible people nowadays have no sympathy. But because we have Germans and Irish in this country, shall we undertake a political movement to persuade them to intermarry with Americans? Or shall we undertake a similar officious and impertinent movement with blacks and whites? To make the next Presidential campaign, as our pamphleteer suggests, turn on the advocacy of marriages between any two classes of our community—Saxons with Celts, fair faces with dark, Northerners with Southerners, Down-East Yankees with Californians—is so absurd as to furnish us another reason for thinking these piquant pages are a snare to catch some good folk for a laugh at them afterward.

We believe the whole human race are one family—born, every individual, with a common prerogative to do the best he can for his own welfare; that in political societies, all men, of whatever race or color, should stand on an absolute equality before the law; that whites and blacks should intermarry if they wish, and should not unless they wish; that the negro is not to be allowed to remain in this country, but is to remain here without being allowed—asking nobody's permission but his own; that we shall have no permanent settlement of the negro question till our haughtier white blood, looking the negro in the face, shall forget that he is black, and remember only that he is a citizen.

But, on the other hand, we do not believe, with this book, that the rebellion arose from prejudice against color—for if the slaves were white, instead of black, their masters would be no less unwilling to give them up; nor do we believe in any forecasted scheme or humanly-planned union of races; nor that the next Presidential election, nor any succeeding one, should have nothing to do with Miscegenation; nor can we see any reason why the Human Family shall exhibit in the future any less diversity of races than now—but more.

Whether or not, according to this anonymous prediction, the universal complexion of the human family at the millennium "will not be white or black, but brown or colored," we certainly believe that the African-tinted members of our community will in the future gradually bleach out their blackness. The facts of to-day prove this beyond denial. Already three-fourths of the colored people of the United States have white blood in their veins. The two bloods have been gradually intermingling ever since there were whites and blacks among our population. This intermingling will continue. Under Slavery, it has been forced and frequent; under Freedom, it will be voluntary and infrequent. But by-and-by —counting the years not by Presidential campaigns, but by centuries—the negro of the South, growing paler with every generation, will at last completely hide his face under the snow.

February 25, 1864.

LYMAN BEECHER AND ROXANA FOOTE.

THE Autobiography of the Rev. Dr. Lyman Beecher, edited by his son Charles, awakens vividly our recollection of a venerable man seen not long ago walking the streets of Brooklyn, or rising to speak in the prayer-meetings at Plymouth Church, or sitting an attentive listener in the great congregation; his silvery hair falling low upon his shoulders; his fine appearance half disguising his infirmities; but his conversation garrulous and wandering, showing a strong man shorn of his strength—a giant withered to a child. We recall also, as if it were yesterday, the tolling of a bell—the gathering of a great assemblage—the funeral discourse—the solemn strain of the organ—the serene face of the dead. Few men who die leave such living names as this old man's. Lyman Beecher will not be forgotten so long as Hopkins, Dwight, Payson, and Taylor are remembered.

The present book is something of a novelty in bookmaking—an autobiography not written by its subject, but snatched from his lips at intervals by his questioning family, and penned on the spot; many of the pages standing in the form of question and answer, the interrogator's name indicated by initials; making altogether an inartistic, loosely-joined, unsatisfactory, yet fascinating record—resembling, in parts, the report of a cross-examination in a law trial.

Through the perspective of such reminiscences, one sees the religious world under far different aspects from those of our own day; going back to a time when Hannah More was the star among religious writers; when Buchanan's travels in the East first awoke among the churches a spirit of. missions; when pious people used to read *The Christian Observer;* when Dr. Mason was the chief pulpit-orator of New York; when Gardiner Spring was beginning to be known as a young man eloquent; and when clergymen, at meetings of association, drank flip to unsteadiness and smoked pipes to blindness. Dr. Beecher's public life stretched through many varying phases of opinion, social, political, and religious. He witnessed the passing away of many bad customs, and the adoption of better; also the fading-out of much that was good in the early days, that has not been since replaced. His own hand helped mightily to work out the beneficial changes which he lived to see accomplished. A power in his day and generation, the witness of his work remains. Never a conservative, nor ever quite a radical, he was a man who stood in the advance, if not in the van, and if not always a pioneer, yet always a leader. Seldom does it fall to a man's lot to exert so much moulding influence on one's times as God permitted to this sturdy minister. Multitudes now living—pillars of the commonwealth—confess that they received from this Christian teacher the solid foundation of their religious training. Reaching with the living voice, through a long life of incessant preaching, an uncounted host of impressible human souls, he set his seal upon them "in demonstration of the spirit and with power." A friend at our elbow, happening in upon us as we write, says: "I owe to Dr. Beecher's preaching more than to that of any other man, living or dead." So his life is not registered merely in this book, but is at this hour an elemental part of the manhood of many of the bravest and noblest men of the land.

But the most interesting personage in this family history (to our own reading) is not Lyman Beecher, but Roxana Foote, his first wife. Her native endowments of mind, her literary attainments, her womanly richness of disposition, and her comeliness of look and mien, made her a fascinating character in all the great circle at whose centre she was set as the fit wife of the most influential minister in New England. Never was a happier marriage—no shadow ever resting on it till the final shadow of death. Her piety was of that serene, exalted, full-hearted kind that so distinguishes naturally-gifted women when once they become touched by the grace of God. Though her strength of mind was such that her husband in later life said she was the only person he ever met whom he considered his match in an argument, yet she was so mistrustful of herself that she could hardly pass through a social company without blushing, and could never muster courage to conduct a prayer-meeting of women. One comes upon the successive traces of her in these pages with the same feeling as in following a lovely heroine through a romance. While living in Easthampton, Long Island, where not a carpet was to be seen in any house in the town, she suddenly surprised the community by weaving one with her own hands, and skilfully painting it with figures of roses—on which her little children walked with never-ceasing admiration ; and in like manner she strewed under their tender feet roses from the garden of the Lord, on which they cease not to walk at this day. As Tintoret had heart to paint his daughter while she lay in death, this heroic mother of a dead babe had strength amid her heart-break to ply her pencil and brush in order to snatch from the grave a likeness which only her own skill could be procured to take.

Riding with her husband one winter night, under a full moon, she said, to his astonishment, "I shall not be with you long;" and, on his asking why, replied, "I have had a vision of Heaven and its blessedness." And when, a few weeks afterward, came a sickness threatening death, she drew nigh the closing hour amid such vivid forelookings toward the other life, that she could hardly sustain their blessed burden upon her soul; saying that if they were continued, she must be overwhelmed. Dying while eight little children wept at her bedside, she then and there gave her sons to the ministry with such a prayer of faith that God could not suffer it to go unanswered.

Such a life, and death, and memory make it no wonder that, forty years after the closing of her grave, the old man, looking back on their letters of courtship, should have written in a trembling hand on the back of one: "*Roxana, beloved still, this December* 5, 1854. *Lyman Beecher.*" Still later, when in a failing hour he lay between life and death, too far gone to recognize the faces or names of his children, and when no word spoken elicited any evidence of consciousness, some one happened to say "Roxana," and that magic name of his first love instantly brought him back out of thick darkness into light! This is an incident not mentioned in these pages, yet it is as beautiful as anything in human life, proving that love is a strength outlasting human weakness, a fire that burns after the flesh has fallen to ashes, a life that conquers death and crowns itself with immortality!

There is one feature in the character of Lyman Beecher,

illustrated in this book, and known without the help of any book, which makes the serious reader rebuke and humble himself at the example. We mean the extraordinary fidelity, earnestness, sincerity, and zeal of this Christian minister, who, in prosecuting his work, exhibited such an activity, pertinacity, and anxiety as would long before have broken down a less fibrous frame, and exhausted a less buoyant spirit. Preaching often nine times a week, with an expenditure of electric force sufficient to conquer and awe down great congregations; unwearied in personal religious conversation with inquirers; attending and managing numberless ecclesiastical councils; maintaining an extensive correspondence with ministers, editors, and college professors; writing constantly for the press, and writing so carefully that he would spend months in preparing a single sermon for publication; riding gallantly in many a joust of theological controversy; suffering many personal bereavements, shattering to the strongest man's strength; making constant battle against poverty; tireless in work, both in-doors and out of doors, in season and out of season; counting not his life dear unto himself:—for all these things, and many more, we look upon him as a model minister of Jesus Christ—as an almost apostolic reproduction of single-minded devotion to the Master's service—as a Christian whose life puts to shame our own barrener lives, and leaves us, after reading this book, in despair of this attainment.

MR. LINCOLN'S GLORY AND MR. JOHNSON'S SHAME.

THE re-inauguration of President Lincoln and the inauguration of Vice-President Johnson were twin ceremonies which we had the fortune and the misfortune to witness last week.

Mr. Lincoln showed a grayer head and a more careworn face than four years ago. A peculiarly sad and thoughtful expression in his eyes, and a quaint and pleasing homeliness in his gestures, gave a touch of undeniable majesty to this singular man. His brief and pithy words—characteristic of their author's home-spun style—were freighted with noble meanings, precious beyond all the earlier utterances of his pen or tongue, and proving not only that his heart has been touched and mellowed by the nation's sorrows, but that his mind has greatened to the task which Providence has assigned him in the nation's struggle. Every succeeding utterance which he gives to the public proves his moral vision to be more and more anointed into a discernment of those great principles of justice and righteousness whereby God governs governments. The old Inaugural of 1861 was, in morals, a generation behind the new Inaugural of 1865. Plant a white lily in the spring, watch it day by day, and its growth seems slow; but measure the stalk at each month's end, and the gardener marvels at the thriftiness. Looking at the government four years ago, and looking at it to-day, we cannot help exclaiming, What hath God wrought! The President of the United States, who at the beginning of his first official term volunteered to return fugitive slaves to their bonds, announced last December his determination to resign his office rather than disgrace it by such a deed, and uttered on Saturday last a sentiment so lofty and prophetic that it cannot fade from the memory of this generation: "If you will," says he, "that the war continue until all the wealth piled by the bondman's two hundred and fifty years of unrequited toil shall be sunk, and until every drop of blood drawn with the lash shall be paid by another drawn with the sword, as was said three thousand years ago, so still it must be said, 'The judgments of the Lord are true and righteous altogether!'" This is the utterance of a man who bends his knees, and who uplifts his face to the heavens for help. So long as such a spirit animates the head of the Government, the President's minor errors may go unchidden of his countrymen. So, once again, we repeat the people's prayer, "God bless Abraham Lincoln!"

And now, concerning the Vice-President and the humiliating spectacle which on that day he furnished to the world, shall we speak, or keep silent? Perhaps there exists some good reason why the sad truth should be suppressed, but no such reason have we yet discerned. We cannot, therefore, join with our three neighbors, *The Tribune*, *The Times*, and *The Evening Post*, in pardoning with silence the great disgrace which Andrew Johnson inflicted on his country at that impressive hour. Had the tables been turned, and a similar offence been committed by Mr. Pendleton, we can hardly believe that these journals would have laid their fingers on their lips in a hush of criticism. As for ourselves, we trust we are habitually slow to speak ill of public men, even of such as deserve dispraise; but if such an appearance as Mr. Johnson presented during his inauguration is to pass without public rebuke, then there no longer remains to the press any duty of impartial criticism of men in official stations.

Once or twice, we have felt it our duty to speak against the excessive use of intoxicating liquors by some of our statesmen. It may be asked, What is the duty of journalists in such cases? It seems to us plain. We hold that if a public man is drunken in a private company, he is not amenable to comment in the newspapers; but if drunken while acting his part on a public occasion, his offence is against the public, and should never be shielded from the just punishment of public censure.

In the Senate Chamber, on the fourth of March, in presence of the Senate, of the House, of the Cabinet, of the Supreme Court, of the Diplomatic Corps, of the newspaper press, of a gallery of ladies, and (during part of the time) of the President of the United States—on an occasion to be for ever historic—the Vice-President elect presented himself to take his solemn oath of office in a state of intoxication.

Not in anger but in sorrow do we chronicle this fact, which we have no just right to suppress.

A few weeks ago, the Speaker of the House of Representatives was commanded by vote of that body to administer a public reprimand to a member who had committed a similar offence with less conspicuous shame. If a member of the House is to be punished for such an act, shall the President of the Senate go unrebuked?

Of course, the Senate will choose its own method of reaching the case—a method which, we trust, will be kind, moderate, and just. But meanwhile, it is the plain duty of Mr. Johnson either to apologize for his conduct, or to resign his office. In the name of an insulted people we demand that so great an affront to the dignity of the Republic shall be made to bear a fit penalty, atonement, and warning.

After the President had delivered his inaugural, and the Vice-President had staggered through his oath; in other words, after the glory and the shame of the day were over; every spectator, as the multitude broke up, turned to his neighbor, and with a look of earnestness seldom seen on all men's faces at one time, exclaimed, "God spare the life of Abraham Lincoln, and forbid that Andrew Johnson shall ever occupy the Presidential Chair."

March 9, 1865

THE EXCURSION TO FORT SUMTER.

EDITORIAL CORRESPONDENCE.

AT SEA, OFF BARNEGAT,
HOMEWARD BOUND, April 20, 1865.

TO THE INDEPENDENT:

HILE the steamer is rolling and pitching, and half the company are queasy in their berths, I, your editor, turned correspondent—a solitary sitter in this deserted cabin, rocking without a rocking-chair, tasting an occasional qualm of mortality, yet sweetly medicined by this confronting cluster of Port Royal roses—force my unwilling pen into a hurried story of the hoisting of the old flag at Sumter, and of our historic sea-voyage that began in joy and ends in grief.

What a memorable party Capt. Gadsden weighed anchor with, a fortnight since, on the Arago! I cannot name them in any accurate order of honor, except that the hero of the expedition was Gen. Robert Anderson, and next in the assigned rank of the occasion was a certain clergyman of Brooklyn, who, having been often taunted with the query, "Why don't you go to the South?" at last answered, "Behold I go!" But the observed of all observers was William Lloyd Garrison, accompanied by his life-long co-worker, George Thompson —noble twins in friendship, and equal veterans in the cause of emancipation in two nations. Then we had Gen. Dix, Joseph Holt, Henry Wilson, Justice Swayne of the

Supreme Court of the United States, Lieut.-Gov. Charles Anderson of Ohio, brother of the General, and himself one of the true heroes of the war, Gen. Townsend of the War Department, Rev. Dr. Storrs of Brooklyn (who preached on Sunday from the capstan as a pulpit), Judge Kelley and Daniel Dougherty of Philadelphia (the latter of whom does whatever is " natural for an Irishman's son "), Abbott A. Low, President of the New York Chamber of Commerce, the venerable Joseph Hoxie, author of an unpublished cyclopedia of anecdotes, and other brilliant gentlemen whose names are just at this moment jarred from my memory by this lurching ship. But I must not forget Gen. Doubleday, and a good story he told. After the surrender of Sumter, a hotel-keeper on Sullivan's Island, whose house had been hit by a stray shot, haughtily accosted Capt. Doubleday, saying, " Sir, why did you fire at my house? a hotel is not a fort." " Well," replied the captain, "you once gave me a squalid room and a villainous bed, and I thought I would take my revenge by putting a hole through your wall! " That answer brevets its author a wit.

South Carolina gave her first kiss to our invading feet at Hilton Head. What a golden morning! What songs of mocking-birds! What wild white roses, and orange blooms! The gay green of the Southern grass, the palmettos, the live oaks festooned with moss, the wondrous magnolias yet unflowered, the cactus and the geranium growing as weeds by the wayside—all these were lustrous reminders how far we had wandered from Yankeeland. Nevertheless, the wonderful sea-beach was Brother Jonathan's Nahant over again, only ampler and grander.

In a strange country the pleasantest thing one's eyes can look upon is the face of an old friend. And who should be the first man to greet us but Colonel Stewart L. Woodford, our former companion on many an anti-slavery platform, and now gallantly bearing his country's eagle on his shoulder! No young man in the nation has a more eloquent tongue or a more knightly heart.

Suddenly General Littlefield made a military arrest of our whole party of fanatics and incendiaries, conveying us in ambulances to Mitchelville—a neighboring village of blacks, and named after that noble astronomer who, ceasing to look toward the stars, dwells now among them. Are negroes competent for self-government? Here is a settlement of three thousand, who choose their officers, make their laws, and regulate their political economy as in a New England town. Nor is New York half so well governed; for a mayoralty according to Murchison, is better than a mayoralty "according to Gunther." A meeting in the chapel brought us face to face with these villagers. Never shall we forget that scene. Never shall our ears lose the remembered music of that day's solemn songs of praise. No soul was unmelted. A company of world-famed abolitionists, speaking for the first time in their lives on the soil of Calhoun, to an audience of tearful, prayerful, thankful, emancipated slaves, presented a spectacle of moral sublimity such as no one of the spectators may ever again behold.

Fort Sumter is a Coliseum of ruins. Battered, shapeless, overthrown, it stands in its brokenness a fit monument of the broken rebellion. Round its base lie innumerable cannon-balls, enough for a bombardment—cankered now by the salt waves, and perishing with peaceful rust. The parapets are ragged as a saw-edge; and one who walks them should have the sure footing of a goat upon the rocks. When the flag ascended, the amphitheatre saluted it with five thousand human voices, and the battlements replied with two hundred guns. How men's hearts cannonaded their breasts! How the joyful blood frolicked in our veins! The fallen honor of the nation was upraised! Straining eyes looked up through tears at the ensign fluttering in the clouds, and grateful hearts sent their thanksgivings to the heavens above. Rent and tattered was the banner, yet amid all its gashes not a star had been stricken out—happy omen that, despite the nation's wounds, not a State shall be lost! A full hour was passed in a merry clamor of patriotism before the jubilant throng could compose themselves for the oration. Finally, Mr. Beecher arose and set his strong voice into a struggle against a sea-breeze that kept whisking his locks and flapping his manuscripts, and threatened at first to wrestle him down, but the man who conquered a Liverpool mob was not to surrender to an east wind. Manly, wise, and eloquent was the speech—of which, good readers of *The Independent*, judge ye, for I here enclose it, word for word. But no speech could rise to the height of that occasion: what *could*, except the flag itself? How wonderful are the ways of that Providence who cast down the nation's flag at Sumter till it should touch the lowly slave of the Carolinas, that it might rise again, and lift him with it to Liberty and Equality.

Charleston is a city of desolation—recalling our early school-book pictures of the gaunt remains of Thebes or Nineveh. It looks the skeleton of its former self. Ten acres are strewn with the ruins of fine houses, brought to ashes by fire-brands of the rebels—in some places not one stone left upon another, while here and there a solitary wall or gable end stands a tell-tale of the general destruction. Of the buildings that remain, nearly half are crippled with gaping wounds from General Gillmore's angels of the swamps.

What havoc that marksman made! Six miles off, he would sight a gun at the rattlesnake's nest, and crack an egg at every shot! Generally a shell would strike a roof, pass downward slant-wise through two or three stories, and come out through the wall—sometimes making a hole big enough to drive a horse through! Eighteen new windows were thus made in the Charleston Hotel; and the Bank of South Carolina was broken a dozen times after its original bankruptcy. In one of the churches a projectile knocked away eight of the ten commandments, leaving these twain: "Thou shalt not steal;" "Thou shalt not commit adultery"—but there was no need of cracking these, for they were broken in Charleston long ago.

Calhoun's grave, spared by missiles, has been hacked by relic-seekers. I have no sympathy with hammerers at tomb-stones. The dead have a right to undisquieted ashes. As my own chief relic of fallen Babylon, I chose to pluck a handful of clover which I found growing among the ruins of Secession Hall.

Gentlemanly, uncertain Governor Aiken's house remains untouched—yet despoiled inside by his own act; for, fearing that the shells would break into his wine-cellar, he sent into the country his unpurchasable three thousand bottles of old Madeira, and his elegant silver plate; and Sherman's thirsty soldiers found the wine and drank it; and an esthetic negro was discovered in the woods frying bacon on the Governor's silver tray! So the negroes now constitute the first families.

How they turned out on Citadel Square to welcome

William Lloyd Garrison and his fellow agitators, escorting us to our hotel by a procession a mile in length, of men, women, and children, unconscious of the curse of Ham, and singing Glory Hallelujah. And how grand were the meetings in Zion's church—a great edifice crowded three times with a congregation of three thousand of the happiest human beings whom we ever saw compacted into one place—each successive meeting outrivalling the other in beauty of spirit.

On the morning of departure, the grateful blacks followed us to the wharf, where one of their number, a true orator, waving a flag in one hand, and clasping his two little children in the other, exclaimed with a sudden inspiration of eloquence, "O men of the North, you now see why I love this flag: it makes my children mine, who never were mine before!" All ears tingled at that speech!

Arm-laden with flowers, the gifts of a hundred hands as we passed through the crowd, we made our parting speeches from the quarter-deck; and as the vessel glided into the stream, the same dark-faced orator knelt at the wharf's edge, holding up the flag in one hand, and pointing fixedly at it with the other—making himself a statue of patriotism—a beautiful and affecting tableau—the last sight we saw of that strange-fated city, whose great men have been humbled and whose lowly have been exalted.

Outward bound, and whither? The Arago returning without us, the swift Suwo Nada (unimpeded by her Japanese name) was to wing us southward to Florida, that we might pluck ancient mosses in St. Augustine. Little did we think, while one flag was rising to the peak at Sumter, how all flags would sink the next day to half-mast! Like an unpredicted eclipse was the awfulness of the gloom. Pleasure withered out of our thoughts and fell a dead leaf, frost-bitten. Straightway our prow plunged homeward-bound. And now on this third sorrowful day since the great shock, it seems as if we were bearing in our sepulchral ship the good man's murdered body, and must hasten to the shore to lay it sacredly in the greenest of graves. Yonder stretches the familiar coast that in one hour more will terminate our clouded voyage. O stricken country!—darkened at noonday, wrapped in the shadow of death, clothed with a funeral pall!—into what grief shall we find thee cast down! May the God of the Pilgrims choose the hour of thy mourning to give thee His benediction of Liberty and Peace!

THE WHITE FEATHER.

"THE decree of a council," said Cotton Mather, "hath no more force than there is force in the reason of it." The National Committee of the Republican party have just issued to the American people an address which, with sorrow, we pronounce repugnant to the moral sense of those American citizens who are inflexibly determined not to compromise Impartial Suffrage. The country is in too critical a condition, the safety of Southern loyalists is too greatly imperiled, the peace and order of the future are too gravely threatened, to permit this address to go forth as representing, as pledging, and particularly as binding, the radical party.

For eighteen months, the daily topic of men's talk has been the reconstruction of the Union. Unanimity of opinion does not prevail. Opposing plans divide the nation into opposing parties, and subdivide parties into opposing sections. The Republican party is divided between the advocates of re-admission without securing the negro's political rights, and the advocates of re-admission only after a guarantee of Impartial Suffrage. At the first trumpet in this war of debate, we took our place under the banner of Equal Rights. We joined the cause not to desert it, not to betray it, not to compromise it, but to fight for it till the victory. It is a sacred cause; the cause of liberty and justice; the cause of honor, magnanimity, and charity; the cause of peace and good will. The noblest men of the nation are its champions; the noblest women are its petitioners to Heaven for benediction upon it. In New England and on the prairies, bereaved families, mourning with proud grief over slain soldiers, recoil in their heart of hearts at any less ample fruition of the war than a settlement just, safe, and final. That settlement must include the political equality of American citizens, without questioning God's wisdom in varying the colors of "the human face divine." Planting their feet on the one true corner-stone of reconstruction, the radical party are not to be driven from it, not to be persuaded from it, not to be beguiled from it. They may, or may not, be a majority of the loyal North; the question of numbers remains to be settled by trial; but, whether they prove a majority or minority, they are not made of the fibre of cowards, and they will never surrender. Seeing their opportunity, they mean to grasp it; knowing their strength, they mean to use it; revering their cause, they mean to win it. At this moment the sky of promise is bright with a sacred light wherein we discern the emblem, "By this sign conquer."

When the National Committee of the Republican party unroll their official scroll, asking us to consent to a compromise of principle, asking us to pledge the Republican vote of next November to a reconstruction on the inadequate basis of the Fourteenth Amendment, asking us to leave the negro's political rights not only unsecured but undemanded, we can only exclaim, Heaven forbid! The Radical party, both North and South, regards the Fourteenth Amendment as no more adapted to be a basis of reconstruction than would be a tariff bill, or a fishery treaty, or a neutrality law. The amendment will not "reconstruct" anything; it will leave things as they are. It will not alter one whit the present relation of the white rebel to the black loyalist. It merely holds out a faint and far-off temptation to the Southern whites to enfranchise the Southern blacks, just as the constitution of 1789 held out, through its three-fifths clause, a faint and far-off temptation to slaveholders to set free their slaves. Slavery was not abolished under the mild influence of temptation, but under the strong influence of compulsion ; and the negro's enfranchisement will not be achieved by such temptation, but by such compulsion. The radical party, North and South, white and black, can assent to no reconstruction short of Impartial Suffrage. Is Congress already committed to a less perfect plan? Not at all. Congress is not committed for or against Impartial Suffrage. It has not tied its hands against the future. It is free to act as the emergency may require. If, next winter, it shall choose to make Impartial Suffrage the condition of restoration, it can do so ; and throughout the world all generous souls will cry Amen. We know personally every prominent member of Congress, and we know that the leaders do not mean to admit the unadmitted States on the mere adoption of the Fourteenth Amendment. Moreover, we know personally the leading radicals of the Republican party outside of Congress, and we know that they have no intention of making this unsatisfactory amendment the final measure of admission. To say, therefore, as the National Committee say, that, on condition of adopting the amendment, as Tennessee adopted it, "the door stands invitingly open" for the ten other States to return, is to make a promise to the ear and break it to the hope. There *is* a door, however, that *does* "stand invitingly open ;" and whenever these States shall choose to enter through this, they will be received with shouts, thanksgivings, and benedictions; it is the golden gate of impartial justice.

Is it asked, Why then was Tennessee admitted on the basis of the Fourteenth Amendment? We answer, Tennessee ought not to have been admitted on such a basis; her admission was a mingled crime and blunder. But the apology which Congress made for her admission was, that her attitude was exceptional — that her case was not to be a precedent for the ten other States. Already the admission of Tennessee without Impartial Suffrage proves the peril of admitting any of the other States except on this basis. Her legislature is about to remedy the deficiency of Congress, by enacting Impartial Suffrage at the next session. The same Tennesseeans who ask for the admission of their State without Impartial Suffrage said at Philadelphia that no remaining State of the ten could be safely admitted except with this guarantee.

We therefore repeat that Congress is not pledged, either by any existing offer of terms to the unreconstructed States, or by the precedent of Tennessee, to make the Fourteenth Amendment the basis of restoration. Even the New York *Times* acknowledges this fact. It says:

"The adoption or rejection of the amendment has nothing whatever to do, as the law now stands, with the admission or rejection of members from the Southern States. A bill providing for their admission on condition of its adoption was rejected by the House, and even if every Southern State should ratify the amendment to-morrow, Congress has not pledged itself in any way thereupon to admit their representatives in Congress."

This is true. To say, therefore, with the Syracuse

Republican Convention, or with the address of the National Republican Committee, that Congress will restore the ten waiting States if these States adopt the Fourteenth Amendment, is to misrepresent the issue.

Admirable is the National Committee's logic, compact and iron-bound, to prove the power of Congress over the whole question of reconstruction. We joyfully assent to the argument. But if Congress, and Congress only, has the right to say what shall be the basis of reconstruction, then what right has the National Committee to make any pledge to the rebels in advance of the action of Congress? In the name of the radical party, whose heart we know and whose voice we speak, we repudiate the Committee's pledge to the South as wholly unauthorized, invalid, and void.

Look at the following passage from the Committee's address:

"'But,' say some, 'the pending amendment is designed to *coerce* the South into according suffrage to her blacks.' Not so, we reply; but only to notify her ruling caste that we will no longer *bribe* them to keep their blacks in serfdom. An aristocracy rarely surrenders its privileges, no matter how oppressive, from abstract devotion to justice and right. It must have cogent, palpable reasons for so doing. We say, therefore, to South Carolina, 'If you persistently restrict all power to your 300,000 whites, we must insist that these no longer balance, in Congress and the choice of President, 700,000 Northern white freemen; but only 300,000. If you keep your blacks evermore in serfdom, it must not be because we tempted you so to do and rewarded you for so doing.'"

Can anything be more humiliating than to see the National Committee of the great Union party thus humbly kneeling at the feet of the aristocracy of the South? Do we employ a National Committee for the purpose of finding arguments against "coercing" the South? Has the Union party no higher duty to the negro than simply to "notify the ruling caste that we will no longer bribe them to keep their blacks in serfdom?" Is the party of Freedom keeping its solemn pledge to its four million allies by now saying to their former masters, "If you keep your blacks evermore in serfdom, it must not be because we tempted you to do so?" If the negro were a white man, instead of a black, the National Committee would never have thought of thus degrading him below the level of a traitor.

Coercing the South, forsooth! Did we not coerce the South into abrogating the ordinances of secession? Did we not coerce the South into repudiating the rebel debt? Did we not coerce the South into ratifying the abolition amendment? Without coercion, would the South have done these things? No. Neither, without coercion, will the South enact Impartial Suffrage. Look at it! This Committee thinks that, in order to achieve Impartial Suffrage, we ought not coerce, but bribe the South! What will history say of the victorious war party of the North, if, after executing a policy of coercion toward secession, coercion toward the rebel debt, coercion toward the Constitutional amendment, it attempted only a policy of bribery toward the negro? Which is of greater consequence in God's sight, the repudiation of the rebel debt, or the enfranchisement of the negro? Are millions of citizens of less consequence than millions of dollars? Is money of more worth than man? Have the National Committee forgotten that two sparrows are sold for a farthing, and that men are of more value than many sparrows?

The unanimous appeal of the Southern Loyalists at Philadelphia, representing the whole ten unreconstructed States, speaks with a pathos that ought to melt all hearts:

"We declare," say they, "that there can be no security for us or our children—there can be no safety for the country against the fell spirit of slavery now organized in the form of serfdom—unless the Government, by national authority, shall confer on every citizen in the States we represent the American birthright of impartial suffrage and equality before the law. This is the one all-sufficient remedy."

Are not these words solemn, noble, and just? Do not they far outshine the tarnished proclamation of the National Committee? Let the Republican party ask itself one thoughtful question: Ought we to reconstruct the ten remaining States so as to protect, or so as to destroy, the lives, property, and happiness of their loyal people? But if these ten States are to be reconstructed in the interest of loyalty, instead of treason, then let the unanimous demand of the Southern loyalists take the place of the less worthy appeal of the National Committee. If, after our pleasant fortune of a week's sojourn at Philadelphia with the noble representatives of the ten unreconstructed States, during which we learned their purposes and gauged their hearts, we had come home only to strike hands with the policy of the National Committee — a policy which the Southern loyalists came to the North to plead against as totally inadequate to their needs — we should account ourselves little less than treacherous to the best-tried and most-suffering friends of the Republic.

We say nothing in criticism of the good men who have

signed the National Committee's address. Some of these signers we honor and revere. How these lovers of justice can assent to such a policy of compromise is undoubtedly excused to their own minds, if not to ours. Horace Greeley gave to this address his revision and his name; but not his heart. His heart is hungry for justice, and craves more than the Committee's husk. Lieut.-Gov. Claflin of Massachusetts signed it; but his honored name is almost a synonym for Equal Rights. It is with heaviness of spirit that we find so many clear-sighted men holding back half their thoughts at a time when the country so urgently needs to hear every voice that can speak for Impartial Suffrage. Will the Republican party be injured by plain speech? No. It will be helped. But, whether helped or hindered, are we to give up to party what was meant for mankind? "Duties are ours," said Phillip Henry, "results are God's." The duty of the Republican party is to reject the pledge made by the National Committee; and the result may be safely left to that Great Disposer "who doeth all things well." O, ye of little faith! Never were thirsty pilgrims so willing to be led to a fountain of living waters, as the loyal party of this nation are now willing to be led to the safe ground of Impartial Justice. "Speak to the children of Israel, that they go forward."

SEPTEMBER 27, 1866.

THE FIRST AND THE SECOND REVOLUTION.

HAVE been walking to-day over the battle-ground of Lexington—the sacred field where our fathers "fired the shot heard round the world." Chipped with frosts and gnawed by time, a piece of perishing granite repeats to the pilgrim their imperishable names. "The blood of these martyrs," says the graven legend, "was the cement of the Union of these States." So thought the fathers who erected this monument in 1799. But this cement of blood did not prove strong enough to keep the States together. They flew asunder—breaking the sanguinary bonds. Henceforth let it be remembered that the cement of the American Union must be something more than the blood which has been shed in its defence. The only cement which can hold the Union together in the future is a vital principle—not buried dust. If men are not animated by justice to the living, they will not be restrained by reverence for the dead. The dead of the late war are as precious a legacy as were the dead of the Revolution. But unless the great cause for which our fresh army of martyrs died shall be placed beyond peril, on the safe foundation of impartial justice, the blood of the heroes of two wars for liberty will unite in crying from the ground.

* * * * * *

Like the rebuilding of Jerusalem, this nation is relaying its foundations. For this sublime task, Providence has given it choice either of the sand or the rock. While yet the nation was shaken of War, it chose the rock. But now that Peace has quieted the tumult, the Government is crumbling the rock into sand.

* * * * * *

The nation is informed from Washington that President Johnson's Administration has no power to impose Impartial Suffrage on the South, because it has no power to impose the same on the North. Is there then no difference between the relation of the Federal Government toward States that have been loyal, and toward States that have been rebel? Look at it. Has the President, for instance, a right to appoint a Provisional Governor for Connecticut? No. But he himself was appointed a Provisional Governor for Tennessee. Has he a right to dictate what Connecticut shall do with her State debt? No. But he commanded his premier to say that every rebel State should repudiate its rebel debt. Has he a right to demand that Connecticut shall ratify the prohibitory Amendment? No. But he gave notice to all the South that it must ratify the same amendment. Is it not effrontery, therefore, is it not mockery, is it not nonsense, to say that he is estopped from propounding suffrage as a condition of reconstruction, because, in order to fix it upon the South, he must at the same time fix it upon the North? If the Government can say to the conquered States, "Nullify your ordinances of secession, repudiate your rebel debt, abolish slavery, ratify the prohibitory amendment"—if it can say all this (and it *has* said all this), then it can also say, in the same breath, and with the same emphasis, "Give the negro soldier his justly-earned franchise." As the Government is exercising the right to fix every other pre-requisite of reconstruction except Equal Suffrage, why does it not fix this also? Is the occasion not yet ripe? When are we to reach the negro, if not now? If the present golden opportunity be squandered, shall Providence make haste to lavish upon us another? A few years ago slavery existed in the Southern States, and the Federal Government had no right to interfere. Even radical Abolitionists recognized the incompetency of Congress to break the slave's chain. War gave the right to emancipate. Except for the changed relations of the slave States by the rebellion, no such Federal authority would have existed. When the rebellious States shall have regained their former status in the Union, the Federal Government will have no more authority over them than it now has over New England or the West. Instead of seeing the Government dictating to the South, we shall then see the South dictating to the Government. If we omit to secure justice to the negro now, it will be too late to secure it by-and-by.

* * * * * *

How will the South treat the free negro? Will it sell him at auction? No. Will it sunder his family? No. Will it hunt him with bloodhounds? No. We answer thus positively, because even Andrew Johnson said to the black regiment, "You are henceforth to enjoy your freedom." But what is the freedom which they are to enjoy? Its sum and substance is (by presidential interpretation) a man's right to work all the week, and to sue for his wages on Saturday night; and, as the Raven said, "only this and nothing more." This freedom—the same which the Austrian has, and groans under; the same which the Hungarian has, and weeps over; the same which the Pole has, and looks to heaven saying, How long, O God, how long!—this is the freedom which the negro is expected to receive with thanks, and to ask for nothing more, because this is enough! How runs the argument? Children are pleased with trifles; the black soldier of Port Hudson is a child; let him, therefore, laugh and be merry over his little fragment of liberty! O bitter logic of insult! If ten white men, good citizens of Maine or Wisconsin, were to stand at this hour as nakedly stripped of their civil rights as the whole four millions of black loyalists at the South, the American people, with a voice unanimous and indignant, would say to the Government, "Right these wrongs!" But if a white man who is oppressed must be protected, shall a black man who is more oppressed be less protected? Shall a Christian government be less just to one man than to another, seeing that the Judge of all the Earth is no respecter of persons? Are we to lose from our veins the manly pulses of that Christianity which exclaims, "Who is offended, and I burn not?" Are we for ever to falsify the beautiful boast of our law that before its bar all men are equal? What is justice, except it be just to all citizens alike? "Do good to all men as ye have opportunity." How sublime, O gentlemen of Congress! is your opportunity. A long-guilty Government standing at last the almoner of delayed justice! A long-oppressed race standing at last the joyful recipient of Equal Rights!

* * * * *

The demand of the radicals has been, and is, that the reconstruction of the Union shall secure, above all things else, justice to the negro. The public debt is of secondary importance compared with this prime duty of the nation. And in thus demanding justice to the negro, the radical party proposes no injustice to white men. On the contrary, the leading radicals have been notoriously temperate in their spirit and purposes toward the leading rebels. More Northern Democrats than Abolitionists have asked for the hanging of Jefferson Davis. More Northern conservatives than radicals have demanded confiscation and severe penalties. The radicals ask for no man's death—for no man's property—for no man's injury—for no man's humiliation. This nation can afford to let its traitors live, though other nations hang such criminals. Life-long abolitionists do not now seek to punish the rebel; they seek only to protect the negro. But they demand inexorably, in the negro's behalf, that justice shall be done, done completely, done quickly, and done for all time.

* * * * *

Making promises only to break them, President Johnson has the boldness to ask if he has ever been perfidious! Promising that treason should be made odious, he has broken his promise by making treason the chief passport to his favor. Promising that rebels should be kept in the background, he has broken his promise by thrusting them into the chief places of honor within his gift. Promising that he would be the Moses of the black race, he has broken his promise by vetoing every bill providing for their safety and happiness. Promising that "loyal men, whether white or black, should alone govern the State," he has broken his promise by setting his foot equally on all loyal men, whether white or black, and selecting instead the enemies of the Republic to be his agents in its government. Promising that his plan of reconstruction was to be only an experiment which Congress might either accept or reject, he has broken his promise by an unparalleled attempt on the part of the Executive branch of the Government to nullify the Legislative. Promising that his quarrels with the Union party should be fought out exclusively within the ranks of that party, he has broken his promise by openly deserting to the enemy. Making all these promises and breaking them all, now at last with an effrontery like that of Charles the First, who lost his head by lying, Andrew Johnson exclaims, "Show me the promise I have ever broken?" To which the American people sadly reply, "Show us the promise you have ever kept."

* * * * *

The former aims of the Republican party are ended. Did it advocate the non-extension of Slavery? That end was accomplished. Did it advocate the prosecution of the war? That end was accomplished. Did it advocate the Proclamation of Emancipation? That end was accomplished. Did it advocate the Prohibitory Amendment? That end was accomplished. All these issues are now of the past. They do not survive. If now the Republican party accepts no new principle, it will have no principle at all. If it have none at all, it will perish. Are we the friends or the enemies of that party, when we warn it against its own destruction? A national party must have a national issue. The next issue before this nation is Impartial Suffrage.

* * * * * *

The slave, a man; the man, a citizen; the citizen, a voter! Is this high ground? No. It is the lowest possible ground—the letter A in the alphabet of Democracy. Faintly is a man baptized into the spirit of American republicanism who does not recognize the principle of political equality as inherent in our institutions. The watchword for the hour is Equal Rights. This is the dictate of Justice—this is the claim of Humanity. Parties must heed it—Administrations must conform to it. Its march shall be as irresistible as Time. It shall sweep with majesty into the National Capitol, and shall seat itself in sovereignty as the Supreme Law of the Land.

* * * * * *

The dwellers in Doubting Castle who now advise the Republican party to wait a few years longer before striking for Impartial Suffrage will be just as unprepared then as now. Minds like theirs never lead, but only hinder, the party of Freedom. They know too little of human nature, too little how to touch the chords of men's hearts, ever to lead the masses. The hearts of a great party are never grandly given to any leaders except bold men. Courage cuts all knots. The Republican party now needs its most courageous men at the front. But the true leaders of parties are the leaders of the leaders; and these are not chosen by ballot; they take their place by self-appointment and divine ordination. Now is the opportunity for men of genius in statesmanship to mould the nation to Equal Rights.

Great occasions greaten men's souls. Let the love of liberty now outrank the love of party. If the cause of the slave had been trusted only to political parties, he would to this day have remained in unbroken chains. Nor even can it be said that for the last eight years a great and victorious political party in this country has been marching by the side of Liberty, helping her forward step by step. On the contrary, Liberty, during these eventful years, has kept her patient place by the side of this tardy party, and continually urged its own halting steps forward to those civil victories by which it now holds the Government. If this party shall now reject its inspiring genius, if it shall prefer to sit still for the sake of place, rather than to go forward for the sake of principle—it will deserve the decay with which Providence shall smite it.

* * * * * *

The blood of the 19th of April, 1775, became the cement of a Union of slaves. Let the blood of the 19th of April, 1861, become the cement of a Union of free and equal citizens.

NOVEMBER 29, 1866.

A PATH TO FORTUNE.

EDITORIAL CORRESPONDENCE.

SHERMAN HOUSE, CHICAGO.

USED to think that Mr. Greeley was ungenerous in advising young men not to seek their fortunes in great cities, but in country districts; particularly as he himself had come from the country to find his fortune in the city. But a winter's travel through both country and city has convinced me that his oft-repeated views on this subject, and his special earnestness in their advocacy, are abundantly justified by facts.

I left behind me in New York thousands of young men, struggling hard to get a footing in the world, earning scarcely enough to keep soul and body together, yet who, if they had the courage to conquer a new country, might easily achieve for themselves that moderate wealth which is always and everywhere the best of good fortune.

Every great American city at the present moment is overrun with applicants for something to do. Chicago, like New York, is crowded with young men who have flocked to it, like moths to a candle, only to be devoured by the flame. The Devil's chief temptation to a young man in the West is to prompt him to keep a merchant's store. "Buy a stock of goods," says the Great Adversary. And of the multitudes who listen to the suggestion, nearly all are ensnared. The prospect appears brilliant; the result proves fatal.

It is an understatement to say that the majority of Western merchants fail, while the majority of Western farmers succeed. A more accurate record would be, that with the exception of a small minority of Western merchants, all fail; while, with the exception of a small minority of Western farmers, all succeed. In view of these undisguised and warning facts, it is astonishing to see so many young men who, on coming from the East to the West to begin a career, wreck themselves at the outset by deliberately following the wrong channel to success.

I was walking with an experienced merchant around the market-square of a Western town, to whom I happened to put the question, "How many of the hundred and twenty business firms around this square do you personally know?" "I know them all," he replied. "How many of them are thrifty in their business?" "Only three." He then explained that these three were growing rich; that a dozen others were earning a living; but that a majority of the remainder must sooner or later, one after another, drop into bankruptcy. On the contrary, almost every old-established farmer whom I have met in the West has said to me: "I came here ten (or perhaps fifteen) years ago, worth five hundred dollars (or perhaps nothing); and now I could sell my property for fifteen or twenty thousand dollars." Thus it almost seems as if a store were an open gate to failure, and a farm an open road to success.

It requires an unusual aptitude of mind to conduct mercantile business. This aptitude is possessed by so few that every beginner ought to take for granted that he does not hold the talisman, until he finds by an unmistakable instinct that he is really one of the few and fortunate masters of the knack. I do not say that a man who cannot be a merchant can be a farmer. Mother Earth is a good judge of men; she will not yield her crops to the shiftless and inefficient. But the farmer runs fewer risks than the merchant. The farmer gives a safe credit to God and Nature; the merchant gives an unsafe credit to Man. The seed-time knows that its promise will be fulfilled by the harvest; but a promissory note of hand never can know whether its promise is to be broken or kept.

I am aware that farming in the East is a poor business; Eastern farmers work hard all their lives, and die poor. But farming in the West has something royal in its rewards. Western farmers, who work hard, grow rich. The West is the garden of the Republic. The prairies, with proper provocation, can grow wheat and corn enough to feed all the hungry mouths of the human family. Thousands of the most beautiful prairies on which the sun's eye has ever winked, lie yet untrodden of man's foot. A bag of money lies hidden under every acre, to reward whatsoever laborer shall dig for the treasure.

Travelling through such a country, I have repeatedly said to myself, "Why should fifty thousand strong-handed young men be working for beggarly wages in New York, when they might come hither and be noblemen in the newer States?"

There is a foolish notion among Western young men that mercantile business is more respectable than farming. This was not the opinion of George Washington. Nor is praise meant for the English when they are called a "nation of shopkeepers." One of the redeeming features of Southern life is, that it dignifies the vocation of the planter. But in the West, particularly among young men of Eastern birth, there is a strange undervaluing of the farm, and a strange overvaluing of the store. This false notion becomes a public calamity in view of the fact that a large majority of Western men must necessarily adopt either the one or the other of these two employments—merchandising or farming. Too many make the wrong, too few the right choice.

A young man, for instance, who has served with distinction in a Western regiment during the war, and who enjoys a local reputation since his return, fancies that his few hundred dollars of saved money will open to him a better position in society through a mercantile than through an agricultural employment. So he stocks a store on credit, means well, works hard, expects success and reaps disappointment. Not dexterous in the manipulation of business, he soon finds that his burden is greater than he can bear, falls under it, and is crushed by it. Since the war, hundreds of such failures have occurred; hundreds more are yet to occur.

It is sad to notice the present tendency of the American people to rush into cities. The population of our cities is growing lamentably faster than the population of the country at large. This tendency is spasmodic, unhealthful, and perilous. A haste to be rich is an American temptation; and a belief that a city is the charmed place for winning riches is a national delusion. Of course, it is idle to offer advice on such a subject; nobody will take it. The majority of men have a pleasing habit of regarding themselves as starred to good luck. Every ticket-holder hopes to draw the opera-house. But let the word of warning be given, that beginners in the art of fortune-making should choose, not the employment which has the most brilliant possibilities, but which has the fewest risks. To invest ten years of life in a mercantile pursuit in the expectation of great gains, and then to fail, is a worse choice than to have invested the same years in the slower yet surer rewards of agricultural prosperity.

A Michigan merchant said to me a day or two ago, "Twenty firms in my town will be blotted out before the end of this year." But probably not twenty farmers in all Michigan will be "blotted out" in the same interval of time. And yet Michigan is not so remunerative a State to a farmer's toil as Illinois or Iowa.

I am not casting any imputation on Western merchants. Western merchants as a class are as safe, solid, and substantial as the Eastern. But, judged in the light of undisputed facts, mercantile business, whether East or West, is the most hazardous and uncertain of all American occupations. Statistics show that even in Boston only three merchants out of a hundred avoid bankruptcy. Like school-teaching, mercantile business is overcrowded with competitors. Too many men attempt to be merchants, who, instead, ought to follow some other occupation. The West to-day has too many merchants; it makes a loud call for manufacturers; but its chief and greatest need is of farmers. Its millions of unplanted acres yearn for the plough. I have an increasing respect for the American farmer. He is the central pillar of the Republic. His farm is the highway over which the nation is to make its safest progress toward the future.

In a crowded community like a great city, a young man without means or position has almost no claim to social consideration. He walks a daily round among a multitude of strangers. The mass of his fellow-citizens neither know nor care whether he lives or dies. But in the country, or in a country town, every neighbor is known to every other; a young man takes immediate rank in the community; he has every incentive to win the good opinion of his fellows; and, as a consequence, he soon developes a manly and positive character. In the great cities, where the mass of men have no special opportunities for winning a fair rank in the community, personal ambition becomes more aimless, and personal character less decided. Such an opportunity as the Western prairies now offer to humble, hard-working, and economical men is far more rewarding and enobling than any similar opportunity now offered by the Eastern cities.

If a brave and brawny young man, who cannot get along at the East because he can find no open door, will go to the West, put his hand to the plough, and look not back, he will find himself at the end of ten years an owner of property, a chief citizen of his neighborhood, an esteemed member of society, and (what is better than all) every inch a man.

I know that other writers have said all this, over and over again; and no man so unwearyingly as Mr. Greeley. But the testimony needs constant repetition, that it may lead the feet of many disappointed throngers of city streets to make a pilgrimage to green fields. This is the path to fortune.

December, 1866.

MY NEW HOUSEKEEPING.

EDITORIAL CORRESPONDENCE.

OUT WEST.

AS I notice that the question "How to live?" is now frequently on the lips of rent-paying citizens, let me mention my experience in living on a new plan.

I have taken lodgings for the winter in a railroad car, and partake of daily bread at the railroad stations.

Under this plan, rent is high, and fare poor; but fuel is gratis, and washing useless.

I have ascertained that a gentle dyspepsia can be purchased for eighteen cents—which brings that luxury within the reach of all classes.

My house is furnished according to Gen. Butler's plan for the reconstruction of the Union—that is, "with all the modern improvements"—water, light, bath-room, and bed-chamber. I must confess, however, that the apartments are generally too dusty either to evince good housekeeping, or to show their plush and damask furniture to the best advantage. But then I have a great deal of company, and all housekeepers know that this interferes with the best attempts at keeping things "to rights." But I am troubled with neither flies nor cobwebs. The spider who, according to Solomon, builds her house in kings' palaces, gets no chance to settle in comfort here.

It would do your heart good to see the sights from my

windows; for I have more extensive grounds around my present residence than any of my late townsmen on Clinton Avenue in Brooklyn, or Murray Hill in New York. Moreover, my grounds have been beautifully laid out by the best and greatest of architects—the many-minded Maker of the world's beauty. My trees are now bare but not desolate; my grass brown, but still bewitching; my brooks are wrinkled along the edges with ice, but still leaping merrily down rocks and dams; and my young winter wheat has the color of Mr. Chase's national currency, looking forward to be turned into gold.

A great advantage of living in the country is that a man can keep a cow. But what is one cow? By my present plan I have several hundred thousand cattle, and more sheep than bore fleece to Abraham, Isaac, and Jacob. This morning, in the rain, their fleecy sides look dark and weather-beaten, like house-fronts of Caen stone when wet; but the storm is breaking away, and my flocks will soon be white as snow. No, not exactly. Our common expressions for colors are seldom correct. Sheep are never white—their nearest approach to the raiment of sainthood is a velvety gray. Some of them served in the Confederate army.

My woodlands are immense—almost interminable. They furnish such a supply for the stove in the corner, that I sometimes am roasted. The man who builds the fires keeps his own precious self cool by spending most of his time in lounging over the iron-railings on the front stoop. Very few people in this world feel for us exactly as we feel for ourselves.

Housekeepers say that three moves are as bad as a fire. But what is house-moving once a year to house-moving every day! All my real estate, though it extends as far as the eye can reach, does not give me half so much trouble as my personal property, though this consists only of a carpet-bag and umbrella. A carpet-bag is one of the serious cares, and perhaps one of the needful disciplines, of this earthly life. As to the umbrella, let me mention a fact worth knowing. An old green umbrella is the safest for a traveller to carry; for nobody will have the hardihood to purloin it. The records of crime show no instance of such an umbrella as mine having ever been stolen.

The daily papers are left regularly at my door. I buy each that comes along, and read them all, whether Democratic or Republican. Then, after comparing both sides, I usually end in agreeing with neither, and doggedly settle down in a confirmed radicalism. Just a moment ago my eyes fell on a paragraph concerning my venerable friend, Thaddeus Stevens. He says, "I was conservative last winter, but I mean to be radical for the remainder of my days." May his days be long in the land!

I occasionally turn for solace to my library—which consists chiefly of the latest volume of the Railroad Guide. Profound respect is due to any American citizen who can learn anything from a Railroad Guide. If intelligence is to become the test for suffrage, I suggest that the citizen who presents himself at the ballot-box shall be required to tell the time of any Western train by looking at the Railroad Guide. Let the advocates of a restricted franchise ponder this suggestion.

I live on one floor—which saves running up and down stairs. In fact, in my present position, to occupy two floors would prove me as double as the Irishman who came over in two ships. My house, it is true, has a second story, containing a row of small attic-windows for ventilation; but as these are never kept open, they might as well not be there.

Frescoes and unique paintings adorn my walls—done in a style unattempted by any ancient master. It was Paganini's delight to play on one string. It seems to have been the ambition of the artist who executed these works to produce a series of fascinating landscapes by the use of one invoice of vermillion paint. Joyfully (if I knew his name) would I give it publicity; but there is no "pinxit" appended to his works. Raphael was not solicitous of fame, and Shakespeare disdained it.

I live like the first families of Virginia—have not a carpet in my house. There is an oil-cloth, but this is on the ceiling, not on the floor—so placed, I suppose, to be ready for use in case we get turned upside down.

I have only to add that the cost of my present arrangement is a fair average of fifteen dollars a day. If this seems extravagant, you must remember that I am compelled to pay a heavy mileage, after the manner of my bleeding country to her Congressmen.

And now, dear friends, I would invite you to my new quarters, except for the trouble you might have in finding the street and number. But, in case a happy chance should bring any of you to my door, I will keep a sharp "look-out when the bell rings."

December 6, 1866.

THE SOCIAL LIFE OF THE WEST.

HAVE seen during a winter's travel that the East is not the country; New York and New England are but the thumb and forefinger; the West is the rest of the hand.

No people in history have developed in so short a time so many differing types of character as the Americans. The New England character is distinct from any phase of mankind which the world has before seen. The Yankee is a new product among the races. Even Shakespeare has left no sketch, no hint, of any such creature as Brother Jonathan. But the Brother Jonathan of the comic papers is not the Yankee. I have never seen this picturesque Yankee, except in the pictures; I do not believe he exists in reality. But the New England character of today is just as individual—just as unmistakable—just as original—as the Brother Jonathan of the caricatures. A Boston man cannot, if he tries, conceal the marks of having been brought up in Yankeeland. Equally noticeable is the Southern character. You know it at a glance. It reveals itself in the manners, the gait, the hair, the complexion, the pronunciation. And it has its admirable excellences as well as its entailed deformities. But the Western character is the most representative of all American types, and best expresses what is called the American idea. The Western is the newest of American characters. It is a flower plucked from the rocks of New England and transplanted in the prairies. "*Qui trans-*

tulit, sustinet." But the present Western character is to undergo great changes—greater than the Southern or the Eastern. The typical and final Western man does not yet exist; for the best Western men are, as yet, partly Eastern. Many of them were born, reared, and married at the East. But climate influences character. Western skies, lands, and lakes are busy at work moulding the souls of the Western people. The process is now going forward—the result cannot be guessed. The flatness of the prairies has not yet had time to lay its dead-level on the Western mind. The absence of sea-board salt from the inland air has not yet begun to mitigate the energy of the Western will. Meanwhile the geographical breadth of the great West imparts (like the sea to the sailor) a noticeable nobleness to the Western character.

A new comer in the West finds a Scotch welcome. Jostle an Illinoisan in the street, and at once you are acquaintances; meet him the next day, and you are old friends. A shake of the hand in Kansas or Minnesota has more grip in it than anywhere between New York and Bangor. Child of the East, the West is the chief crown of the parent. The universal New England element westward is not only the best part of the West, but the best part of New England; for only the courageous, the energetic, and the conquering have had the will to quit Eastern homes for Western prairies. Thus the early Pilgrims *to* New England have their truest sons in the later Pilgrims *from* New England. A Yankee does not come to his fullest stature in Yankeeland. At the East he is a geranium in a pot, thrifty and prim; at the West, he is a geranium in a garden, exuberant and generous. Thus do new countries greaten men's souls.

I have lately crossed the thresholds of nearly one hundred Western homes. I look back upon those pictures of domestic life with more pleasure than I should look back upon the pictures of the Louvre. Nothing in this world is more beautiful than a happy home. My pilgrimage has given me a new sense of the great amount of domestic happiness enjoyed by the American people. It is no wonder that men are willing to fight for their firesides; nothing else is so well worth fighting for. The American's house is his castle.

Domestic life in the West is more self-centred than in the East; that is, a home in the West must of necessity find its sources of enjoyment more within itself, and less in its surroundings, than a home in the East. The West furnishes fewer advantages of well-settled communities, of old neighborhoods, and of long-established friendships. A Western farm-house generally has no neighbor nearer than a horse-back ride. Accordingly, the farmer and his family spend their evenings at home. A visit requires the labor of a journey. Social life—that is, life among neighbors—becomes possible only in villages, towns, and cities. Within the region west of the Alleghany Mountains and north of the Ohio there are at least two hundred towns and cities which have five thousand people and upward. In all these places—with a few unhappy exceptions, over-given to money getting—there is a delightful social life, particularly in winter. In many of these towns almost every well-reputed family knows every other. Moreover, there is no aristocracy; and thus one of the chief curses of modern society is removed. The rich and the poor meet on equal terms for the good reason that the rich were lately poor, and the poor may be quickly rich. A social evening spent in a Western man's house is as warm-hearted a season as one can desire.

There is very little of that cold formality which sometimes (though I know not why) passes for politeness. If the farmer's daughters can sing, they sing without making mawkish excuses. If they can act charades, they plunge into the sport without unnecessary objection. Frosty manners are a grievance to genuine souls.

I had not expected to see cottage-architecture illustrated by so many specimens of beauty as I have encountered in these remote regions. The ideal New England roof has no projecting eve — no rich shadow to bedeck the weather-boards; but in most of the new cottages of any pretension in the West one notices a happy touch of the picturesque. Particularly have I been struck with the architectural prettiness of many of the station-houses along the railroads—showing many ingenious adaptations of the Swiss roof by making it project over the platform for the shelter of passengers from sun and shower. Some of these modest buildings are of exquisite proportion, and here and there I have seen one so absolutely perfect that I have been patient with the belated train out of respect to the beauty of the passenger-station. These models have had much influence on the taste for cottage-building in the thriftier Western towns. But I cannot hold my peace concerning Western brick. The color is ugly and abominable. I do not mean the Milwaukee tinge, which is pleasant and (to a stranger) novel; but I mean the Jersey-mud complexion of the ordinary red brick of the West. Houses built of such brick ought to be either painted into a cheerful appearance, or else veiled with growing vines. Left raw, I believe they tend to corrupt the public morals. An ugly house helps to make a perverse man.

Personal beauty is not so common in the West as in

the East. It is not common anywhere. But I have observed that the inland atmosphere of the Western States lacks the magic by which the salt air of the seaside adds roses to a woman's cheek. Western men are finer looking than Western women—a fact which I attribute to their frequent journeyings on business from climate to climate. Moreover, take a thousand Western children gathered into an audience (an experiment which I have had many opportunities to witness), and their cheeks show less bloom than the cheeks of children by the Atlantic. Still, I find that in the West as elsewhere, one's own children are regarded the handsomest in the world.

I cannot see why household music need be so scarce in Western well-to-do families. In the hundred houses which I have mentioned, I did not see five good pianos, or hear ten good players. But, as music has been the tardiest of arts to make its way through the great world, so it is peculiarly the tardiest of arts to make its way into a new country. Very little good singing is heard in the Western churches. I call no church singing good which is not done by the congregation. The Methodist church is the Christian song-bird of the West. But the Sunday-schools of every sect are rapidly teaching the children to sing. There will come a day when the Americans will be as musical as the Germans: and the credit of the change will belong to the Sunday-school system. I believe that the Sunday-schools of the Republic are of far more importance to its welfare than are all its churches. "A little child shall lead them."

There is more hilarity among Western than among Eastern people. Work is more of a play here than at home. More than half the laughter done by the American people falls from the mouths of Western men. And a good deal of it, of late (I grieve to say), has been at the expense of his Excellency Andrew Johnson, President of the United States.

I marvel that Western women do not cultivate more house-plants. Their dwellings never have so many flower-pots in the windows as an Eastern man sees at home. The household geranium—dear, sacred plant!—seems to have few rights which Hoosier housekeepers are bound to respect. And yet, by common consent, it has a fee-simple, a clear title, an undisputed right, to live in every good woman's house in all the land. Of course, the prairies are full of flowers in the summer; but this is all the more reason why the prairie-cottage should be full of flowers in the winter. I shall never forget a certain cottage on the Illinois prairie at Princeton, into which, after a long walk through the snow, I entered to find a whole bower of summer green inside! Such a house offered hospitality, not only to the body, but to the soul. And I afterward met, in a university town, a law professor in whom the sweet charities of life abounded to such a degree as to be totally inexplicable by anything belonging to his dusty and mouldy profession; and I should have gone off without an explanation had I not happened to detect his face all aglow while in the act of watering his plants! "He that watereth shall be watered also himself."

I may be pardoned for mentioning that a good woman now living in Abraham Lincoln's home at Springfield, planted, before his martyrdom, a handful of morning-glory seeds at the foot of a pillar by the rear piazza, and was surprised to find the mass of growing vines flowering into three distinct stripes of color—red, white, and blue; not from any design in planting, as she told me, but from mere accident of growth; a patriotic freak of nature, made as if to give a beautiful proof of the indigenous loyalty of the West—the very soil of the Martyr's garden testifying what flag ought to wave over the land!

How much a bountiful storm of snow contributes to a winter's happiness! Less snow falls in the West than in the East. In Kansas a sleigh-ride is an unusual treat. In Michigan sometimes a whole winter comes and goes without the jingling of a sleigh-bell. This winter there has been snow in abundance. But I am annoyed that so many sleighing-parties go to their sport without sleigh-bells. It ought to be held a misdemeanor to sadden a sleigh-ride by omitting the bells. The cheery snow, the crisp air, the merry blood, all call for the accompanying music of the bells. This winter has yielded me some of the grandest of sleigh-rides, set to the tinkle of the gladdest of bells. All which has been some compensation for losing the happiness of crossing the East River on a fool's bridge of ice.

Cultivated people at the West—particularly Eastern women who are fresh residents on the prairies—yearn for New England, and weep in secret at their separation from it. But these same Eastern women, as soon as they become Westernized, partake of the same pride in the West that animates Western men. Certain fashionable people, who prefer to be ladies rather than women, and who flourish in the large Western cities, regard it as a compliment to be told that no one would suspect they had not lived all their days at the East. But when you see a Western Yankee girl who after five or ten years' residence in Illinois cannot be told from an Eastern woman, she may be excellent and admirable, but she is not the best whom the West can produce. I say this with downright positiveness. The true Western woman, though perhaps born at the East, would not give a sixpence to be thought fresh from Beacon street, or Fifth avenue. Moreover, I venture the prediction that the first State in the Union to acknowledge the political equality of men and women is a State west of the Mississippi. I mean Iowa. Let the golden day speed swiftly—for I want Horace Greeley to see it before he dies.

One thing more. I am told by friendly critics at home that I draw my Western pictures in over-colors. No. I endeavor always to understate, rather than overstate, my admiration of the West. It is a majestic region. Its people belong to the nobility of mankind. Its prospective growth is beyond calculation. Its soul is of fire. Its ambition is to rule the land. Its opportunity is not far in the future. The West is to be the Dictator of the Republic.

FEBRUARY 12, 1867.

MR. SEWARD'S GARDEN.

S I peered into Mr. Seward's garden at Auburn, and saw the snow and ice cloaking his trees and shrubs, I could not but think of the still more chilling blight that has winter-killed his green old age. Of course, I do not refer to his domestic bereavements. God forbid that any criticism of a public man's character should go untempered with sympathy at a moment when his critics are looking at the shut windows of his half-empty house whose recent and chief household lights lie quenched in the grave. The late mistress of this mansion was one of the noblest women of America. I have never heard Mr. Greeley praise the character of any other woman as I have heard him always praise the character of Mrs. Seward. A few days after her death, he wrote the noblest tribute which any public pen paid to her memory.

Gazing, therefore, at this shadowed house through the haze of this irresistible sympathy, I could not but recall tenderly my early boyish enthusiasm for Mr. Seward—when I thought him the greatest of statesmen, and bravest of leaders; when I believed that he loved liberty better than power, and sought justice rather than office; when his calm, pure, limpid eloquence flowed like a fountain undefiled; when I ranked him as the foremost of American statesmen, and one of the chief pillars of the anti-slavery cause; and when I shed foolish but actual tears at his rejection by the Chicago Convention, and the nomination of Abraham Lincoln instead.

After one has built so much upon another as many a young man, years ago, built upon Mr. Seward, only to be cheated in the end by the favorite whom he trusted in the beginning, there arises within one's mind toward such a betrayer an unconquerable and abiding emotion of repugnance—compounded of mingled affection, pity, and scorn.

The Secretary of State still boasts that he is the policy-maker of the President; and so, all the calamities inflicted on the nation by Mr. Johnson are to be registered against Mr. Seward. What a catalogue of mingled blunders and crimes! Macaulay said of Antony Astley Cooper that "every part of his life reflected infamy on every other." In like manner, the impartial historian will say of Mr. Johnson that every measure of his administration reflected infamy on every other. To all this record of humiliation, the premier stands pointing his finger, saying, "This handwriting is mine!"

Mr. Seward is one of twins. His other self is Thurlow Weed. These twain are like Jacob and Esau; you know the one by his voice, the other by his hand. The one now possesses a great office; the other a great fortune. But each has earned a very unsuccessful success. "There is a way that seemeth right unto a man, but the end thereof is death."

If Mr. Seward, since 1861, had inscribed against his name such a public record as that of Thaddeus Stevens —faithful, instead of faithless—what a grand renown might have been his to-day! What loving enthusiasm the American people would have manifested toward the great anti-slavery senator of New York! What bountiful accompaniments of old age would have been his portion—" reverence and troops of friends!"

To outlive one's fame is a pity; to outlive one's usefulness is a calamity; to outlive one's conscience is a disgrace. Mr. Seward has brought upon himself this pity, this calamity, and this disgrace.

Melt, snows of Auburn! and unveil the great man's garden once again to the sun; but his pleasant plants, when they renew their leaf and bloom, shall only mock their master's laurel, which shall not again be green!

March 28, 1867.

AN EDITORIAL SOLILOQUY.

AMONG the movings of May-day—with its rattle of furniture-carts and its racket of tumbling boxes—we expected to see our neighboring sidewalks cluttered with a strange package, received by the Eastern train, and labeled "*The Boston Recorder*—handle with care." We knew that this literary invoice was anxiously looked for by that genial poet, the Rev. Dr. Ray Palmer; from whose pen we had hoped to see a sonnet on the event. But our friend watched in vain for a glimpse of the ancient type-cases, the dusty files, the thin subscription-books, the lists of delinquent subscribers, and the personal carpet-bags of those distin guished strangers, the Rev. Mr. Marvin and the Rev Mr. Tarbox. The package did not arrive. At first we feared it was detained at the depot by non-payment of freight; and we were about to ask our fellow-craftsmen of *The Observer* and *The Evangelist* to join with us in a subscription to relieve our Bostonian friends from their limbo. But we now understand that the Rev. Mr. Marvin, before venturing on his journey, made a precautionary examination of the antique and disjointed furniture of *The Recorder* office, and found that it needed only the jar of a freight-train to shake it entirely to pieces. As Oliver Wendell Holmes had already made known the serious consequences of a similar accident to the "One Hoss Shay," the Rev. Mr. Marvin and the Rev. Mr. Tarbox abandoned the trip. Accordingly, like the State House, the Common, and the Long Wharf, *The Boston Recorder* still remains in Boston.

But the proposed loan of a Congregational newspaper by Boston to New York has elicited remarks from two distinct classes of our personal friends: first, from those who hope that we will render such a new journal unnecessary by remodeling *The Independent* so as to fill the supposed gap; and, next, from those who beg that no fear of a rival journal will induce us to put back the spreading oak of *The Independent* into the acorn of a sectarian sheet.

Let us, therefore, now and here, say something of ourselves.

The Independent is sometimes called an organ of the Congregational denomination. People who thus speak of it know little either of that sect or of this press. Congregationalism, by its very genius, repels any and every organ—except of the musical kind, such as we now enjoy in Plymouth Church. Denominations which are ecclesiastically organized may have ecclesiastical organs. But the Congregational denomination, rejecting all such organizations, rejects all such organs. *The Independent* was started, however, to be an organ—a mouth-piece—an exponent of the Congregational churches. In carrying out this aim, it was ably edited by three well-known Congregational clergymen—the Rev. Drs. Bacon, Storrs, and Thompson. No three—no twenty—ministers could have more fitly spoken for the Congregational denomination—provided only that this denomination would consent to be spoken for. But it is the nature of Congregationalism, having a multitude of living tongues, to let every man speak for himself, and to suffer no man to speak for all. So, notwithstanding the eminent ability of its first conductors, a dozen years of their editorship left this journal forty thousand dollars in debt. This statement is strictly accurate. The account of *The Independent* with its proprietors, at the close of those twelve years, showed an aggregate outlay of $40,000 over and above the aggregate income of the paper; and this too at a time when the cost of making a newspaper was less than half as great as it is now. We make this statement not at all to the disparagement of the original editors; the fault was not in the men, but in the plan. Moreover, the money was paid ungrudgingly, out of a rich exchequer, in the hope that it was the sunken but certain and solid foundation of what afterward was proven an impossible thing—namely, an organ of the Congregational denomination. For our part, we rejoice that the Congregational denomination would not support any organ—not even *The Independent*—and not even though *The Independent* (as conducted in those days) was confessedly the ablest denominational paper in the United States.

Under the ensuing editorship of Mr. Beecher—owing not only to the indisposition of the Congregational churches to accept any man for their mouth-piece, but owing still more to the eminently unecclesiastical and catholic tone of his mind—the paper was not administered as the organ of the Congregational churches, but as the organ of its Editor-in-chief; which is the only proper theory for the conduct of a vital journal, secular or religious. Mr. Beecher had a grand idea of the true function of the religious press—just as he has grand ideas of other things. And *The Independent*, in his hands, was a noble power. With grateful pride we look back to our joint connection with that great man, in this journal, as a golden period in our life and labor.

When providentially his editorial pen was bequeathed to our hand, we harbored no thought of bending back *The Independent*—no, not for an hour!—into its original shape as a Congregational instrument. Inflexibly Congregational as we are—expecting to live and die in the membership of a Congregational church—revering the Pilgrims, and their heritage of church polity—standing uncovered by the graves of our fathers, and counting ourselves honored to be numbered among their sons—we nevertheless value the inherent principles which animate the Congregational polity so far above that polity itself, that by the very force of these principles we cherish an ingrained and ineradicable repugnance to sectarian propagandism and denominational championship. We do not disparage sectarian journals. They have their uses; they have many able pens in their service; they do great good in the world; but let such journals be edited by men who feel called to such tasks. As for ourselves, we have no inclination or spirit to embark in any such enterprise for our life's work; and *The Independent*, if we should attempt to make it an ecclesiastical or sectarian journal—our hearts all the while set on higher things—would necessarily become nothing but a weekly bundle of chaff. "Whatsoever ye do, do it *heartily*, as unto the Lord." We have far more disposition to earn a livelihood by sawing wood—which we can do well, for we have tried it!—than for editing a Congregational or any other sectarian journal—which we cannot do at all, and never mean to try.

Nevertheless, we know that among our quarter of a million readers there are some ministers, some deacons, and some grandmothers of these, who would relish *The Independent* better than now, if only it would add to its customary flavor a strong, green-tea taste of ecclesiastical stringency. It was for the sake of seeing these friends gratified that we were preparing to heap coals of fire on the head of the Rev. Mr. Tarbox for his laudable endeavor to get semebody else to establish, in order that he himself might edit, here in Babylonian New York, a paper with the genuine green-tea title of "The Organ of Puritan Congregationalism in the United States." Of course we had no wish that the Rev. Mr. Marvin and the Rev. Mr. Tarbox, or either of these venerable but unsophisticated men, should lose forty thousand dollars of borrowed money. But we knew that Mr. Barnes the bookseller, Mr. Holmes of the Scovill Company, and Mr. Pettengill the advertising agent, were abundantly able to contribute ten thousand dollars a year each, for the sake of compensating the blower and the player of a Congregational organ. Our only dubiousness was whether the blower and the player (after getting their salaries) could possibly induce the Congregational denomination to face the music; for it is very disheartening, as Robert Browning's gypsies found out,

> "To go on with the grinding,
> * * * * * *
> Up and down, and nobody minding."

Now let us mention another matter.

We have lately been bullied and brow-beaten (affectionately, of course!) by some Congregational clergymen because we have invited into our columns such writers as William Lloyd Garrison, Lydia Maria Child, Charles Sumner, Thomas Wentworth Higginson, and others. These writers have been solemnly and warningly described to us as "infidels." Shame, messieurs critics! Remember the words of King David: "Who can stretch forth his hand against the Lord's anointed, and be guiltless?" It makes one sorrowful to witness the pitiful bigotry which can consent to write the word "infidelity" over the *faithfulest* men and women of this age! Personally, we do not agree with the religious views of these writers. Nor, to take another instance, do we agree with the religious views of our familiar contributor, Mr. Greeley. But shall we, on this account, shut the doors of *The Independent* in the faces of these friends? Shall we blot from our hymn-books one of the sweetest and noblest of modern hymns, "Nearer, my God, to Thee!" because its author was a Unitarian? Shall we imitate the last number of the *Congregational Review*, and fiercely charge one of the most Christian of American women, Mrs. Harriet Beecher Stowe, with "denying the fundamental doctrines of the Bible?" Shall we make these columns an *Index Expurgatorius*, for the sake of keeping a catalogue of such men as may be allowed to speak, and of such others as must be kept silent? Shall we shrivel *The Independent* into a pious tract for weekly distribution by the American Tract Society? God forbid!

We hereby announce to the theological critics of William Lloyd Garrison and Horace Greeley, Lydia Maria Child and John G. Whittier, Charles Sumner and Wendell Phillips, Thomas Wentworth Higginson and Edmund Quincy, Anna Dickinson and Frederick Douglass, that when the time shall arrive for the exclusion of these men and women from *The Independent* on the ground of their infidelity, heterodoxy, and religious unsoundness, we shall proudly retain what measure of self-respect we now possess, and retire in their honorable company.

The Independent once expressed an editorial opinion (not written by ourselves, nor by our predecessor) that William Lloyd Garrison was "a degraded infidel," and that Oliver Wendell Holmes was a "moral parricide." The Dog Noble now respectfully announces that he has quit barking at that ancient hole!

Once for all, then, let us frankly set forth the one and central aim of this journal—for this world, and for the next. Originally named *The Independent*, both because of the ordinary signification of that manly word and also because the same term technically denoted a "Congregationalist," we now retain the name, no longer on account of its Congregational, but solely on account of its moral meaning. Whatever this sheet may have been in the past, it is henceforth not a denominational, not a sectarian, not a Congregational, but a *religious* journal: a religious journal aiming at a higher, ampler, and grander ideal than can ever possibly be realized by any sectarian or denominational sheet. We base these columns on the broad foundation of the Christian religion—not on the narrow platform of a Christian sect. Devoutly, unalterably, and humbly, we hold to the fundamental principles of Christianity. These we shall endeavor to teach, illustrate, and enforce. But as far as the East is from the West, we shall banish from these pages all unprofitable disputations on minor points of doctrines and creeds. So many men possess worse creeds and yet better characters than ourselves, that we totally despair of forcing the whole world into moral goodness through the narrow method of one prescribed belief. We are thoroughly determined to conduct this journal, not according to the Westminster Catechism, not according to the Burial Hill declaration of faith, but simply according to the plain and undisputed principles of Christian ethics. Our epitome of theology is short—consisting simply of the two tables of stone—love to God and love to man; but we beg to remind our brethren that "on these two commandments hang all the law and the prophets." Since the Founder of Christianity thought this simple creed an amply sufficient statement of Christian doctrine and duty, we have not the hardihood to make any unnecessary additions to this perfect rule of faith and practice.

These columns, therefore, are consecrated to God and man; to religion and civilization; to liberty, justice, and equality; to the family, and the sweet human charities; to literature, art, and industry; in a word, to human progress! With the full measure of our strength, we have heretofore endeavored to render some service to our down-trodden fellow-men, in the hope that we were thereby rendering our best service to our Father in Heaven. With the full measure of our strength, we shall pursue the same course in the future, whether good men grumble or applaud. This is our idea of Christian duty in the midst of a perverse generation; this is our idea of a religious newspaper in the midst of a time-serving press. We are constantly criticized for meddling with politics by men who do not understand the first principles of religion. Against these half-enemies, we array a legion of the noblest friends that ever formed the constituency of an American journal. We have seen their generous faces; we have grasped their hearty hands. "Behold, they that be for us are more than they that be against us!" Among the 75,000 registered subscribers to this journal, 8,000 are clergymen; these are of every denomination; and to judge the whole number by the hundreds whom we met during a winter's travel through twelve States, a preponderating majority are men under forty years of age. They are in the prime of life. Their brows yet glitter with the dew of their youth. They are kings of men—pillars of the church—apostles of the age. God be with them!

Now the antiquated managers of ecclesiastical conventions, and the alms-collecting editors of mediæval religious journals, will be as powerless to control the young blood of this rising ministry as to ask the sun at morning to turn back the day! Moreover, every noble young man of America—whether in the pulpit or out of it—carries in his heart an unquenched fire of liberty which was kindled by the war for the Union. The battle of blood is over: the battle of ideas proceeds. The trumpet now sounds a new onset. "Whoever," cried Garibaldi, "is in love with cold, hunger, wounds, and death, let him follow me!" So, whoever welcomes calumny, criticism, misrepresentation, and sneers, let him be a comrade with ourselves! Falter who may, follow who dare!

May 9, 1867.

AN IMBECILE PULPIT.

IN a sermon before the New School Presbyterian General Assembly at Rochester, the Rev. Dr. Samuel H. Hopkins declared that the Episcopal denomination of the United States had "an imbecile pulpit." The remark was made by the retiring moderator of the Assembly, in his official capacity, and in a city that had recently welcomed the Episcopal bishops with the same hospitality which the citizens were at that moment showing to the Presbyterian commissioners. On the Assembly's "sea of upturned faces," this squally remark blew up a general ripple of dissent. The daily papers of Rochester urged an official retraction by the Assembly, as due to the dignity of that body. This, however, was awkward, and not to be done. But the pastor of the church in which the Assembly held its sessions contrived to make a neat public reference to the offensive remark, and in a semi-official way to disavow it. But it still stands in the official reports, and will not fade from men's memories: an illustration of the Chinese proverb that "an ill word, once out of the mouth, cannot be brought back by a coach and six."

We refer to the incident, not for its importance, but for its suggestiveness.

Has the Episcopal Church "an imbecile pulpit?" Is Dr. Tyng, amid the ruins of St. George's, reduced to "an imbecile pulpit?" Does Bishop McIlvaine pursue his bishopric in "an imbecile pulpit?" Has Dr. Schenck come from Baltimore to Brooklyn to fill "an imbecile pulpit?" Did Bishop White wear out his long and saintly life in "an imbecile pulpit?" Did Dr. Milner bequeath his unforgotten name to be linked with the memory of "an imbecile pulpit?"

No. The remark of Dr. Hopkins was a bitterly distilled drop of the quintessential tincture of sectarianism. The fact that such a remark fell from the lips of so eminent, able, and noble a clergyman, shows how unconsciously yet how insidiously and irresistibly a sectarian spirit bewilders the judgment and good taste of men whom the Church would make broad, but whom a Sect keeps narrow.

The question arises, What *is* "an imbecile pulpit?"

It is a pulpit that lacks genius, courage, and fire; a pulpit submissive to follow, instead of bold to lead, public opinion; a pulpit inefficient toward the stirring questions of the time, and hesitant to incur the reproach of teaching advanced ideas; a pulpit that cringes to the pew, and lowers the manly independence of the ministerial office; a pulpit moulded by the very men whom it is sent to mould. There are thousands of such American pulpits. They belong to all denominations. They rustle their silks in every diocesan convention, and utter their platitudes to every synod. They are the self-appointed censors of nobler men who, whether in pulpits or out, are seeking to serve God in their day and generation. They bring the Church at first into weakness, and at last into reproach. Against all such pulpits, if the pulpiteer of the General Assembly will uplift his voice, we will join in the protest. But let him not attack the Episcopal, and shield the Presbyterian denomination. Let him administer his judgment equally upon all the guilty.

What is the present tone and character of the American pulpit? There was a time when the great body of the American churches, of all denominations, and both pulpits and pews, lay under the ban of complicity with the hideous crime of Slavery. An eloquent voice in one of the ablest of Presbyterian pulpits startled the country with the declaration that "the American Church was the chief bulwark of American Slavery." It is sorrowfully and unpardonably true that during the anti-slavery agitation, when the struggling cause first cried aloud for the help of all good men, the majority of ministers and church-members, even in the North, were the abettors of human bondage. But in process of time, as the Northern churches were split asunder by the indriven wedge of the all-penetrating question, every church thus cleft in twain let in upon itself a great light. During the war the Northern churches girded the imperiled government with a stalwart league of defence. The Northern pulpits "spake as with tongues of fire." Never in the religious history of this country did the American clergy so nobly fulfil their mission as during the war. Mouths that had for years been dumb toward Liberty, then had a voice. Hearts that never before had beaten for the slave, then yearned for him in prayer. The ears of this generation never before heard so many good and so few poor sermons as during the war—not merely on public topics, but on the whole range of pulpit topics. Ministers never before stood so near to God, for the reason that they never before stood so near to man. The holy oil of consecration with which that struggle anointed the Northern clergy still remains on a thousand brows. If "there were giants in those days," there are giants in these next-succeeding days. It is our deliberate conviction that the religious bodies of the country—its conferences, councils, and assemblies—have for the last three or four years exerted more influence on our chief national questions than has been exerted by all the political caucuses and conventions of the same period. For instance (speaking of the New School General Assembly), we recall with delight the scene which we witnessed in that body when it met in Brooklyn two or three years ago, and gave a unanimous vote for Impartial Suffrage before any political convention of equal magnitude had uttered a word on the subject. Without the help, sympathy, zeal, and co-operation of the Northern churches, the War for the Union would have been a failure. But if the nation had need of her churches then, she has equal need of them now. What this Government lacks is moral quickening; religious ideas must penetrate political statutes; Christian principle must take the place of party expediency.

A church that has no influence on the times in which it stands, might as well have belonged to a former age. It is a happy omen that the American churches, which for twenty years were dead, have arisen to newness of life. Nevertheless, God forbid that we should settle down into the easy and smooth-tongued business of praising these churches or their pulpits. Our religious, like our civil, institutions—our religious, like our civil, leaders—are equally full of faults and flaws. Both alike need God's grace and man's forbearance. The church, like the state, ought to be pruned with a busy knife of criticism to keep its branches fruitful and its leaves green. "Shall not judgment begin at the house of God?" Yea, verily.

And when one Christian denomination compliments itself and defames its rival, it is generally a sign that both equally deserve the same condemnation.

Let every minister—whether in the Episcopal Church or the Presbyterian, whether in the Baptist or the Methodist—ask himself whether or not he stands in an "imbecile pulpit." If a man ordained for the ministry is without a sacred passion for his work, certain it is that he makes an "imbecile pulpit." If his heart burns not with love toward all his fellow-creatures, high and low, then no matter what culture may sit upon his lips, he is the weak master of an "imbecile pulpit." If he is ashamed or afraid to declare "the whole counsel of God," he is a poor prisoner in an "imbecile pulpit." If he is an idolater of his own creed, holding that every man who believes something different is a heretic and infidel, he is an unanointed babbler from an "imbecile pulpit."

It may be that a Presbyterian moderator, in taking the trouble to slander a single denomination, has spoken a measure of truth of all. If so, it were better for those who felt the scourge of small-cords in the Master's hand driving them from the temple, than for those whom His divine indignation frowns upon, blasts, consumes, and shrivels in an "imbecile pulpit."

Arise, John Knox! and preach before the General Assembly! Awake, Martin Luther! and burn the Pope's bull before the General Association!

O for a *stalwart* pulpit!—a pulpit muscular with the strength of strong men!—a pulpit to shake the land, and be itself unshaken!—a pulpit to fight the general enemy, and not to stab its faithful friend!—a pulpit to deliver the bolt of God's wrath, and yet utter the "still, small voice!"—a pulpit to fling down or pick up the gauntlet of defiance to all evil!—a pulpit to keep unrolled the perpetual banner of the Holy War!—a pulpit clothed with the shadow of the Cross of Christ!—a pulpit covered by the wings of the Unseen Dove!

May 30, 1867.

AN OUTRAGE ON THE CHRISTIAN RELIGION.

IT is the glory of Christianity that it stoops to the lowly. The proud exalt the proud. The great flatter the great. The strong make fellowship with the strong. The rich rank themselves with the rich. But Jesus Christ was the Messiah of the poor. Born in a manger, he made the lowliest roof sacred. The son of a carpenter, he made the commonest calling honorable. Having not where to lay his head, he took from poverty its disgrace. Condescending to men of low estate, he made pride of rank for ever despicable. Taking the form of a servant, he thereby invested human nature with a dignity which forbids the strong man to oppress the weak, forbids the high class to scorn the low, forbids society to divide itself into castes, and forbids the government to outrage its citizens.

In contravention of the Christian religion, the President of the United States has once again set his heel on the necks of the lowly. Andrew Johnson's late Message is the greatest affront to the Christian spirit of this age which has been given by any presidential manifesto since the iniquitous Fugitive Slave law. With scorn and indignation, with sorrow and shame, we have read the dull, stony, and cruel argument which the Chief Magistrate of a Christian republic has pointed against a class of citizens whom he ought to exalt rather than to degrade, and whom he ought to clasp with the hand of fellowship rather than to smite with the gauntlet of scorn. This state paper is without parallel and without excuse. It is out of harmony with the Christian era. It is three thousand years old. It is the product of a Pagan brain. By the side of the Roman Emperor who kept in his girdle a bodkin to pierce flies, let posterity place an American President who kept in his inkstand a pen to stab negroes.

This new document from the Whited Sepulchre is filled with dead men's bones. It crushes at a stroke not merely a multitude, but a race, of victims. It rolls like Juggernaut over the rights of one-sixth portion of the American people. It re-lights the dying fires of that martyrdom which the black race on this continent has suffered for generations, and ought to suffer no more. It begins again the cruel persecutions which all mankind lately supposed were drawing to an end. Not even Horatio Seymour were he governor, nor Fernando Wood were he mayor, would have written at this late day a message so bitter in its accusations against the most docile race in the Republic. The man who promised the black-faced millions that he was to be their Moses; the man who wrote to Governor Sharkey that all negroes who could read and write ought to vote; the man who said to Major Stearns that negro suffrage was to be fostered in Tennessee; the man who assured the black regiment that this Government was not for white men alone:—this man, forgetting his pledges, forgetting his duty, forgetting his origin, has shocked his own nation, and astonished mankind, by putting forth, under the solemn seal of the Executive Department, an official re-utterance, in the year 1867, of the satanic slanders against the negro which disgraced the year 1856.

During the peril of the Republic the negro was a loyalist; his master a traitor. The negro was the nation's defender; his master, its assassin. The negro succored Union prisoners; his master starved them to death. Yet now, after this history, the President proposes to deliver the negro, bound hand and foot, to his late master! He argues that black loyalists should have no political rights, and white rebels no political disabilities. He asks for the repeal of all that Congress has done toward reconstruction, in order that Southern whites may immediately be re-invested with power over Southern blacks. He declares that impartial suffrage is worse than military despotism. He intimates that black men are unfit, not only to share political power with their white brethren, but even to govern themselves. He believes that foreign immigrants should have more privileges than native-born citizens. He insists that no calamity has ever yet befallen the Republic equal to the danger which will ensue from what he calls Africanizing one-half the country. He maintains that what is stigmatized as negro supremacy in the South will cost two hundred million dollars a year. He pretends that the ballot in the negro's hand will paralyze all mercantile business south of Mason and Dixon's obliterated line.

How strangely this message will fall on the ears of thoughtful Europeans! One President of the United States issues a proclamation emancipating slaves; and another writes a message asking practically for their rendition to slavery. How the beginning of 1863 puts to shame the end of 1867! How the silent sepulchre at Springfield rebukes the babbling Executive at Washington.

Spiritual wickedness prevails in high places. What is

the remedy? Spiritual purity must prevail all the more in other places. When the government is base, the people must be noble. When the state is false, the church must be faithful. The conscience of this nation ought to be so sensitive that such a message from the President would sting twenty million loyalists to indignation, and cost its author his immediate impeachment. The sentiment of justice ought to prevail among the people to such a degree that a chief magistrate who should speak against the just rights of the weakest citizen would raise as great a tempest about his head as would an archbishop who should publicly assail the 39 Articles. A nation that quietly looks on while its ruler tramples a negro, shall be one day trampled itself by the same tyrant.

This nation needs to be re-baptized in the fountain of political equality. To this end, the Christian pulpit must re-preach St. Paul's sermon on the one blood of which God hath made all the nations of the Earth. Citizens who love liberty must kindle anew its altar-flames in their breasts. Good men's lips must learn how to say, "Who is offended and I burn not?"

We want to see tyranny swept out of the land. We want to see the civil and political rights of all American citizens established on a rock of adamant. We want to see justice done alike to rich and poor, high and low, white and black. We want to see the Christian religion victorious over men's pride of birth and prejudice of skin. We want to see a truer value set upon that human nature which the Lord thought worthy of redeeming at so high a price. We want to see the Gospel leveling no class down, but all classes up. We want to live under a government which fears God, and respects its citizens. We want to see an awakening church leading the sluggish state. We want to hear thirty thousand clergymen proclaiming with an eloquence heretofore unheard by the ears of this generation, the inherent equality, nobility, and immortality of all mankind! O, for a baptism of fire!

December 12, 1867.

A FOLDED BANNER.

SPECTATOR in Washington just now finds that three personages are jointly challenging and bewildering the public attention: First, the Chief Justice of the United States; second, the President of the High Court of Impeachment; and, third, the Hon. Salmon P. Chase.

If the American people, at Judge Taney's death, could have foreseen that his successor (whoever he might be) would be called to preside over a trial for the impeachment of the President of the United States, such as is now going forward, and over a trial of the President of the Southern Confederacy, such as may go forward next month, they would have urged upon President Lincoln, still more earnestly than they did, the appointment of Mr. Chase as the one man who, above all others, was most signally fitted for the high post and its great duties. But, though Mr. Chase took his supreme seat amid the plaudits of half the nation, yet, ever since he was gowned, there has been an impression on the public mind that he would rather be off the bench than on it.

It is remarked of Mr. Chase more frequently than of any other statesman that he is ambitious for the presidency. Of course, it is idle to murmur at a great and good man for no better reason than because he wants to be President. "He that desireth the office of a bishop desireth a good thing." If the church can sanction an ambition for a bishopric, surely the state can sanction an ambition for the presidency. Nevertheless, a man of great aspirations ought to beware of "the last infirmity of noble mind." A hope of the presidency is like a gossamer in the air: he who runs too pantingly after it always blows it away with his own breath.

Of Mr. Chase's desire for the presidency we have no comment to make, except to say that, during our long acquaintance with him, we never once heard him utter a word or drop a hint which could be construed as the expression of such a thought. If others among his admirers can give a different testimony, this at least is all that we ourselves can give. If Mr. Chase has kept a presidential hope within his breast, he has carried it like a hid treasure, which he may have exhibited to other friends, but which he never once laid before our own eyes.

Nor have we any voice to lend to the clamor against Mr. Chase for his rulings during the present trial. Mr. Sumner, the other day, made an able argument—one of the most masterly of his minor speeches—to prove from parliamentary precedents that the Chief-Justice, in presiding over the Senate as a Court of Impeachment, is not entitled to any vote, even in case of a tie. Mr. Chase, on the other hand, believes that as he takes the place of the Vice-President of the United States, who is President of the Senate, and who has a casting vote, he himself as Chief-Justice shall in like manner have a casting vote; a view which, though it may not be in accordance with the precedents, is nevertheless in accordance with good sense. But the question whether the one or the other of these views is correct, or whether Mr. Chase during the trial shall be addressed as "Mr. Chief Justice" or as "Mr. President," seems to us of far less practical importance than the learned lawyers would have the world regard it.

For years past, we have earnestly and often advocated Mr. Chase's nomination to the presidency. This advocacy now ends. Without crediting the fables of the scandal-mongers who say that Mr. Chase has abandoned the party of which he was lately the chief ornament, and has practically joined the Democracy, we are nevertheless constrained to say that the Republican party can no longer with propriety look to Mr. Chase to be one of its leaders, and least of all to be its chief. A short time ago, we thought the greatest gift we could offer to the coming Chicago Convention was Mr. Chase's illustrious name. We now have reason to believe that Mr. Chase would not accept the Republican nomination, even if it were tendered. We have equal reason to believe that he would accept the Democratic nomination, if it could be tendered on a platform not inconsistent with his well-known views of Negro Suffrage. No one who knows the man will expect him ever to change, modify, or compromise his life-long and ineradicable convictions in favor of Liberty, Justice, and Political Equality. Solemnly and earnestly he holds now, as he has held always, to the equal civil and political rights of all American citizens, without distinction of color, and (let us add also) without distinction of sex. Nor have we any doubt that he will remain, in his own judgment, sacredly true to those great and high convictions during the rest of his life. But, as the fact is now evident that Mr. Chase no longer links his political future with the Republican party, we have no right any longer to solicit the Republican party to unfurl the banner of his name.

Of course, these remarks are not designed to state the position, or indicate the views, or hint the purposes of Mr. Chase—an office which we have neither authority, nor knowledge, nor wish, nor right to assume; but solely for the sake of honorably informing the Republican party that *The Independent* unequivocally recalls its long-maintained nomination of Mr. Chase for the presidency.

If at this late day it were not wholly useless to substitute another name, it might be that of Charles Sumner, or Schuyler Colfax, or Benjamin F. Wade, or Gen. Butler. But the Chicago Convention will go pell-mell for Gen. Grant. Nevertheless, we shall go on dreaming our day-dream of the happy time when a great statesman shall preside over the Great Republic.

April 16, 1868.

THE SOILURE OF A FAIR NAME.

GREAT man's honor, if unsullied, is a coronet on his head, to mark him a prince among men. But this diadem is not of gold, that no rust can corrupt; nor of jewels, that no mould can blight. Borrowing its lustre solely from virtue, it can be stained by any touch of baseness. Fortunate is he who, amid the world's temptations, keeps his honor lustrous and unspotted; wretched is he who, in the battle of life, finds that some evil blow has struck from his brow the emblem of his kingliness; despicable is he who, with deliberate purpose, uplifts his own hand to discrown his own head.

Mr. William M. Evarts, counsel for Mr. Andrew Johnson, has pawned his honor for a lawyer's fee. The charge is grave, but true. Let us substantiate it.

A conspicuous actor in Republican conventions, a trusted adviser in Republican councils, an ambitious orator before Republican assemblages, a once-beaten but still aspiring Republican candidate for a United States senatorship, a leading Republican member of the recent New York State Constitutional Convention—Mr. Evarts was summoned to the President's defence, not because he was a shining light in the legal profession, but because he was an influential leader of the Republican party. The President did not go to the bar of New York to hire its most skilful advocate, but to buy its most serviceable politician. If Mr. Johnson had been simply in quest of a great lawyer, he would have forgotten Mr. Evarts and remembered Mr. O'Conor. But Mr. O'Conor was a Democrat, and the crafty President wanted a Republican. It was not Mr. Evarts' legal ability, but his political influence, that Mr. Johnson bargained for, purchased, and secured. But Mr. Evarts, in thus making a traffic of what, among honorable men, is too precious to be merchandise, parted with what no man can ever sell except by throwing into the bargain his good name.

Let us do no injustice to Mr. Evarts. If, in looking forward to the Impeachment Trial, he could have had his choice of sides, he undoubtedly would have chosen the prosecution; he would have preferred to act *with* his party, rather than *against* it. If the managers of the Impeachment, desiring outside help, had asked this thin, bloodless, and ambitious man—this frail Cassius—to fill the stalwart part assumed by General Butler, he would probably have undertaken, however humbly he might have executed, Cæsar's task. But with a lawyer's itching to connect his name with the greatest trial in our annals, Mr. Evarts, seeing that the opportunity was tempting, seeing that the position was unique, seeing that the emolument was great, stipulated with his conscience that, since he had no opportunity to serve on the right side, he should therefore be justified in serving on the wrong.

Compare Mr. Evarts's too pliable moral sense with the stiffer self-respect of some of his nobler peers of the bar. For example, does any one imagine that Charles O'Conor could have been induced for any fee to *prosecute* the President? Or will any one dare to hint that William Curtis Noyes, if now alive, could have been tempted by any bribe to *defend* the President?

Look at it! Here, on one side of the Senate, sit the

managers of the Impeachment: would any interpretation of professional obligation or propriety have induced George S. Boutwell, a Massachusetts abolitionist, to plead for Andrew Johnson's escape from justice? Yonder, on the other side, sit the counsel for the defence: would any consideration of reward or distinction have moved Mr. Groesbeck, an inflexible Democrat, to plead for the President's removal by a Senate of Republicans?

No. It was reserved for Mr. Evarts, with a too facile conscience and a too easy virtue, to be equally ready to advocate one side or the other; not in a common suit at law, but in a case without parallel in law or history, and involving not only his party's success or failure, but his country's honor or shame.

If it be answered that a lawyer may lawfully take either side of any litigated question, we do not say nay. We have no present quarrel with any general rule of the profession, even though some of its rules are not defensible in morals. Certainly no criminal can be too guilty to deserve a fair trial; and a fair trial cannot be had without counsel for the defence. Lord Brougham has taught the bar of two countries to believe that the guiltiest man's lawyer must do his utmost to prove his client guiltless— a view, however, which many lawyers refuse to accept. But, whether this view be correct or not, our criticism of Mr. Evarts is not at this point. If he had undertaken to defend the lowest villain who ever stabbed a fellow-creature in a midnight brawl, his act would have had the general sanction of his profession, and should have been exempt from censure here. He would then have been simply following the strict line of his professional duty. But, on the other hand, when Mr. Evarts lent himself as a loyalist to the guilty task of shielding a rebel President from the righteous judgment of an offended people, he undertook an act outside of his professional obligation; an act shocking to the finer senses of upright men among his brethren of the bar; an act indefensible in ethics; an act of which he himself seems to have privately doubted the propriety; an act concerning which he was anxious to know the opinions of his personal friends before venturing to commit it; an act for which, in the exordium of his argument, he publicly apologized; an act inconsistent with an honest fealty to the great party of which he claims to be a chief; an act hostile to the welfare of his country.

No President of the United States—not Tyler, who violated his pledges; not Fillmore, who re-enslaved the escaping negro; not Buchanan, who surrendered the nation's honor without striking a blow to maintain it:—not all these illustrious criminals, taken together, rivalled in crime this one man Johnson, who, more signally than Tyler, betrayed his friends, more wantonly than Fillmore trampled on the negro's rights, and more traitorously than Buchanan leagued himself with rebels against the Government.

From our previous high estimate of Mr. Evarts's patriotism and public spirit, we would as soon have expected to see him taking a commission from the Copperhead party in 1863 to prosecute President Lincoln for high treason, as to see him taking a commission from the same source in 1868 to defend President Johnson for "high crimes and misdemeanors."

When Warren Hastings was impeached for misgoverning India, Thomas Erskine, the greatest of English advocates, refused point-blank to undertake the criminal's defence. This refusal was given in spite of many temptations to accept. The impeacher was Edmund Burke;

and, above all other ambitions, Erskine longed for an opportunity to cross swords with Burke in Westminster Hall. If the case had been of any other character than one involving the conflicting policies of opposing parties —if Erskine could have undertaken the task without espousing the cause of his political opponents—he would have given his right hand for the unequalled opportunity which the trial was to afford. But happily his willingness to serve his country proved greater than his desire to profit himself; and he refused to purchase professional distinction at the price of political treachery. If Erskine could once more open his mouth, what words of rebuke he would let fall on Mr. Evarts, who, for the sake of figuring in a famous case, consents to counterwork both his party and his country!

Mr. Evarts had a noble opportunity not merely to repeat Erskine's example, but to stamp it into an abiding and irreversible precedent for the profession. If he had said, "I will go as far as any lawyer may or ought for the defence of any criminal; I will see that no undue advantage is taken of him on his trial; I will shield him against every cunning stratagem of his accuser; I will claim for him his fullest rights under the law; but I will not utter a lie in any man's defence, even though he be a President impeached; I will not advocate in open court a political policy which I abhor in my secret heart; I will not betray my party, or imperil my country, by championing the common enemy of both:"—the whole world would have applauded the utterance; and the unseduced advocate would have written his name on the scroll of the honored and proud. On the other hand, the fact that Mr. Evarts, at one of the most critical moments of our political history, in derogation of his professional honor, and in antagonism to the public welfare, hired himself for lucre to be the defender of Andrew Johnson, is as great a shock to the moral sense as if James Otis had been bribed by George III. to defend the Writs of Assistance, or Patrick Henry had accepted a fee to justify the Stamp Act of 1765.

Grandson of a signer of the Declaration of Independence, Mr. Evarts has put his little measure of Roger Sherman's blood to an unwonted blush by bartering for a price the safety of the Republic.

Sing to him Robert Browning's song:

> "Just for a handful of silver he left us,
> Just for a ribbon to stick in his coat."

May 7, 1868.

THE TONGUE OF FIRE.

THE Queen of England, in her published diary, occasionally refers to some particular sermon which has pleased her fancy or touched her heart. We quote her Majesty's gracious allusions to a couple of distinguished Scotch clergymen whom not only queens and princes, but scholars and critics, might well afford to praise.

"OCTOBER 29, 1854.

"We went to the kirk as usual at 12 o'clock. The service was performed by the Rev. Norman McLeod, of Glasgow, son of Dr. McLeod, and anything finer I never heard. The sermon, entirely extempore, was quite admirable; so simple and yet so eloquent, and so beautifully argued and put. The text was from the account of the coming of Nicodemus to Christ by night—St. John, chap. viii. Mr. McLeod showed in the sermon how we all tried to please *self*, and live for *that*, and in so doing found no rest. Christ had come not only to die for us, but to show us how we were to live. The second prayer was very touching. His allusions to us were very simple, saying, after his mention of us, 'bless their children.' It gave me a lump in my throat; as also when he prayed for 'the dying, the wounded, the widow, and the orphans.' Every one came back delighted; and how satisfactory it is to come back from church with such feelings! The servants and the Highlanders *all* were equally delighted."

* * * * * *

"October 14, 1855.

"To kirk at 12 o'clock. The Rev. J. Caird, one of the most celebrated preachers in Scotland, performed the service, and electrified all present by a most admirable and beautiful sermon, which lasted nearly an hour, but which kept one's attention riveted. The text was from the 12th chapter of Romans and the 11th verse: 'Not slothful in business, fervent in spirit, serving the Lord.' He explained, in the most beautiful and simple manner, what real religion is; how it ought to pervade every action of our lives; not a thing only for Sundays, or for our closet; not a thing to drive us from the world; not a 'perpetual moping over good books;' but 'being and doing good,' 'letting everything be done in a Christian spirit.' It was as fine as Dr. McLeod's sermon last year, and sent us home much edified."

Not to speak of the Queen's genuine motherliness of feeling evinced by that "lump in her throat" at hearing blessings invoked on her children, it is pleasant to know the good lady's English admiration of her Scotch divines. Those temporary "court preachers" preached to a better purpose than the obsequious flattery which once characterized "court-preaching." They chained the attention, stirred the heart, and "sent home much edified" the chief lady of Europe. Perhaps those sermons, so working on the Queen's heart, may through her have worked a little, (though, we fear, a very little) on the harder heart of that great government of hers which knows how to be just to England and unjust to the rest of the world. The Queen's journal proves her to have grown so thoroughly in love with the Scotch preachers whom she heard and the Scotch people whom she met, that we wish she would now, in like manner, make a trip to Ireland, listen to the Irish clergy, and open her heart to the Irish people; from both of whom, we venture to say, she would hear such a tale of oppression and misery as, more than ever, would bring a "lump in her throat."

But we quote the Queen's journal for the sake of its royal testimony to extempore preaching. This is the only royal preaching. All sinners, from sovereigns to beggars, are more moved by it than by the best of Sunday-morning essay reading. One sermon preached from a brief is worth three sermons read from a manuscript. We hope Congress will lay as high a tax on sermon-paper as on whisky—in conformity with Napoleon's rule, that the vices should be taxed high.

Dr. Chalmers, and a few great men like him, have proved themselves able to make even a manuscript burn and glow in the pulpit; but as a general thing, the life in a minister's manuscript is like the voice in Balaam's ass —it requires a miracle to make it speak.

The habit of reading from the pulpit tends not only to make the delivery dull, but to make the preaching metaphysical. If a sermon is full of hair-splitting, it is certain to have been written word for word beforehand. If it is to contain a whole body of divinity, accurately stated, it must of course be nicely fashioned at the pen's point. But if it is to be (as it generally ought to be) on some plain, homely, and vital truth of the Gospel, why should it be written? The pen oftenest preaches to the head; the tongue to the heart. A lady lately said to us, in speaking of a distinguished clergyman who had made himself a bond-slave to a manuscript, "He has a great faculty for preaching religion *out* of people." This same minister is one of the most expert of theologians. But, if he had been less addicted to discussing theological distinctions, and more addicted to emphasizing practical religious duties, he might have become an excellent extemporaneous preacher. If Paul himself had tried to put into his sermons all the theology which he reserved for his epistles, he too would have been reduced to a manuscript, suffered a second thorn in the flesh, and become in "his speech" more than ever "contemptible." Imagine Christ delivering the Sermon on the Mount from a bundle of papyrus!

Many of our theological seminaries seem to forget that their students are to become not merely theologians, but orators. The chill of the seminary has quenched the natural fire out of the tongue of many a young man who might have been a speaker, but who becomes only a reader. A minister said to us mournfully, "I charge upon the seminary where I was trained the entire crushing out of all my early tendencies to extemporaneous speech." Now and then a strong man, in spite of such early training, achieves a signal success in revolting against his manuscript—as, for instance, the Rev. Dr. Storrs, of Brooklyn, whose recent practice of extemporaneous preaching is the delight of his congregation. But most ministers are never able to outgrow their seminary. It follows them, clings to them, and governs them, through life. They throw off the yoke, but the stiff neck remains. It is as happy a day when a minister gets rid of his manuscript as when a church gets rid of its debt.

A lawyer does not read, but speaks. Is a sermon a piece of closer reasoning than a law-argument? The majority of sermons, considered as efforts of reasoning, are not equal to the majority of law-arguments. If a lawyer can get along without writing, certainly a minister ought to do the same. Where is the fault? It is not in the minister's vocation; it is not in his constitution; it is simply in his training. The oratorical gift may be fairly presumed to belong, in a reasonable degree, to every man who feels within himself a strong predisposition toward either the pulpit or the bar. The difference between a young lawyer and a young clergyman is this: the one fans his native spark by speaking; the other smothers it by reading. Let a young minister, whose temptation is manuscripts, tumble them into his study-fire. They will flash new lustre on all his subsequent preaching. The devil is fond of written sermons, but trembles at the living voice.

The Queen's delight in hearing the Rev. Norman McLeod (who had not then won his spurs in divinity) reminds us of the equal delight with which the same preacher was heard by a friend of ours who lately returned from Europe. "I would give a hundred dollars," said our friend—"yes, two hundred—if I could hear another sermon which would do me as much good as the only one I ever heard from Dr. McLeod. I shall never forget it. He did not look at a scrap of paper from beginning to end. But he took hold of me with a grip which he has never let go to this day." This is the right kind of praise which the right kind of sermon elicits from the right kind of hearer.

The true ideal of a preacher is one whose sermon is *in* him and not in *front* of him; who speaks, not reads; who allows no "middle-wall of partition" to arise between him and his congregation; who has less desire to utter rounded sentences than to utter glowing truths;

who gloves himself with a gauntlet of strong English for the sake of striking terrible blows. The New England pulpit is altogether too chirographical in its speech. The Christian ministry everywhere needs "the tongue of fire."

WOMAN'S INFLUENCE ON LITERATURE.

THE purest passion of human nature is love for children. In disinterestedness, unselfishness, and consecration, no other love is equal to it. A babe's breath against its mother's bosom fans the holiest flame that ever kindles her heart. Even an Esquimaux drudge, sitting in Arctic darkness, brightens her dull eye with a sacred fondness for her offspring. Round the world, mother-love is next to God's love.

It may seem strange, then, that so small a share of the world's poetry has turned on this keen and eager passion. Every other love has been a thousand times celebrated in royal verse, except this one perennial pulse that out-beats them one and all. Why has not love for children taken that high place as a lyric and dramatic theme in literature which it takes as a passionate reality in life?

The answer is plain: this love, though well expressed by man, is best expressed by woman; and against woman, until a comparatively recent period, the gates of literature have been shut. To the whole world's cost, woman was too long denied the pen. She has only lately learned to write. The Elizabethan poets, many-sided as they were, lacked a woman among their choir, to be not merely their peer but their counterpart. In later days, since woman has ventured to lift a pen, she has found it a Moses-rod, smiting a rock whose fountains have been hitherto sealed. The noblest use to which woman has put her new-found literary function has been to express those peculiar phases of human experience which man can never so pathetically state, because he can never so exquisitely feel. Many literary critics doubt whether women can ever become great writers. This doubt is born of a superficial knowledge of human nature. Sooner or later great women must inevitably become great writers, if for no other reason than that God leads woman into a sacred realm of human life whose secrets no one knows, or ever can know, except herself. The Elusinian mysteries were not half so mysterious as the common daily experiences that women attain in the birth and death of their children. This is a chord of life that can be made to vibrate in literature only by woman's hand. This is a lore that can be written only out of woman's heart. It is not by saying well what men say better, but by saying authoritatively what men cannot say at all, that women are to become (and cannot help becoming) profound writers. No reason exists why women should not become the very chief of those heart-revealing poets " who learn through suffering what they teach in song."

Indeed, during the quarter of a century since woman's pen has been busy in English literature, it has already contributed to our poetry many sweet records of love and grief which our language cannot afford to lose, and which posterity will not willingly let die.

When Macaulay first began to write, it was the literary fashion of his age to sneer brilliantly at woman's authorship; and he himself was among the brilliant sneerers. But side by side with his own great fame there grew up a name in English literature which, though a woman's, now serenely outshines his own. We mean the name of Elizabeth Barrett Browning. Without forgetting her many faults as a writer—faults in structure and expression—faults in which her husband is still faultier—nevertheless to Mrs. Browning is due the high praise of giving to motherly affections and yearnings and prayers such an expression as no other poet has ever set in hallowed verse. And other women have since followed and will follow in her train, uttering their full hearts like nightingales. The literature of the nineteenth century owes its finest specimens of artistic structure to men, but owes its noblest utterances of the affectional and religious nature to women.

It has occurred to us to transcribe three or four poems written by women, which fathom a depth of feeling not attained by men. They shall all relate to one theme—the death of children. Let the first be "Little Mattie," by Mrs. Browning—a strain to which many hearts have given a loving response, and at which many eyes have shed tender tears:

"Dead! Thirteen a month ago!
  Short and narrow her life's walk;
Lover's love she could not know
  Even by a dream or talk:
Too young to be glad of youth,
  Missing honor, labor, rest,
And the warmth of a babe's mouth
  At the blossom of her breast.
Must you pity her for this
And for all the loss it is,
You, her mother, with wet face,
Having had all in your case?

"Just so young but yesternight,
  Now she is as old as death.
Meek, obedient in your sight,
  Gentle to a beck or breath
Only on last Monday! Yours,
  Answering you like silver bells
Lightly touched! An hour matures:
  You can teach her nothing else.
She has seen the mystery hid
Under Egypt's pyramid:
By those eyelids pale and close
Now she knows what Rhamses knows."

"Cross her quiet hands, and smooth
Down her patient looks of silk,
Cold and passive as in truth
You your fingers in spilt milk
Drew along a marble floor;
But her lips you cannot wring
Into saying a word more,
'Yes,' or 'No,' or such a thing:
Though you call and beg and wreak
Half your soul out in a shriek,
She will lie there in default
And most innocent revolt.

"Ay, and if she spoke, may be
She would answer like the Son,
'What is now 'twixt thee and me?'
Dreadful answer! better none.
Yours on Monday, God's to-day!
Yours, your child, your blood, your heart,
Called . . . you called her, did you say,
'Little Mattie' for your part?
Now already it sounds strange,
And you wonder, in this change,
What He calls His angel-creature,
Higher up than you can reach her.

"'Twas a green and easy world
As she took it; room to play,
(Though one's hair might get uncurled
At the far end of the day).
What she suffered she shook off
In the sunshine; what she sinned
She could pray on high enough
To keep safe above the wind.
If reproved by God or you,
'Twas to better her, she knew;
And if crossed, she gathered still
'Twas to cross out something ill.

"You, you had the right, you thought
To survey her with sweet scorn,
Poor gay child, who had not caught
Yet the octave-stretch forlorn
Of your larger wisdom! Nay,
Now your places are changed so,
In that same superior way
She regards you dull and low
As you did herself exempt
From life's sorrows. Grand contempt
Of the spirits risen awhile,
Who look back with such a smile!

"There's the sting of't. That, I think,
Hurts the most a thousand-fold!
To feel sudden, at a wink,
Some dear child we used to scold,
Praise, love both ways, kiss and tease,
Teach and tumble as our own,
All its curls about our knees,
Rise up suddenly full-grown.
Who could wonder such a sight
Made a woman mad outright?
Show me Michael with the sword
Rather than such angels, Lord!"

Mrs. Maria White Lowell wrote very little, but she wrote one tender and true poem which her husband (perhaps our chief American poet) was proud to publish side by side with his own works—a little, unpretentious, and doubtless unpremeditated strain, which has had a strange popularity, and which, slight as the structure is, nevertheless has proved itself strong enough to bear up the heavy load of many a mother's grief:

"We wreathed about our darling's head the morning-glory bright.
Her little face looked out beneath, so full of love and light,
So lit as with a sunrise, that we could only say,
She is the morning-glory true, and her poor types are they.

"So always, from that happy time, we called her by their name,
And very fitting did it seem, for sure as morning came,
Behind her cradle-bars she smiled to catch the first faint ray
As from the trellis smiles the flower, and opens to the day.

"But not so beautiful they rear their airy cups of blue,
As turned her sweet eyes to the light, brimmed with sleep's tender dew,
And not so close their tendrils fine round their supports are thrown,
As those dear arms, whose outstretched plea clasped all hearts to her own.

"We used to think how she had come, even as comes the flower,
The last and perfect added gift to crown love's morning hour,
And how in her was imaged forth the love we could not say,
As on the little dewdrops round shines back the heart of day.

"We never could have thought, O God, that she must wither up
Almost before a day was flown, like the morning-glory's cup;
We never thought to see her droop her fair and noble head,
Till she lay stretched before our eyes, wilted and cold and dead.

"The morning-glory's blossoming will soon be coming round,
We see their rows of heart-shaped leaves uprising from the ground,

The tender things the winter killed, renew again their birth,
But the glory of our morning has passed away from earth.

"O earth! in vain our aching eyes stretch over thy green plain,
Too harsh thy dews, too gross thine air, her spirit to sustain;
But up in groves of Paradise, full surely we shall see
Our Morning-Glory, beautiful, twine round our dear Lord's knee."

Not to multiply quotations, let us add only one more; and it shall be from Adelaide Anne Proctor, who lived and died a Roman Catholic, and whom we would not (if we could) have persuaded to be a Protestant—at least not until after she had written these exquisite and immortal lines:

"Our God in Heaven, from that holy place,
To each of us an Angel guide has given;
But Mothers of dead children have more grace—
For they give Angels to their God and Heaven.

"How can a Mother's heart feel cold or weary
Knowing her dearer self safe, happy, warm?
How can she feel her road too dark or dreary,
Who knows her treasure sheltered from the storm.

"How can she sin? Our hearts may be unheeding,
Our God forgot, our holy Saints defied;
But can a mother hear her dead child pleading,
And thrust those little angel-hands aside?

"Those little hands stretched down to draw her ever
Nearer to God by mother love:—we all
Are blind and weak, yet surely she can never,
With such a stake in Heaven, fail or fall.

"She knows that when the mighty Angels raise
Chorus in Heaven, one little silver tone
Is hers for ever, that one little praise,
One little happy voice, is all her own.

"We may not see her sacred crown of honor,
But all the Angels flitting to and fro
Pause smiling as they pass—they look upon her
As mother of an angel whom they know,

"One whom they left nestled at Mary's feet—
The children's place in Heaven—who softly sings
A little chant to please them, slow and sweet,
Or smiling strokes their little folded wings;

"Or gives them Her white lilies or Her beads
To play with:—yet, in spite of flower or song,

They often lift a wistful look that pleads
And asks Her why their mother stays so long.

"Then our dear Queen makes answer she will call
Her very soon: meanwhile they are beguiled
To wait and listen while She tells them all
A story of Her Jesus as a child.

"Ah, Saints in Heaven may pray with earnest will
And pity for their weak and erring brothers:
Yet there is prayer in Heaven more tender still—
The little Children pleading for their Mothers."

We appeal to any thoughtful reader who knows these poems, or who will take the pains to know them (for a genuine poem cannot be properly weighed by merely reading it once, or twice, or thrice), whether these do not possess a subtle quality that places them just as far beyond man's expression as they are beyond man's experience. Indeed, what man could have written either of them without losing from the verse the unmistakable womanly quality which constitutes its predominant charm?

Woman's influence on English literature is growing stronger and richer every day. Already many of the sweetest hymns used in our churches are the compositions of women—as, for instance, "Nearer, my God, to Thee," written by Sarah Flower Adams. In certain qualities of mind, the greatest novelist of our time is a woman—the author of "Adam Bede" and "Romola." Next to "Bunyan's Pilgrim," no book has made a profounder impression on mankind than Mrs. Stowe's "Uncle Tom." A Frenchman once wrote an essay to assert a woman's right to the alphabet. What a beautiful use she has made of her A B C's!

And the time is nigh at hand when woman is to exert as refining an influence on politics as already she has exerted on literature.

KAULBACH'S ERA OF THE REFORMATION.

ALL the world has heard of Kaulbach's frescoes on the walls of the Berlin Museum:—the crowning works of a master who first became famous half a century ago, and who now, in ripe years, stands as undisputedly at the head of the living artists of his country as Albert Durer did at a former day.

These frescoes, six in number, represent respectively "The building of the Tower of Babel," "The Nations of Greece listening to the Songs of Homer," "The Battle of the Huns," "The Destruction of Jerusalem," and, finally, "The Era of the Reformation." Of the whole series, the last is regarded by the artist's friends (and by the artist himself) as his *chef-d'œuvre*. The cartoon was sent to the Paris Exposition, where it received the highest prize, after which it was purchased by au American citizen, who has brought it to New York, and lent it to the Somerville Gallery.

Taking this cartoon as the favorite illustration of the artist's genius and style, one glance is enough to detect in it the regulated riot of a frolicsome fancy, and the curbed gallop of a restive hand. Here are ingenious figures, striking attitudes, and dramatic situations. Here are illustrative costumes, allegorical emblems, and poetic accessories. Here are flowing lines, antithetic lights and darks, and (doubtless in the fresco) animating surprises of color. But, notwithstanding many brilliant beauties that compel admiration, and notwithstanding many truthful uglinesses that command respect, the composition in several vital points is so demonstrably inadequate that we wonder at its extraordinary popularity among critics.

We shall endeavor to render some reasons for believing that it is estimated beyond its desert.

What is its theme or moral? This is not readily discovered. A picture called "The Era of the Reformation"—with Martin Luther for its central figure, holding up in both hands an open Bible, while round him are grouped Melancthon, Calvin, Zwingle, and other reformers—might be supposed to represent the struggle and triumph of Protestantism. But this plausible theory is contradicted by the inclusion of many personages who lived and died Roman Catholics, and who are here represented not merely in no antagonism to Luther and his comrades, but in undissenting harmony with his great movement.

If the cartoon by its ecclesiastical title, its open Bible, and its fiery-tongued preacher, be still assumed to indicate a religious theme of some kind, this interpretation is spoiled by the fact that one large section is devoted to art, another to literature, another to science, and another to discovery; so that, on the whole, the picture is like a religious newspaper—almost entirely full of secular topics.

If the aim be (as probably Kaulbach would acknowledge) to give a comprehensive representation of religion, art, science, literature, and politics, as these flourished during, or in consequence of, "The Era of the Reformation;" and if, in carrying out this scheme, he desired to make his picture do honor to religion by visibly elevating this above all other human concerns; and if, still further, he desired to testify that, among the many grand events which form the pageantry of the cartoon, he thought the grandest of all was Luther's illustrious crusade:—then we cannot help saying that this glowing idea does not seem to be animating the great convocation itself, and, as a natural consequence, is not made to enkindle the breast of the spectator. In fact, a majority of the stately personages here depicted seem to be occupied with almost every other thought than of Luther and his proclaimed Gospel. Of the 112 figures in the cartoon, only *one* seems to be paying any heed to the Protestant Bible; and this is a Roman Catholic, Sir Thomas More! In fact, we can count only four persons in the entire congregation who seem aware of Luther's presence. No street-missionary preaches to the vagabonds of the Five Points without attracting greater attention than the illustrious leader of the Reformation is here eliciting from this worshipful company of the world's worthies. There is a general turning of backs upon the great preacher, which is all the more noticeable because he himself is represented in the earnest attitude of calling the whole world's attention to the emancipated Gospel; a call to which there is so little response from any quarter of the picture that the proclaimer seems deserted and alone—"the voice of one crying in the wilderness." In striking contrast with this neglect of the Bible by the very priests, sages, and martyrs, whom the artist has convened to celebrate it, we notice the eager interest awakened by a copy of Homer's Iliad, which Petrarch has taken out of an ancient tomb, and is showing to Shakespeare, Cervantes, and others. Of course, in thus introducing these two representative books—the one sacred and the other profane—the artist has shown a pious intent to exalt the Bible over the other literatures of the world; but, in so doing, he has unhappily represented it as the least interesting to the noblest classes of mankind. The picture by its wayward accessories, thus becomes unfaithful to its leading intent, and fails to impress the spectator as strongly with its primal as with its minor meanings.

Much good, but some bad, judgment has been shown in the selection and rejection of representative characters. The artist's *dramatis personæ* are mainly Germans —a fault (if it be one) easily pardoned to a proud partiality for one's own country. But, in choosing his Englishmen, he has strangely omitted Cromwell and Milton, who inherited the very soul of the Reformation, and yet he has included Essex and Burleigh, who add nothing whatever to the theme. If it be said that Cromwell and Milton are too late for "The Era of the Reformation," we reply that the artist makes this era reach into the second century after Luther's death. In fact, among his Englishmen, he has introduced Harvey, the contemporary of the Protector and of his Latin secretary. So too an "aching void" exists in the group of painters, occasioned by the noticeable absence of Titian, who, born before Luther and living after him, reproduced in art more of the spirit of the Reformation than any other artist here given, not even excepting Albert Durer; for to Titian belongs the historic credit of emancipating art from its ecclesiastical bonds. Moreover, how advantageously might Kaulbach have forgotten Von der Tam, to have remembered Grotius; or spared the uninteresting Sebastian Frank, to make room for the world's favorite, Blaise Pascal; or chosen Arminius, the luminous teacher, instead of Barneveldt, his reflecting disciple; or preferred Servetus (who was of sufficient importance to be burned) to some of the obscurer lighters of his fire.

In "The School of Athens," by Raphael, notwithstanding the extraordinary intellectual activity that animates its eager groups—the figures being in the varying attitudes of sitting, stooping, and standing; writing, reading, and listening; holding globes, measuring distances, and carrying books—yet how adroitly the great draughtsman has kept all these figures from crowding, elbowing, and jostling each other! What room, and what freedom to move about in it, he has given to each! How evidently the ground plan of his groups would admit of the figures transforming themselves from mere painted shapes, existing on a flat wall, into rounded statues, filling an actual temple! In "The Hemicycle," by Delaroche, although all the canvas is compactly occupied, yet such is the sense of remaining roominess that, in addition to the 75 figures already there, it seems as if 40 more might suddenly glide into that majestic company without disturbing its convenience or order. But similar praise cannot be justly given to "The Era of the Reformation," which, with its 112 figures (just twice as many as Raphael introduced), looks uncomfortably crowded, not to say impossibly full; and a helter-skelter air pervades the composition, as if the artist had fixed his moment of time just after the various groups had arrived in the cathedral, and before any one common purpose had begun to unify the convocation.

Raphael's groups being on two planes, separated by a stairs of only three steps; and Delaroche's on two planes, separated by only two steps; the figures in the rear, in both these pictures, are neither so far above nor so far behind the figures in front as to make a marked difference between their comparative heights; but in Kaulbach's there are four distinct ranks of figures, receding behind and rising above each other through all the great space existing between the floor at the entrance of the cathedral and the distant and lofty organ-gallery. As a consequence, the inexorable law of perspective mercilessly keeps cutting down the size of a human being in each successive rank, and thus irretrievably wastes the impressiveness of a composition whose chief interest must be in its recognizable portraits. For example, the leg of Hans Sach, who sits on the floor in the foreground, is twice the length of the whole body of Luther, and yet Luther stands in the very next plane behind him; while behind Luther are two other swiftly-dwindling ranks, in the more distant of which the half-length bodies, seen above the rail of the choir, are no longer than the sole of Hans Sach's unforeshortened shoe. This multiplication of planes and distances is not only fatal to a just equality of honor among the personages, but actually reverses many of the obvious preferences which the artist seeks to indicate. For instance, although he undoubtedly means Luther to be the one commanding figure, yet by placing him on a distant rostrum, high above the great groups of the foreground, he has been compelled by an unavoidable exigency of perspective to belittle his hero into secondary importance. In fact, not Luther, Calvin, Zwingle, Melancthon, all taken together, are as prominent, impressive, and interesting as the solitary old Hans Sach, cobbler and poet, who, with a leather apron on his lap and a pen in his hand, is altogether the most picturesque and loveable figure in the whole composition. Kaulbach's Hans Sach is twin to Raphael's Diogenes.

Among the portraits, many of which are life-like and almost satisfactory—as for instance, Melancthon, Macchiavelli, Reuchlin, and Vesalius—the chief failure is Shakespeare. The authentic data for a correct portrait of Shakespeare are not abundant; but such as they are, they do not warrant this fancy sketch—which resembles neither the Droeshout, the Chandos, the Jansen, nor the Felton portrait, nor the Stratford bust, nor the cast after death. The artist seems to have used the common Parian head with which crockery-stores insult the finest skull of all time, and to have invigorated the brow, eyes, and mouth into the look of a man of intense outward activity rather than of inward fecundity—a Knight Templar who would have handled a rapier more dexterously than a pen. Lord Bacon is here totally unrecognizable at first; and even after one detects in his hand the *Novum Organum*, one cannot discern in his face anything betokening either the greatest or the meanest of mankind. And Columbus, as he here looks, is as much a piece of guess-work as if he had been meant for Abraham, Isaac, or Jacob.

On the whole, we prefer many other designs by this artist to the generally preferred "Era of the Reformation."

Let us add that these candid criticisms on one of the most famous works of art produced during the present century are put forth in a spirit of profound respect for the genius, character, and career of Wilhelm von Kaulbach; who by universal acclaim is one of "the choice and master spirits of this age;" and who falls short only of that superior greatness which God has given to no modern artist in equal measure with Ghiberti and Angelo, or with Raphael and Titian.

THE CHURCHWOMAN'S BALLOT.

IN years gone by, the chief offender against the negro was the church. "The American church," said Albert Barnes (while the conflict was raging), "is the bulwark of American slavery." Let us be thankful that the American church, which did so much to rivet the negro's chain at first, did so much to break it at last. But the same American church that once bound the negro, still binds woman. Mr. Barnes's proverb might be re-stated thus: The church is at this day the chief bulwark of woman's bondage. Let us be thankful, for every sign witnessed among our churches, of the sundering of woman's yoke of oppression.

The woman question, like the negro question, must be fought inch by inch through the church before it can come to victory in the State. The church to-day offers a more hopeful battle-ground than the State for fighting the question to a speedy triumph. Church suffrage and State suffrage are identical in principle. Win one, and you have won the other. The church and the State are like the calf and the ox of the fable. Begin by carrying the calf, and you will have strength to carry the ox; but, haply, if you undertake the ox first, you may afterward need to wait awhile for breath to carry even the calf. Of course, we do not mean that the agitation of the woman question should not go forward in the State at the same time as in the church: there should be a "continuous firing all along the line;" but we earnestly advocate (as a consideration too greatly overlooked) the equal importance of carrying forward this noblest, purest, and grandest of public questions just as vigorously in the church as in the State. Woman never forgets that she is a member of the church, and seldom remembers that she is a citizen of the State. She can always be more easily reached through the church than through the State. The chief obstacle to woman's suffrage is woman herself. Permit her to vote in the church, which she is already willing to do, and you have thereby half taught her to vote in the State, which she is yet half unwilling to do. Every movement toward woman's suffrage in the church is prophetic of woman's suffrage in the State.

Church suffrage for women lately gave rise to an animated debate between two opposing parties in a Congregational church in Chicago; a debate which derives an added significance from the fact that its two opposing leaders were two colleague professors in the same theological seminary.

In this controversy it was argued that "Female suffrage stands opposed to all the authorities of Congregationalism for 250 years;" a statement which, if true, would sooner or later bring Congregationalism itself into disrepute and decay. But such a statement never was, and never will be, true. Congregationalism is a system which, if faithful to its own genius, requires not only that each individual church, but also that each individual church member, shall stand on a common equality with all other Congregational churches and all other Congregational church members. Now two-thirds of all the Congregational church members of the United States are women. To deny female suffrage in a Congregational church is to put the government of a majority into the hands of a minority—a proceeding which flagrantly violates the Congregational polity. But even if the tables should be turned, and a majority of church members should happen to be men instead of women, every woman would still (according to the principles of Congregationalism) be sacredly entitled to every church prerogative of man. A Congregational church that denies suffrage to *any* of its members, male or female, few or many, repudiates the essential features of the Congregational polity. Nay, more: Congregationalism — the simplest of all church polities—makes it not only the right, but also the duty, of every church member to exercise all those church functions which are summed up in church suffrage.

What would be thought of a proposition to deny to woman the right to church membership? But to admit woman to church membership, and then to deny her the suffrage which accompanies such membership, is practically to say that woman is unworthy of a full, but only of a partial, footing in the church. And yet women are the best part of every church. If any class, in any church, ought to be denied suffrage, it should not be women, but men. A church without women would soon degenerate into a mere monastery, or a theological seminary.

Prof. Samuel C. Bartlett's argument that woman's suffrage in the church is opposed to Congregationalism is as futile as Stephen A. Douglas's argument that negro suffrage in the State was opposed to the Declaration of Independence. Female suffrage does *not* stand "opposed to all the authorities of Congregationalism." On the contrary, properly speaking, the "chief authorities of Congregationalism" are the majorities in each of the many individual Congregational churches. These majorities, in almost every case, are women. Female suffrage, so far from being opposed to "the chief authorities of Congregationalism," represents the very chiefest of these "chief authorities."

Prof. Joseph Haven, who bore the lance for woman's suffrage against Prof. Bartlett, is one of the ablest thinkers of the West. The very fact that such a man—studious, contemplative, and retiring—shrinking from public controversy, and given to the cloister—should have stepped before the public in championship of female suffrage, is an evidence that the most just, sound, and philosophic minds of this country are no longer debating, but have already decided, the question of the rightful equality of men and women in church and State. Prof. Haven's argument was conclusive with the church to which it was addressed. He overthrew Prof. Bartlett as gallantly as one knight unhorses another. The final vote was an overwhelming majority in favor of an equal church franchise for all classes of church members. This was a just decision. Any other would have shown a lack of faith by Congregationalists in their own congregational polity—a system which, when unwarped from its true idea, aims to secure an equitable Christian democracy.

St. John was called the "woman of the apostles." The more a man's moral and spiritual nature is like a woman's, the better fitted he is to teach religion to a worldly-minded generation. "Woman," says George William Curtis, "is the conscience of the race." We respectfully submit, that as woman is the strong pillar of the church, it is time that she had a vote in the church meetings.

APRIL 2, 1868.

EDWIN M. STANTON.

N Tuesday, May 26, 1868, Edwin M. Stanton, Secretary of War, addressed the following note to his friend and office-companion, Major-General Townsend, Assistant Adjutant-General:

WAR DEPARTMENT,
WASHINGTON CITY, May 26, 1868.

GENERAL:—You will take charge of the War Department, and books, papers, archives, and public property belonging to the same, subject to the disposal and direction of the President.

(Signed) EDWIN M. STANTON,
Secretary of War.

Brevet Major-General E. D. Townsend, Assistant Adjutant-General.

On the same day, Mr. Stanton addressed the following note to Mr. Andrew Johnson, President of the United States:

WAR DEPARTMENT,
WASHINGTON CITY, May 26, 1868.

SIR:—The resolution of the Senate of the United States of 21st February last, declaring that the President has no power to remove the Secretary of War, and designate any other officer to perform the duties of that office *ad interim*, having this day failed to be supported by two-thirds of the senators present and voting on the articles of impeachment preferred against you by the House of Representatives, I have relinquished the charge of the War Department, and have left the same, and the books, archives, papers, and property heretofore in my custody as Secretary of War, in care of Brevet Major-General Townsend, the senior Assistant Adjutant-General, subject to your direction.

(Signed) EDWIN M. STANTON,
Secretary of War.

To the President.

This action was characteristic of the promptness, clear-headedness, and manliness of its author. After the failure of the Senate to convict the President, no better disposition of Mr. Stanton's case could possibly have been made than he thus made of it himself. It will be noticed that the war-portfolio was not returned directly to the President. The Secretary simply ordered one of his own subordinates to take charge of it, and then notified the President of this fact. As Mr. Stanton for many months had held the War Office against the wish of the President, and only in conformity with the wish of the Senate, there would have been an impropriety in his surrendering the office directly to the President. Mr. Johnson might then have put the War Department immediately into the hands of some weak tool of his own, without "the advice and consent of the Senate." The Secretary's relinquishment to the Assistant Adjutant-General—a trustworthy officer, who had been confirmed by the Senate—left the department just as much under the Senate's watch and care as if Mr. Stanton had still continued to hold it himself. The Secretary thus handsomely relieved his own disagreeable position, without compromising or embarrassing the Senate.

Long before his retirement, Mr. Stanton, having performed the labors of Hercules, desired to be relieved from his wearying and wearing duties, and, for "tired nature's" sake, to seek repose. Had Mr. Lincoln's successor been a patriot instead of a traitor, the Secretary of War would two years before have gladly escaped from his office, taken a sea-voyage for health and recreation, and visited the Pyramids. But when Andrew Johnson undertook to continue the work which Jefferson Davis was compelled to abandon, the newly-imperilled nation shuddered at the mischief which a treacherous President might accomplish through an unrestricted control of the War Office. Mr. Stanton, against every desire of his own, except his single desire to serve his country, remained at his post to counterwork the renegade. For a long time the President did not dare remove him, and the Secretary (at the unanimous desire of the Republican leaders) refused to resign. Anxious men, who at one time feared that the President would actually attempt an armed rebellion, felt that the country was safe so long as the key to its arsenals was in Mr. Stanton's hands. When at length, with unparalleled audacity, the President instituted the extraordinary measures which finally resulted in his impeachment (and which ought to have resulted in his conviction), it was still more apparent to thoughtful observers that Mr. Stanton was the main bulwark between the President and a conspiracy against public liberty. Had not the Secretary's wisdom, patriotism, and courage mastered his master at every step, it is impossible to say how completely the Federal Government would have been betrayed to the enemy. The Senate's resolution of February 21st, 1868, declaring that the President had no power to remove the Secretary of War, made Mr. Stanton's duty to retain his office still more imperative and obligatory. From that time to his retirement his retention of the War Department must be regarded as the act, not of himself, but of the Senate. The legitimate and only consistent consequence of the Senate's resolution would have been the conviction and removal of the Senate's defier. But, since the High Court of Impeachment, partly through cowardice and partly through corruption, failed of the requisite majority to convict, Mr. Stanton had no alternative except retirement.

The Republic is not ungrateful, yet full justice will not be done to Edwin M. Stanton during his life-time. The great events in which he nobly figured, the gigantic combinations of which he was the master-spirit, the magnificent energy with which he impelled the war forward to victory, the incorruptible integrity which has kept his public (like his private) life untainted with a breath of suspicion: —all these qualities will make him loom up hereafter as the one great, controlling mind of the War for the Union, and as one of the truest patriots in all our country's history.

From an intimate acquaintance with most of the conspicuous men who now occupy high places in various departments of the Government, we have no hesitation in saying that, for those peculiar qualities which make a safe, wise, courageous, and victorious director of great affairs, we have never met a man who, on the whole, seemed equal in greatness to Edwin M. Stanton. The Federal capitol abounds in men who can *think*, men who can *talk*, and men who can *vote*, but not men who can *act*. Even among men who pass for great statesmen, the executive quality is rare. But Mr. Stanton possesses this quality in so unwonted a degree that a generation may elapse before a cabinet office shall again be filled by so masterful a cabinet officer. We believe that, after the passions of the day shall have quenched their flames, and when calm judgment shall have taken the place of excited prejudice, Mr. Stanton will finally rank as the most gifted, illustrious, and successful war minister, not only of this, but of any other country.

At present he is, perhaps, the least popularly understood and appreciated of any of our first-class statesmen. He is so careless of his reputation, so unambitious for his own distinction, so thorough a despiser of the common arts by which famous men keep their names green and fragrant before the people, that only those who know him intimately, who have been joined with him in patriotic work, who have sat with him in council, and who have detected the inner movements of his mind, know how great and grand a man it was whom Abraham Lincoln put into his cabinet, and whom Andrew Johnson cast out. Nature gave to Mr. Stanton a frame of iron, and filled it, like a furnace, with a soul of fire; so that, with such a body and such a soul, he is perpetually forging those inexhaustible and irresistible energies which make him, like Bismarck, the equal of ten common-place great men. During the war he outworked all his subordinates, compelling them all occasionally to rest, but compelling himself incessantly to work. His ability to look at a complicated case, to comprehend in a few minutes all its details, to give a just and happy decision on the spot, and so to be done with the matter forever, is a genius which he possesses in so remarkable a degree that, to the slow-working minds of smaller men, his action often appears rash and precipitate; whereas it results from that superior sagacity which is called intuition. No police officer was ever more quick than he to discover at a glance the distinguishing marks of a rogue or of an honest man. It took a rare scoundrel to deceive the Secretary of War. Sudden and tempestuous wrath fell on any man whom he caught defrauding the Government, or enriching himself at the public expense. Impartially just, he showed no whit more of favor to his admirers than to his critics.

But the greatest of his virtues was the one least common to American statesmen; that is, courage. Never did it fail him. When was he known to quail at a critical moment? Who, in leaning on this man, ever found him a broken reed? He never despaired of the Republic. In the darkest days, though he was oftentimes full of sorrow, and sometimes full of agony, yet his steady nerve never trembled; his stout heart never played the coward.

Gentle and affectionate as his own little children, he is nevertheless capable of those volcanic and fiery angers which are the tokens of a great nature, and which are oftentimes the weapons of great achievements. Violent outbursts of passion are generally to be reckoned among men's failings; but they sometimes belong to men's virtues. It must be a mean-spirited man who does not admire General Washington's towering rage during the battle of Monmouth, or who would have substituted for that storm the greater calmness which would have indicated less majesty of soul. King David's imprecations are an immortal warrant for a strong man's wrath at a critical hour.

Mr. Stanton retires to private life shattered in health. Grandly has he earned the rest and relaxation which he has long greatly coveted, and which he may now quietly enjoy. No greater privilege can be granted by Providence to any mortal than to have served one's country as signally as Mr. Stanton has served it. The good-will of his countrymen is his just and freely-rendered reward. Thousands and tens of thousands of good wishes follow him out of his office, and shall hover over him like a cloud of blessings as long as he lives.

Cheerfully and eagerly, as part of our duty toward the public opinion of our day and generation, we set down, in the most conspicuous manner, our solemn belief that this nation owes to Edwin M. Stanton a greater debt of gratitude than to any other living American citizen.

June, 1868.

MATTHEW ARNOLD'S EXAMPLE.

T is always with delight that we read anything and everything written by Matthew Arnold—a man so true, so sincere, and so cultivated that one finds, in any single effort of his masterful pen, a clear proof of a fine genius and a Christian heart. "Sweetness and Light" are his favorite words, and they well describe his writings; for his style is sweet as honey, and light as day. But Matthew Arnold's friends in this country grieve to find him espousing the conservative party in England, and opposing popular liberty:—committing the old offence which, for three centuries, has been common with erudite professors whose learning has proved greater than their wisdom.

For illustration, take the Irish Church question. It is just as criminal in the British Government to force the English Church on Ireland as it would be in the American Government to force the Romish Church on Connecticut. If there had been but one elegant writer in England to uphold and defend Mr. Gladstone in his just and righteous position on this question, Matthew Arnold ought to have been that one. But Matthew Arnold's present views on the disendowment of the Irish Church are about like Robert C. Winthrop's former views on the abolition of American slavery. In fact, Mr. Arnold is a model for a polished and compromising Massachusetts politician. He ought to be adopted into the Adams family.

Take, again, the popular custom of mass meetings.

Our Constitution expressly forbids Congress to make any laws "against the right of the people peaceably to assemble and to petition the Government for a redress of grievances." What if some first-class American writer should argue in *The Atlantic Monthly* against the right of the citizens of New York to hold a "monster meeting" in Union Square? American readers of the ocean-cable dispatches for the last year have frequently noticed brief and pithy accounts of great popular demonstrations at which Mr. Bright has spoken. These items of intelligence have always been hailed in America as signs of a better future for England; signs of the elevation of the people; signs of the progress of political equality. But Mr. Arnold astonishes us by saying, "that monster processions in the streets . . . ought to be unflinchingly forbidden and repressed." And yet a government which would forbid its loyal and honest (albeit humble) citizens "peaceably to assemble and petition for a redress of grievances," has no right to be a government, and ought to be pulled down by the very people whom it would repress.

Take, again, the English marriage question. Several years ago, the Rev. William Morley Punshon lost his wife. Afterward, finding in his deceased wife's sister a fit and congenial companion, he sought her in marriage. But the ecclesiastical law of England forbids a man to marry his deceased wife's sister. Accordingly, Mr. Punshon, in order to be lawfully married, came to the hither side of the Atlantic. Of course, we know that America is the best of all places to be married in, still we cannot think that an English clergyman ought to be exiled from his native shores merely because he wants to marry his deceased wife's sister. An eminent Presbyterian clergyman in New York, who wanted to marry in the same way, simply did it; and no sensible person on this side of the ocean has held him in any less respect for so doing. But the marriage of either of these clergymen would now be pronounced in England unlawful and incestuous. Mr. Punshon will have a storm to face on his return. Meanwhile, liberal pens and presses in England are arguing against so supercilious, meddlesome, and tyrannous a law. The American friends of Matthew Arnold naturally expected that, if he took any side at all on such a question, he would take the right side. But this son of his father, this student of history, this reformer of society, is lending his influence, not for the repeal, but for the perpetuation of the antique wrong.

Take, again, the delicate but solemn question brought lately to public attention by medical and other scientific men, and by many outspoken clergymen and religious bodies;—we mean the murder of children before their birth. Abortion is almost a fashion in our best society. Indisputable evidence proves that thousands of respected and refined families are in the habit, like Herod, of murdering the innocents—only the victims are not the first-born, but the unborn. But this is true of rich men's rather than of poor men's families. In fact, we have a current phrase, "the virtuous poor;" but the world has not yet found need for a corresponding phrase, "the virtuous rich." The small (and constantly diminishing) number of children born in well-to-do families is ground for public sorrow and alarm. Society, both American and British, vitally needs a public sentiment which would revive and make fashionable the olden praise and honor attaching to the parents of many children. But Mr. Arnold, writing of the poor people of East London—a class with whom he mingles too little, and from whom he shrinks too much—adds to their poverty an elegant gentleman's unintended insult, by chiding them for the too great number of their children. Mr. Arnold's rebuke was directed against the wrong end of London.

Take, again, such a service as Mr. Beecher rendered to his country in England in 1863—a service such as few men have ever had the happiness to perform. Is not a generous breast stirred at the spectacle of a patriot pleading the cause of his country before a mob of enemies in a foreign land? The supreme hour of Mr. Beecher's life was when he stood before the miscreants of Liverpool, and demonstrated to them in his own person the spirit of the unconquerable North. But how did he appear to Mr. Arnold? The English professor called the American orator "a heated barbarian." And yet, what is there in Mr. Arnold's civilized indifference half as noble as in Mr. Beecher's barbaric fire? A certain one of our own poets (now abroad) took occasion, some time ago, to characterize Mr. Greeley as "a very unnecessary kind of man." And yet this gilt-edged critic has never yet succeeded in making his own dainty self half so necessary, or half so useful to his countrymen, as Mr. Greeley is bravely doing every day. If, two hundred years ago, any two British popular leaders had held the same sympathetic relation to the struggling people of England as Mr. Beecher and Mr. Greeley have long sustained toward the toiling millions of America, does any one suppose that John Milton, scholar above scholars, and poet above poets, would have called the one "a heated barbarian," or the other "a very unnecessary kind of man?"

We might mention other instances in which Mr. Arnold, and other modern scholiasts of whom he is a type, exhibit a perversity of judgment on practical questions of profound importance. But we do not care to multiply citations. Our sole purpose in referring to Mr. Arnold's views on any subject whatever is to deduce a moral. That moral is, *the danger accruing to learned men from studying books too much, and studying humanity too little.*

The wave of that Christian democracy which is sooner or later to flow under and uplift all nations, is now beginning to heave and swell once again in England almost as when Cromwell and Milton were its attracting sun and moon. What then becomes the present duty of English literary men? In England, as in America, every man whose lips can speak, or whose pen can write, belongs by divine appointment to the party of progress. What the university scholar borrows from books he should repay to the people. If a man of letters uses his gifts, not to urge forward popular rights, but only to anchor existing institutions still deeper in the mud-bottom of conservatism, he might better never have learned the alphabet. A plantation negro who does his best to make South Carolina a republican commonwealth is more useful in his day and generation than an erudite philosopher who would force a church of one faith upon a people of another. Mr. Arnold (perhaps without egotism) mentions that he has read the Iliad in its original tongue twenty-two times from beginning to end. But there is many a man who has never opened Homer, yet who out of his English Bible can teach this conservative scholar the first principles of political equality, of national greatness, and of human happiness. Thoreau said nobly of John Brown that "he might have slanted a Greek accent the wrong way, but would have righted a fallen man." Mr. Arnold slants his Greek accents the right way, but keeps back his helping hand from the down-trodden masses. And yet an elegant essayist might better have a brotherly heart filled with yearnings toward the lowliest of his countrymen, than to have a Greek skull filled with the dust of a dead language which keeps him speechless for living duty.

In the long course of human history, everything has come by turns to its due honor, save only man. Kings, priests, scholars, poets—all these have had their "recompense of reward." But Man, simply as man—man without a crown to make him a king—man without a robe to make him a priest—man without a scroll to make him a scholar—man with nothing but the fee simple of his humanity—man with no other credentials than his ignorance and immortality—this is a creature who still waits, in all nations, to be lifted to his true station, as the peer and equal of all the children of God.

The dignity of human nature, the inherent nobility of the meanest of mankind, the divinely crowned regality of the squalid poor of East London, and of the Five Points:—to understand these things is a high and superior lore, more important to be learned than Homer's Greek. "Though I speak with the tongues of men and of angels, and have not charity, I am become as sounding brass, or a tinkling cymbal." Is it not written—yea, and in Greek too—that "God is no respecter of persons?" Oxford learning is good, and East London ignorance is bad; but the Judge of all the earth looks upon the student of books and upon the carrier of coals with an impartiality awful to be contemplated by men who allow their learning to become their pride. "Studies," says Lord Bacon, "teach not their own use." Their noblest use is to inculcate the brotherhood of the human race. Nature creates many a man a radical, and afterward some university perverts him into a conservative. Every Erasmus is half a coward. A British Parliament composed of Oxford professors, or an American Congress composed of Boston literati, would be nothing but a meadow of reeds bending before every wind. Of course, over-education is not so common in America as in England. Nor is it very common anywhere. But now and then, on either side of the sea, it sucks the blood out of some great man. This is a sufficient reason of warning. Many a scholar sets out with enthusiasm to float his bark on the current of progress, but runs aground on the quicksands of too many books. Just now, anybody seeking for the whereabouts of Matthew Arnold will find him shelved on a bar somewhere off Salamis in the Ægean Sea.

We trust that Mr. Gladstone will disendow the Irish Church, that the workingmen of England will pour forth in mass meetings to cheer John Bright, that the families in East London will have a numerous offspring, that the Rev. Mr. Punshon will find great happiness with his deceased wife's sister, that Mr. Beecher will not become a heated barbarian, that Mr. Greeley will prove himself a very necessary kind of man—and all this, while Mr. Matthew Arnold shall be reading the Iliad in Greek for the twenty-third time.

August 17, 1868.

A FALLEN OAK.

T is hard to pen in a few words as much as our heart prompts us to say of Thaddeus Stevens—now at last in his grave. Any other President than Andrew Johnson would have announced his death in an official bulletin—as Abraham Lincoln announced Edward Everett's. But the grand old Roman needs no tribute from the Punic traitor of the White House. Nay, a President who could step down to a drunken mob, and ask them to hang Thaddeus Stevens, had no right to intrude a chaplet upon the dead statesman's bier. White flowers were strewn upon the coffin-lid by black hands—which was a greater honor. Henceforth, like a dew, the blessings of the lowly shall keep green his grave,

> "And Freedom shall awhile repair
> To dwell a weeping hermit there."

Called the Great Commoner, like the elder Pitt, Mr. Stevens was also like him in parliamentary sway; like him in quickness of attack; like him in power of blistering sarcasm; like him in the scorn and contempt which he could express by his countenance and forefinger; like him in arrowy directness of argument; like him in whiteness of unspotted honesty; like him in that self-abnegation which substituted for personal interest a passionate pride of country; and like him, above all things else, in illustrious devotion to liberty.

Of course, we are far from saying that Thaddeus Stevens

was gifted with that majestic eloquence which, if tradition be true, made Lord Chatham the Demosthenes of modern times. But it must be remembered that Mr. Stevens rose from a local into a national reputation, not by efforts made in the prime, but in the decline of life. Not sent to Congress till he was already a veteran, his best battles had been fought and won long before the nation saw him lift a spear in Washington. In his ashes lived his wonted fires, but the earlier blaze was brighter than the later embers. If during his whole career, instead of during a mere fragment of it, he had been an actor on the national stage; if, like Palmerston, he had been a life-long gladiator in his country's chief arena; his colossal abilities would have achieved for him a colossal reputation. At the death of Coleridge, it was said that "a great man had died, leaving behind him no adequate memorial of his greatness." Of Mr. Stevens it must be said that he leaves behind him no speeches, no measures, no achievements (great as some of them are) which afford an adequate measure of his extraordinary powers. "I shall soon die," said he to us recently, "and shall then be soon forgotten." Such a man can never be entirely forgotten. But there are some statesmen—as, for instance, Burke and Jefferson—who live more vividly after death than before; whose names grow more and more authoritative, and whose influence more and more potent; but Thaddeus Stevens does not belong to this immortal class.

The supreme hour of his life occurred a third of a century ago, in April, 1835, when, with a single speech, spoken with a fiery vehemence that melted all opposition, he conquered a Pennsylvania legislature which had been elected on the express issue of repealing taxation for the support of schools—actually persuading his political opponents to violate the instructions they had received from their own constituents—establishing for ever the cause of popular education in that State—and earning for himself the proudest of all his titles, "The Father of the Pennsylvania Common Schools." We have recently read this most famous of his speeches. Certainly, as it stands in the coldness of the printed page, although strong and unanswerable, and although in parts nobly eloquent, yet, on the whole, it is not a masterpiece of composition. Still, the true test of a speech is not its style, but its effect. Thus judged, this was one of the greatest speeches ever uttered by American lips. A writer in the Washington *Chronicle* (whom we take to be Colonel Forney) was present on the occasion, and thus describes the orator's great victory: "Never," says he, "will the writer of these lines forget the effect of that surpassing effort. . . . . . . All the barriers of prejudice broke down before it. It reached men's hearts like the voice of inspiration. They who were the most ready to take the life of Thaddeus Stevens a few weeks before were instantly converted into his admirers and friends. During its delivery in the hall of the House at Harrisburgh, the scene was one of dramatic interest and intensity. Thaddeus Stevens was then forty-three years of age, and in the prime of life; and his classic countenance, noble voice, and cultivated style, added to the fact that he was speaking the holiest truths and for the noblest of all human causes, created such a feeling among his fellow-members that, for once at least, our State legislators rose above all selfish feelings, and responded to the instincts of a higher nature. The motion to repeal the law failed, and a number of votes pledged to sustain it were changed upon the spot, and what seemed to be an inevitable defeat was transformed into a crowning victory for the friends of common schools."

Mr. Stevens always felt that he never afterward rose to the height of that one crowning occasion. In Congress, after winning the leadership of his party, he might perhaps have achieved similar feats, except for a diminution of that physical energy which is needful to invigorate the mind. During the war, Mr. Stevens had a working allowance of health; but during the reconstruction, if well on one day, he was sick the next. One morning, when expecting to speak on one of his reconstruction bills, he said to us: "I shall try to stir that sluggish House to-day; but you see how shattered I am!" and then, rising like an old lion from his lair, he suddenly exclaimed: "But if I were something else than a rack of bones—yes, Sir, if I were only as young as you, I could settle this business of reconstruction in the one and only way that God Almighty points out." The old man, who remembered what he had done in his younger strength, grew more and more dissatisfied with his best efforts in Congress. When some admiring newspapers would speak of him as "the leader of the House," he would bitterly smile—sometimes in scorn of his cowardly followers, and sometimes in contempt of his enfeebled self.

Courage—the American statesman's "lost art"—was this man's crowning virtue. He had enough iron in his single will to stiffen the "wood, hay, and stubble" of a whole Congress of falterers. How dauntlessly he defied the opinions both of foes and friends! When did he ever hesitate to speak his mind openly? Who ever knew him to equivocate? What Republican or Democrat ever reproached him, saying: "Sir, you cheated me!" Intrigue had no lodgment in his lordly nature. Compromise he scorned. Honesty was his policy; and like Benjamin Franklin in Paris, he accomplished more by blunt directness than others by artful diplomacy. Open and not covert attack was his method; and like Alexander at Arbela he disdained to win a victory in the dark. Whoever else was plotting in a corner, whoever else was lobbying in a committee-room, whoever else was bargaining with the White House, Thaddeus Stevens with cleaner hands was performing all his acts "before all Israel and the sun."

Hopelessness—a half-despair—was the prevailing mood of his mind. How early in life the steel-spring was broken we do not know. Certain it is that, during his declining years, he seldom looked on the bright side of affairs. But perhaps this was from an old man's natural dimness of eye—not from any original defect of constitution. It was always touching to talk seriously with him, and to find how little expectation he entertained that his cherished measures would be carried. "No," he would say, "the bill will be voted down; there is not virtue enough in the House to pass it." He thought the Republican majority in Congress destitute of nerve. "These men are made of pulp," he said. He was no flatterer of his parliamentary peers—no rose-colorist of the political situation—no eulogist of human nature. Often have we known him to bow down his head like a bulrush, and, distrusting measures and men alike, to utter his despair of the Republic.

Wit is a parliamentarian's sword of victory: he who can wield it is a conqueror in defeat. Thaddeus Stevens carried this weapon—a Damascus blade that could cut a hair or split a helmet. His jests were coarse or fine, polite or vulgar, gentle or terrible, according to the company and occasion. His best repartees were jewels of the first water. A book of them—but they have never been preserved—would report him to the next generation, "a wit among lords, and a lord among wits." Bitter as John Randolph, and cruel as Tristam Burgess, Mr. Stevens, unlike either of these serpent-tongued men, never felt more than a momentary malice. He harbored no unkindness to any human being. In fact, we happen to know that he had not a particle of ill-will even toward Andrew Johnson. To the credit of human nature what more can be said?

His private life was not a good example. His habits included the offences common with many English statesmen of a quarter of a century ago, and too common with some American statesmen of to-day. We do not believe in eulogistic lies—least of all in the solemn presence of death. A living man's vices cannot become a dead man's virtues. During his life, Thaddeus Stevens was no saint; nor, after his death, ought he to receive canonization. Sister Loretta's baptismal drops on his brow did not wash away any soilure from his character. Writing of him here as his faithful friend, we know that, could he now so frame these words of ours as best to suit his own wishes, he would command us to paint him truthfully as he was, and forbid us to omit the necessary shadow of the picture. But we have noticed, as an occasional phenomenon in morals, that public spirit sometimes becomes all the more a passion with men who have lost something of private virtue—as if human nature, having stained itself on one side, sought all the more bravely to keep itself bright on another. To all who knew Thaddeus Stevens beneath the surface, it was plain that, having many years ago parted with his proper pride of personal character, he sought to make perpetual atonement to his higher nature by a substituted Platonic fidelity to his country's honor; and so this old man loved the Republic as purely as Florizel loved Perdita. But the few men whose private errors may thus become public benefits, and who can say with Luther, "I thank God for my sins," are none the less to be condemned for those failings which thus "lean to virtue's side." Nevertheless, there is sometimes one spiritual compensation to such men; for hidden within their breasts are solemn sorrows, or what Wordsworth calls "majestic pains," by which their natures receive a purification as by refining fires. Such inward processes as these long ago made Thaddeus Stevens a better Christian than many a slave-hunting clergyman who will take occasion of his death to sneer at his life.

Not many months ago, on learning that the cemetery in Lancaster, in which he hoped to be buried, would not admit the bodies of negroes to burial, he indignantly sold his lot, and purchased one in another ground where, in the common dust of God's acre, all men might be equal:—and so, even in his grave, we may still salute him as "The Great Commoner." Brave soul!—champion of Liberty, Equality, and Fraternity—hail and farewell!

August 20, 1868.

THE HARVARD ENGRAVINGS.

T is not widely known that in a certain crowded alcove in the library of Harvard College a multitude of precious engravings lie shrouded in linen cloths, coffined in stately portfolios, and sepulchred between oaken shelves, whereon like the dead of the catacombs they rest layer above layer, undisturbed except as some permitted visitor, breaking into their tomb, awakens them into an occasional hour of resurrection and light.

We have just been visiting this alcove—or, rather let us call it, this little palace-royal—which, though hardly big enough to swing a cat in, is nevertheless richer than the enchanted castle that held the sleeping beauty; for here the imprisoned beauties are a thousand instead of one.

It was with no profane step that we crossed the threshold of the "Gray Collection," and troubled the venerable curator (to whom the task seemed a joy) to lay open before our gaze the best copies of the best engravings of the best paintings in the world.

When Mr. Gray of Cambridge died and left his portfolios to the University, the bequest was coupled with the condition that they should remain under the charge of the only man in this country thoroughly competent to be their historian and critic. That man is Dr. Louis Thies, who has spent a long life not only in collecting such works, but in investigating their history, in cultivating the personal acquaintance of engravers, and in gathering materials for an elaborate catalogue of important engravings. He was the personal friend of Mauritz Steinla, and spent many a day with that great engraver while the Sistine Madonna was in process. It is perhaps not too much to say that no man even in Europe is more learned in the bibliography of steel-plates than Dr. Thies. The catalogue on which, with several assistants, he is now laboring daily, will be something like Richardson's Dictionary, except that it will quote pictures instead of words. Dr. Thies has the inestimable advantage of making his notes and comments not from memoranda or recollections, but from the whole world's finest specimens which he can at any moment outspread before his eyes. We have had the happiness to examine the yet unfinished manuscript of a part of his volume, particularly the interesting pages devoted to the Sistine Madonna. No connoisseur can look into this careful and painstaking record without a profound respect for the life-long studies which have gone to its preparation. To the great public (who are more pleased with half a dozen quails picking lady-bugs from a cucumber-vine than with the twelve disciples sitting at the Last Supper) this *con amore* cyclopedia of Dr. Thies will seem a monument of superfluous learning; but to the small (yet happily increasing) number of Americans who possess fine copies of European engravings, the announcement that this most experienced of collectors will publish the results of his half century of investigation must be hailed as a promising fore-token of an American literature of art.

In this collection, one has a rare opportunity to compare the two (and only two) great engravings of the Sistine Madonna. The first was by Müller—that young enthusiast who worked himself to insanity and death, and whose finished proof-sheet was brought from the press just in time to be hung over his bier, like the unfinished Transfiguration over Raphael's. The second was by Steinla, which is more popularly known because it has become the basis of all the photographs and cheap woodcuts that everywhere vilify the original painting. Müller's work is regarded by a few critics as the one supreme engraving of the world, although other voices speak for Steinla's as more literal and accurate. Müller copied Madame Seidelmann's drawing, except that he re-drew with his own pencil the faces of the mother and child; Steinla, on the contrary, worked from a drawing which he trusted no hand but his own to make. Müller's rendering is deeper in color, Steinla's airier in movement; Müller's more substantial, Steinla's more spiritual; Müller's more majestic, Steinla's more pure. Raphael himself would probably have preferred Steinla's, since the proportions of the prototype are better preserved in this than in the other. Then, too, Müller's is cut off at the top, shorn of the curtain-rod and rings which run across Steinla's—an omission explained by the fact that, in Müller's time, the painting (unbeknown to its keepers) was imprisoned in a frame which concealed not only several inches of the canvas, but an explanatory part of the design. An English magazine, in a recent critical reference to Müller, mentions that, much against his own taste, and acting under the spur of Rittner, his publisher, he made his shadows so positive that he considered them too dark to be in harmony with the celestial light that everywhere shines through the original. Whether this statement has any foundation we cannot say; but it is evident that Steinla, who, while working on his own engraving, kept Müller's hanging on the wall before his eyes, took infinite pains to avoid this dark effect, as if he meant to fill the spectator with suggestions of that glory which is "above the brightness of the sun." The best copy of Müller's ever printed is in the Gray Collection; the best of Steinla's is in a private collection in Brooklyn. A comparison between these two copies is like a dispute between the rose and the lily as to which is the fairer. The truth is, each engraving has a peculiar and chief beauty of its own; and to go from each to the other is to make the spectator equally in love with both.

The Gray Collection contains the finest copy we have ever seen of Toschi's "Madonna della Scala" (after Correggio), a transcript which, like the original, makes no attempt to express divine dignity or supernal glory, yet which for motherly tenderness and childish simplicity is certainly (or, at least, we sometimes think so) the most winsome, captivating, and altogether lovable engraving in the whole compass of art.

Here, too, Raphael Morghen's "Transfiguration" (after Raphael) is seen in an impression so much more brilliant than the numbered subscription-copies that bear the engraver's autograph, as to appear a totally different work; showing that, except Longhi, no engraver more than Morghen needs to be seen in one of the earliest of proofs rather than in a later print, if one would catch him before his glory fades.

Here is Longhi's "Espousals" (after Raphael), a print which, as exhibited in the print-shop windows, is always cold, dull, and gray, but which in Dr. Thies's impression glows with such a silvery light that the whole composition is looked at (as every bridal ceremony should be) through an atmosphere of enchantment.

Here are costly relics of the handiwork of Marc Antonio Raimondi, who, in Raphael's own house, and under Raphael's own eye, engraved Raphael's own designs.

Here is Rembrandt's famous "Hundred Guilder Piece"—not the identical impression for which a London nabob lately paid enough to buy a house in West End, but a "next best" copy, good enough to show that neither this nor any other etching by Rembrandt can justly take rank with the greatest engravings after the Italian school; for certainly, to a true, trained, and classical eye, Toschi's "Spasimo" (after Raphael), or Sharp's "Fathers of the Church" (after Correggio), or Morghen's "Parce Somnum Rumpere" (after Titian), ought to be worth many guilders more than the "Hundred Guilder Piece."

Here, in many forms, is Albert Durer—that grand, sad, and reverend man, who needed only to have lived in Italy, instead of Germany, in order to have become the peer of the four great masters of Christian art—Raphael, Angelo, Leonardo, and Titian.

Here is Holbein—that good, honest soul, whose portraits always told the plain, unflattering truth, and whose famous Burgomaster's Family (as one sees it in Steinla's other masterpiece) is all the more interesting because the faces are so bewitchingly homely.

Here, also, impossible to be now mentioned, are many other of those rich and precious jewels of art which "sparkle on the stretched forefinger of all time."

The Gray Collection shows that, of all the great artists, Raphael loses least, and Titian most, when reproduced by engraving. The reason generally assigned for this is, that Raphael's greatest merit consists in his lines and proportions, and Titian's in his colors and shades. But, although this is a correct statement of the chief contrast between these two painters, it is not a sufficient explanation why one should generally be engraved so much better than the other. Why may not Titian be as well rendered as Raphael? Is not the engraver's art just as powerful in lights and darks as in lines and proportions? Long ago, Raphael Morghen proved that he could express Titian as well as Raphael. In our own day, Mandel has achieved a greater success with Titian's "Bella" than with Raphael's "Madonna of the Chair." But it is absolutely necessary that the engraver of Titian should not desire to make distinct what the artist purposely left dim, nor attempt to find what the artist endeavored to lose. Schiavoni, in his engraving of Titian's "Assumption of the Virgin"—a painting which Gilbert Haven called the chief artistic splendor of all Europe—partly obeyed and partly violated this necessary law; and his engraving reminds one of the famous criticism on Pope's Iliad: "A great poem, but not Homer;" a great engraving, but not Titian. Connoisseurs ought to regret that neither Müller, nor Toschi, nor Desnoyer, engraved Titian's "Entombment of Christ"—a painting which, although its lines melt entirely away in its colors, nevertheless shows itself even in Masson's timidly stippled translation (which does not represent this merging and dissolving beauty) as one of the noblest of all works of genius. Mandel's "Bella" makes us hope that he will attempt the "Entombment." No other living man is so competent to the task; for Dupont, his only rival (and truly his peer), does not incline to the positive and striking chiar oscuro which only Titian could paint, and only Mandel can engrave.

The Gray Collection (we are sorry to say), is a light under a bushel. The genius of our institutions forbids the hiding of our public art-treasures in a cloister as the monks sequestered their illuminated missals. The Harvard engravings should be accessible not only to a few favored eyes, but to every person who desires to study them—just as accessible as the poor oil-portraits which cast their dismal but interesting gloom through the white refectory where the alumni dine and wine. There ought to be somewhere in this country—and, with this collection for a nucleus, there might be at Cambridge—a complete gallery of first-class specimens of all the memorable engravings and etchings known to art. The Gray Collection is a grand beginning to such an end; it is the broad foundation of the pyramid. A universal collection would be the accretion of years. But it could easily be made—in fact, it would almost make itself. Some of the best specimens of famous engravings exist in private families in this country—impressions of which, in many instances, the Gray Collection has no equally fine duplicates. In the course of time, many of these private treasures, like those of Mr. Gray himself, would find their way by last will and testament to Harvard College—particularly if a proper hall were there waiting to give them a hospitable welcome. A long, low gallery, two stories high, and with a glass roof, should be immediately constructed—convenient in design, and not necessarily costly in execution—where, under a full down-streaming flood of the sun's light, these engravings, slenderly framed and not too crowdedly hung, should remain on perpetual exhibition. If such a gallery were founded by some rich son of his Alma Mater, other collections would from year to year fall into it, like ripe fruit into a basket. For instance, we know of a Bostonian who possesses a noble collection of etchings—perhaps the most comprehensive in the country—who means to bequeath them to some public institution, and would undoubtedly select Harvard if that university afforded comfortable lodgings for such dainty strangers. In fact, we have not a little questioned our own heart as to the future and final disposition to be made of our "Morghens," our "Steinlas," our "Mandels," and certain other engravings, which, while they are not too heavenly for the earth, are just a little too earthly for heaven. All life-trustees of precious "artists' proofs" would rejoice at the erection in Cambridge of a little Louvre of engravings. Who will lay the corner-stone?

A LOTUS-EATING LAWYER.

IT is always so agreeable to our feelings to see a deserving man honored that we are thankful to those who honor him. But his garland ought to be for his unspotted, not for his tarnished acts. Moreover, when a guild of men, like the lawyers of New York, join in a public tribute to one of their brotherhood, as in giving a public dinner to Mr. William M. Evarts, they ought to take care that their plaudits to their comrade re-echo no ridicule to themselves.

The lawyers who invite Mr. Evarts to dine say rashly in their invitation that the highest possible compliment which can be paid to the New York bar is the fact that the President of the United States chose one of its members for Attorney-General. Now, what President chose Mr. Evarts for Attorney-General? Andrew Johnson—an escaped criminal! Nor, in choosing him, did the wily rogue mean thereby to compliment the New York bar, but only to settle with Mr. Evarts for services rendered. Mr. Johnson had no money, but could pay his lawyer with an office; and his lawyer, needing no money, ambitiously accepted the office. This transaction, in the judgment of a bevy of New York lawyers, reflects distinguished honor on the New York bar. But unless the law has ceased to be the noblest of professions, the honor of the New York bar ought to be so bright that a compliment from Andrew Johnson would fall on it as a stain. "Praise from Sir Hubert Stanley is praise indeed;" but praise from Mr. Evarts's guilty client is opprobrium and shame.

But why, under any President (even a respectable one), should the New York bar consider that the summit of professional ambition is the Attorney-Generalship? The Attorney-General is never selected because he is a lawyer, but only because he is a politician, or haply in some rare instance (not the present) because he is a statesman. If it were a rule to give this greatest of legal offices to the greatest of legal minds, Mr. Evarts would have small claim to it; he would stand shaded into inconsequence at the side, for instance, of Mr. O'Conor. Certainly, to thoughtful and discreet auditors, Mr. Evarts's argument in the Impeachment Trial was flimsy, prolix, and vague. In the judgment of many eminent and fatigued listeners during those four Evarts days—"the saddest of the year"—the advocate's performance, when at last it ended, left the lustre of his professional reputation rusted rather than scoured. His prairie-level of commonplace had flattened all the salient points of his prestige. The unwearied but wearying talker proved himself another Garret Davis in the Senate Chamber. In fact, both there and everywhere, Mr. Evarts, though never without a brief, has always been without brevity. But, withal, he is one of those happy men who have the halcyon fortune to get themselves popularly estimated at their own self-appraised value. He not only thinks highly of himself; but, with a fine gravity, decorously solicits his friends to think highly of him also; and, as we New Yorkers are a fraternity of mutual admirers, we all cheerfully acquiesce in our friend's self-complacent request. Accordingly it long ago became a pleasure to us all to pay a more than ordinary deference to our gentle Roman's meagre greatness.

But even if he were, in point of intellect, superior to his superiors, what a precious piece of humbug it would be, and is, to say that because Mr. Evarts, or any other New York lawyer, happens to receive from an impeached President a fee in the form of a cabinet appointment, he thereby makes himself a conduit for conveying to the New York bar the pure water of the greatest compliment which it can possibly deserve? When Henry Stansbery, an abler lawyer than Mr. Evarts, was made Attorney-General, did the bar of Ohio meet, and dine, and wine, and say that because the first law-officer of the Government was chosen from their number, they themselves, the unchosen remainder, had thereby received the highest of professional distinctions? When Caleb Cushing, an abler man than either of these two, was made Attorney-General, did the bar of Massachusetts go into prandial fervor over President Pierce's supposed compliment to their happy selves? When Jeremiah Black, a still more eminent advocate than either of these three, was made Attorney-General by President Buchanan, did the lawyers of Washington stand flushed with rose-colored pleasure, as if under a sudden sunburst of glory to their whole bar?

Then, too, if the New York lawyers give a dinner over the President's appointment of Mr. Evarts, why should not the New York merchants give a dinner over the President's appointment of Sheridan Shook?

Now, if Mr. Evarts's professional brethren want to honor him for his professional skill, let them say so, and nobody will object—since, alas! nothing now remains of Mr. Evarts worthy of honor except his professional skill. But no such tribute was meant by the signers of Mr. Evarts's dinner-warrant. They simply say that since

Andrew Johnson has paid to the New York bar the highest fee of flattery which it ever received, they will cheerfully contribute *pro rata* for a dinner to Mr. Evarts in celebration of an honor which Mr. Johnson thus conferred, not on that gentleman, but on themselves. In other words, the smile which the President bestowed on Mr. Evarts was of such a diffused sweetness that it bathed in lavender all the attorneys of New York!

But, of course, under the surface and down at the bottom, the proposed Evarts dinner, like the proposed Fessenden dinner, is meant to be one of those political tributes occasionally offered to a frost-withered politician by way of reviving him into hot-house bloom. In fact, when a public man goes into moral decline, what is there left for him but a public dinner? Did not a great company of New York tuft-hunters give Andrew Johnson himself a public dinner? Will not Horatio Seymour, after his defeat, be sure to get a public dinner? Every clever knave, sooner or later, gets his public dinner. Even John Quincy Adams will have one in due time.

Mr. Evarts, for the approaching dinner, has two distinct claims to what the Western people call a "square meal." First, it was as morally base in a Republican leader like Mr. Evarts to be bribed with a lawyer's fee to plead for Andrew Johnson's acquittal as it would have been in James Otis to have been bribed with a lawyer's fee to defend King George's Writs of Assistance, or in Patrick Henry to have been bribed with a lawyer's fee to vindicate Lord North's Stamp Act. Next, it was as politically traitorous in a Republican like Mr. Evarts to accept an Attorney-Generalship under President Johnson as it was in Mr. Johnson himself to betray the Republican party, or in Mr. Seward to be the guilty partner of the President's crime.

It is the glory of a public man to wear the ornament of public virtue. Mr. Evarts, once a Republican candidate for a United States senatorship, and always a conspicuous orator in Republican conventions, ought to have had spirit enough to spurn the gift of any office from the tainted hand of Andrew Johnson. Even those morally blind men who saw no wrong in Mr. Evarts's loan of his weary tongue to the President's cause when that traitor was impeached, have no excuse for excusing Mr. Evarts's unmanly acceptance of a privy-counsellorship to the Wickedest Man in the United States. Think of Charles Sumner, or any other unsullied patriot, throwing his supporting arms round a presidential neck that had just escaped the axe of justice! Mr. Evarts's acceptance of a minister's portfolio under President Johnson is no less repugnant to a proper moral sense than would be his acceptance of the same office under President Seymour—Heaven save the mark!

Alas! for human consistency! Mr. Evarts—the man who at Cooper Institute denounced President Johnson as a public enemy—now kisses his hand every Friday in cabinet meetings! When the ghostly little Attorney shall come back from Washington to New York to sit down to his public dinner, how much besides his meat and drink he will have to swallow! After his table is spread, let some one set before him, in an earthen dish, the familiar diet which he now partakes at the President's table — that legendary fruit which makes the men who eat of it forget their country.

October 29, 1868.

THE ELLIOTT COLLECTION OF PORTRAITS.

NOW that Charles Loring Elliott lies in his grave, and black crape hangs round his portrait in the Academy, one cannot but think tenderly of the fine genius which he himself (being his own and only enemy) perpetually held back from its highest development. His pictures in the present exhibition illustrate palpably his many merits and many faults. He always painted dextrously, always showed the free stroke of a master, always proved himself one of the greatest men of his profession; but, on the other hand, he rarely painted with that high and solemn devotion to his art which is the only mood of mind out of which the greatest works can spring. It is not possible to look at the best specimens of his handicraft—as, for instance, the two Hammersley heads—without an involuntary admiration of the great vigor, power, and masculinity of his style; but, after all, we have never seen a portrait by Elliott which, on a calm judgment, could be pronounced truly great. Certainly the dozen or twenty representative heads which his death has brought together, show nothing that will send up his name to be registered in the small list of the great modern masters. In fact, we know of but one American who can be said to belong to the whole world's pre-eminent portrait painters, and that is Page.

It ought to be known that no man in America was a more sincere admirer of Page than Elliott himself. Shortly before his death, Elliott went to Page, and proposed that each should paint the other's portrait—a proposition to which Elliott's great competitor gave a hearty assent; but the grave suddenly opened between the friendly rivals before either of the pictures was begun. We greatly regret that Elliott's fine face and beard—almost the face and beard of Reubens over again—could not have been painted by the one hand that would have given the picture an immortal permanence in art.

As to Elliott's various portraits of himself (almost as numerous as Rembrandt's), they are like all his other works, in that they give only the outside picturesque look and not the inside native character of the subject. Baker's portrait of Elliott, with its pinched and dwarfed features, is not a satisfactory likeness, notwithstanding the great cleverness of its execution. We prefer the untouched photographs to any other likenesses of Elliott. The camera always treated him well—better than he was treated by his own brush; for he usually gave himself more prettiness than strength, whereas Nature gave him a countenance not only handsome but majestic.

The question now is, What is to be his final rank in art? It is not easy to answer. But we can justly say that, despite his life-long failure to realize his full degree of native power, he still stood above all the portrait painters of his time, except the one greater man whose superiority he himself was too clear-sighted not to see and too candid not to acknowledge. Looking one day with great admiration at a picture by Page, Elliott said to a comrade, "Ah! my friend, the Devil don't interfere with *him*, as he does with *me*." We believe that we are to assign to Elliott's sad infirmity, and to no other cause, the striking fact that he never was able to paint the more delicate qualities of "the human face divine." For instance, he signally failed in painting portraits of women; all his female heads are soulless; he wanted a bluff, hale, well-fed man of the world, with a touch of healthy English red in his cheeks. But we have always believed that Elliott possessed, by Nature's gift, the ability to paint as subtly and spiritually as the most gifted of men. It is a regretful reflection that he foolishly trifled away this original inheritance. Genius is a sacred talisman which God never gives to any man outright, but only lends to him on trial; and, if the "one man in a million" on whom the Divine partiality bestows it makes a misuse of it, the magic sooner or later fades out of the amulet. Elliott's mind was endowed with an artistic ability far greater than his best works evince, as his finest skill was early and irrecoverably snatched away from him by that enemy which men put into their mouths to steal away their brains. His life, in its promise and its failure, illustrates Tennyson's immortal lines:

> "The powers that wait on man
> Cancel a sense misused."

The Elliott collection, as it stands in the Academy, festooned with sombre crape, affords a new and touching evidence that a man's genius is not a prolonged and unwasting possession for a life-time, but a corruptible gift, quickly capable of soilure and rust.

"How is the fine gold become dim!"

DECEMBER, 1868.

ELIZABETH CADY STANTON.

ONCE watched an artist while he tried to transfer to canvas the lustre of a precious stone; but, after his utmost skill, his picture was dull. A radiant and sparkling woman, full of wit, reason, and fancy, is a whole crown of jewels; and a poor, opaque copy of her is the most that one can render in a biographical sketch.

Elizabeth Cady, daughter of Judge Daniel Cady and Margaret Livingston, was born November 12, 1816, in Johnstown, New York—forty miles north of Albany.

Birthplace is a secondary parentage, and transmits character. Elizabeth's birthplace was more famous half a century ago than since; for then, though small, it was a marked intellectual centre; and now, though large, it is an unmarked manufacturing town. Before her birth, it was the vice-ducal seat of Sir William Johnson, the famous English negotiator with the Indians. During her girlhood, it was an arena for the intellectual wrestlings of Kent, Tompkins, Spencer, Elisha Williams, and Abraham Van Vechten, who, as lawyers, were among the chiefest of their time. It is now devoted mainly to the fabrication of steel springs and buckskin gloves. Like Wordsworth's early star, "it has faded into the light of common day."

A Yankee said that his chief ambition was to become more famous than his native town; and Mrs. Stanton has lived to see her historic birthplace shrink into a mere local repute, while she herself has been quoted, ridiculed, and abused into a national fame.

But Johnstown still retains one of its ancient splendors —a glory still as fresh as at the foundation of the world. Standing on its hills, one looks off upon a country of enamelled meadow lands, that melt away southward toward the Mohawk, and northward to the base of those grand mountains which are God's monument over the grave of John Brown. In sight of six different counties, Elizabeth Cady, a child of free winds and flowing brooks, roamed at will, frolicking with lambs, chasing butterflies, or, like Proserpine, gathering flowers—"herself a fairer flower." Hanson Cox, standing under the pine tree at Dartmouth College, and gazing on the outlying landscape, exclaimed, "This is a liberal education!" Elizabeth Cady, in addition to her books, her globes, her water-colors, and her guitar, was an apt pupil to skies and fields, gardens and meadows, flocks and herds. Happy the child whose foster-parents are God and Nature!

The one person who, more than any other, gave an intellectual bent to her early life, even more than her father and mother, was her minister. This was the Rev. Simon Hosack—a good old Scotchman, pastor for forty years of a Presbyterian Church in which the Cady family had always been members, and of which Mrs. Stanton (though she has long resided elsewhere) is a member to this day; a fact which her present biographer takes special pains to chronicle, lest otherwise the world might be slow to believe that this brilliant, audacious, and iconoclastic woman is actually an Old School Presbyterian. The venerable Scotch parson—snowy-haired, heavy-browed, and bony-cheeked—was generally cold to most of his parishioners, but always cordial to Elizabeth. A great affection arose between this shepherd and his lamb. What she could not reveal to either father or mother, she unbosomed to him. Full of the sorrows which all imaginative natures suffer keenly in childhood, she found in this patriarch a fatherly confessor, who tenderly taught her how to bear her little burdens of great weight, or, still better, how "to suffer and be strong." Riding his parish rounds, he would take Elizabeth with him in his buggy, give the reins into her hands, and, while his fair charioteer vainly whipped the mild-mannered mare, would put on his spectacles, and read aloud from some book or foreign review, or, when not reading, would talk. The favorite subject, both for reading and talking, was religion—never the dark, but always the bright side of it. Indeed, religion has no dark side. The fancied shadow is not in the thing seen, but in the eye seeing. "If the light that is in thee be darkness, how great is that darkness." Seeking to fill the girl's mind with sunshine and glory, her minister kept always painting to her young fancy fair pictures of paradise and happy saints. Peregrinating in his antique vehicle, the childless old man, fathering this soulful child, taught her that the way to heaven was as beauteous as a country road fringed with wild roses and arched with summer blue.

"My father," she says in one of her letters, "was truly great and good—an ideal judge; and to his sober, taciturn, and majestic bearing, he added the tenderness, purity, and refinement of a true woman. My mother was the soul of independence and self-reliance—cool in the hour of danger, and never knowing fear. She was inclined to a stern military rule of the household—a queenly and magnificent sway; but my father's great sense of justice, and the superior weight of his greater age (for he was many years her senior), so modified the domestic government that the children had, in the main, a pleasant childhood."

The child is not only father of the man, but mother of the woman. This large-brained, inquisitive, and ambitious girl, very early found her whole nature sensibly jarred with the first inward and prophetic stirrings of the great problem to which she has devoted her after years—the elevation and enfranchisement of woman.

"In my earliest girlhood," she writes to me in a letter, which I have liberty to quote, "I spent much time in my father's office. There, before I could understand much of the talk of the older people, I heard many sad complaints, made by women, of the injustice of the laws. We lived in a Scotch neighborhood, where many of the men still retained the old feudal ideas of women and property. Thus, at a man's death, his property would descend to his eldest son, and the mother would be left with nothing in her own right. It was not unusual, therefore, for the mother, who had probably brought all the property into the family, to be made an unhappy dependent on the bounty of a dissipated son. The tears and complaints of these women, who thus came to my father for legal ad vice, touched my heart; and I would often childishly in quire into all the particulars of their sorrow, and would appeal to my father for some prompt remedy. On one occasion he took down a law-book, and tried to show me that something called 'the laws' prevented him from putting a stop to these cruel and unjust things. In this way, my head was filled with a great anger against those cruel and atrocious laws. Whereupon the students in the office, to amuse themselves by exciting my feelings, would always tell me of any unjust laws which they found during their studies. My mind was thus so aroused against the barbarism of the laws thus pointed out, that I one day marked them with a pencil, and decided to take a pair of scissors and cut them out of the book—supposing that my father and his library were the beginning and end of the law! I thought that if I could only destroy those laws, the poor women would have no further trouble. But when the students informed my father of my proposed mutilation of his volumes, he explained to me how fruitless my childish vengeance would have been, and taught me that bad laws were to be abolished in quite a different way. As soon as I fairly understood how the thing could be accomplished, I vowed that, when I became old enough, I would have such abominable laws changed. And I have kept my vow."

After the failure of Elizabeth's novel and original plan of amending the laws with her scissors, a strange ambition took possession of her mind.

"I was about ten years old," she says, "when my only brother, who had just graduated at Union College with high honors, came home to die. He was my father's pride and joy. It was easily seen that, while my father was kind to us all, the one son filled a larger place in his affections and future plans than the five daughters together. Well do I remember how tenderly he watched the boy in that last sickness; how he sighed, and wiped the tears from his eyes, as he slowly walked up and down the hall; and how, when the last sad moment came, and all was silent in the chamber of death, he knelt and prayed for comfort and support. I well remember, too, going into the large, dark parlor to look at my brother's corpse, and finding my father there, pale and immovable, sitting in a great arm-chair by his side. For a long time my father took no notice of *me*. At last I slowly approached him and climbed upon his knee. He mechanically put his arm about me, and, with my head resting against his beating heart, we sat a long, long time in silence—he thinking of the wreck of all his hopes in the loss of his dear son, and I fully feeling the awful void death had made. At length he heaved a deep sigh and said, 'O my daughter, I wish you were a boy!' '*Then I will be a boy*,' said I, 'and will do all that my brother did.'

"All that day, and far into the night, I pondered the problem of boyhood. I thought the chief thing was, to be learned and courageous, as I fancied all boys were. So I decided to learn Greek, and to manage a horse. Having come to that conclusion I fell asleep. My resolutions, unlike most made at night, did not vanish in the morning. I rose early, and hastened to put them into execution. They were resolutions never to be forgotten—destined to mould my whole future character. As soon as I was dressed, I hastened to meet our good pastor in his garden, which joined our own. Finding him at work there as usual, I said, 'Doctor, will you teach me Greek?' 'Yes,' he replied. 'Will you give me a lesson now?' 'Yes, to be sure,' he added. Laying down his hoe, and taking my hand, 'Come into my study,' said he, 'and we will begin at once.' As we walked along, I told him all my thoughts and plans. Having no children, he loved me very much, entered at once into the sorrow which I had felt on discovering that a girl was less in the scale of being than a boy, and praised my determination to prove the contrary. The old grammar which he had studied in the University of Glasgow was soon in my hand, and the Greek article learned before breakfast.

"Then came the sad pageantry of death—the weeping friends, the dark rooms, the ghostly stillness, the funeral cortége, the prayer, the warning exhortation, the mournful chant, the solemn tolling bell, the burial. How my flesh crawled during those three sad days! What strange, undefined fears of the unknown and the invisible took possession of me! For months afterward, at the twilight hour, I went with my father to the new-made grave. Near it stood a tall poplar, against which I leaned, while my father threw himself upon the grave with outstretched arms, as if to embrace his child. At last the frosts and storms of November came, and made a chilling barrier between the living and the dead, and we went there no more.

"During all this time the good doctor and I kept up our lessons; and I learned also how to drive and ride a horse, and how (on horseback) to leap a fence and ditch. I taxed every power, in hope some day to make my father say, 'Well, a girl is as good as a boy, after all!' But he never said it. When the doctor would come to spend the evening with us, I would whisper in his ear, 'Tell my father how fast I get on.' And he would tell him all, and praise me too. But my father would only pace the room and sigh, 'Ah, she should have been a boy!' And I, not knowing why, would hide my head on the doctor's shoulder, and often weep with vexation.

"At length, I entered the academy, and, in a class mainly of boys, studied mathematics, Latin, and Greek. As two prizes were offered in Greek, I strove for one, and got it. How well I remember my joy as I received that prize! There was no feeling of ambition, rivalry, or triumph over my companions, nor any pulse-beat of satisfaction in winning my honors in presence of all the persons assembled in the academy on the day of exhibition. One thought alone occupied my mind. 'Now,' said I, 'my father will be happy—he will be satisfied.' As soon as we were dismissed, I hastened home, rushed into his office, laid the new Greek Testament (which was my prize) on his lap, and exclaimed, 'There, I have got it!' He took the book, looked through it, asked me some questions about the class, the teachers, and the spectators, appeared to be pleased, handed the book back to me, and when I was aching to have him say something which would show that he recognized the equality of the daughter with the son, kissed me on the forehead, and exclaimed with a sigh, 'Ah, you should have been a boy!' That ended my pleasure. I hastened to my room, flung the book across the floor, and wept tears of bitterness.

"But the good doctor, to whom I then went, gave me hope and courage. What a debt of gratitude I owe to that dear, old man! I used to visit him every day, tell him the news, comb his hair, read to him, talk with him, and listen with rapture to his holy words. Oh, how often the memory of many things he has said has given me comfort and strength in the hour of darkness and struggle! One day, as we sat alone, and I held his hand, and he was ill, he said, 'Dear child, it is your mission to help mould the world anew. May good angels give you thoughts, and move you to do the work which they want done on earth. You must promise me one thing, and that is, that you will always say what you think. Your thoughts are given you to utter, not to conceal; and if you are true to yourself, and give to others all you see and know, God will pour more light and truth into your own soul. My old Greek lexicon, testament, and grammar, which I studied forty years ago, and which you and I have thumbed so often together, I shall leave to you when I die; and, whenever you see them, remember that I am watching you from heaven, and that you can still come to me with all your sorrows, just as you have always done. I shall be ever near you.'

"When the last sad scene was over, and his will was opened, sure enough, there was a clause in it, saying, 'My Greek lexicon, testament, and grammar, I give to Elizabeth Cady.'

"Great was the void which the doctor's death made in my heart. But I slowly transferred my love to the books. When I first received them they were all falling to pieces. So I had them newly bound in black morocco and gilt. Dear are they to me to this day, and dear will they continue to be as long as I live. I never look at them without thanking God that he gave me in my childhood so noble a friend."

At the time of Dr. Hosack's death, or in her fifteenth year, her term at the Johnstown Academy was drawing to a close. Among the scholars, whether girls or boys, none could recite better, or run faster, than she; none missed fewer lessons, or frolics; none were oftener at the head of recitations, or mischief. If she was detained from the class, the teacher felt the loss of her cheery company; if she was absent from the out-door games, the boys said half the sport was gone. She who had been the loved companion of a sedate theologian had at the same time remained the ringleader of a bevy of mad romps. A school-house is a kingdom: and Elizabeth was a school-house queen.

After graduating at the head of her class, a sudden blow fell upon her heart, inflicting a grievous wound. She had secretly cherished a hope that as she had kept ahead of the boys, and thus shown more than her equality with the domineering sex, she would be sent (as Johnstown boys were then usually sent) to Union College at Schenectady.

The thought never occurred to her that this institution, like most other colleges, was not so wise and liberal as to educate both sexes instead of one. There will come a time when any institution that proposes to educate the sexes separately will be voted too ignorant of human nature to be trusted with moulding the minds of the sons and daughters of the republic. To shut girls and boys out of each other's sight during the four most impressible years of life is one of the many conventional interferences with natural law which society unwittingly ordains to its own harm. It is a happiness to see that most of our new colleges, particularly in the Western States, are based on a more sensible theory.

Just when Elizabeth Cady's heart was most set on Union College, whither she would have gone had she pleased her father by being a boy, she was told that she must go instead to Mrs. Willard's Female Seminary in Troy, because she had disappointed him by being a girl. Great was her indignation at this announcement—impetuous her protest against this plan. The stigma of inferiority thus cast upon her on account of her sex, and on account of her sex alone, was galling to a maiden who had already distanced all her competitors of the opposite sex. At every step of her journey to Troy she seemed to herself to be treading on her pride, and crushing out her life. Exasperated, mortified, and humbled, she began in a sad frame of mind a boarding-school career. "If there is any one thing on earth," she says, "from which I pray God to save my daughters, it is a girls' seminary. The two years which

I spent in a girls' seminary were the dreariest years of my whole life." Nevertheless, nothing remained for the disappointed child but to make the best of a bad situation. So she beguiled her melancholy by playing mischievous pranks. For instance, in the seminary a big hand-bell was rung down stairs every morning as a call to prayer, and up stairs every night as a call to bed. After the nightly ringing, the bell was set down on the upper floor in an angle of the wall. One night at eleven o'clock, after the inmates had been an hour in bed, Elizabeth furtively rose, stole out of her dormitory in the drapery of a ghost, and solemnly kicked the bell step by step down every flight of stairs to the ground floor! Although everybody in the house was wakened by the noise, and many of the doors were opened, she glided past all the peeping eyes like a phantom, to the general terror of the whole house, and was never afterwards suspected of being the author of the mischief.

Soon, however, the frightener of others was frightened herself. The Rev. Charles Grandison Finney—a pulpit orator who, as a terrifier of human souls, has proved almost the equal of Savonarola—made a visit to Troy, and preached in the Rev. Dr. Beman's Presbyterian church, where Elizabeth and her schoolmates attended. "I can see him now," she says, (describing Mr. Finney's preaching), "his great eyes rolling round the congregation, and his arms flying in the air like a windmill. One evening he described Hell and the Devil so vividly that the picture glowed before my eyes in the dark for months afterwards. On another occasion, when describing the damned as wandering in the Inferno, and inquiring their way through its avenues, he suddenly pointed with his finger, exclaiming, 'There! do you not see them?" and I actually jumped up in church and looked round—his description had been such a reality."

In thus quoting Mrs. Stanton's allusion to my venerable friend Mr. Finney, I cannot help adding that, although high respect is due to the intellectual and spiritual gifts of the Titanic ex-president of Oberlin College, such preaching often works incalculable harm to the very souls it seeks to save. It worked harm to Elizabeth. The strong man struck the child as with a lion's paw. Fear of the judgment seized her soul. Mental anguish prostrated her health. Visions of the lost haunted her dreams. Dethronement of her reason was apprehended by her friends. Flinging down her books, she suddenly fled home.

The good minister of Johnstown, her one and only counsellor, was in his grave. His successor was a stranger whom she could not approach. In her despair, she turned to her father. "Often," said she, "I would rise out of my bed, hasten to his chamber, kneel at his side, and ask him to pray for my soul's salvation, lest I should be cast into hell before morning." At last she regained her wonted composure of spirits, and joined the Johnstown church. "But I was never happy," she writes, "in that gloomy faith which dooms to eternal misery the greater part of the human family. It was no comfort to me to be saved with a chosen few, while the multitude, and those too who had suffered most on earth, were to have no part in heaven."

The next seven years of her life she spent at Johnstown, dividing her time between book-delving and horse-taming; and, having an equal relish for each, she conquered the books in her father's library, and the horses in her father's stable. In fact, she would sometimes ride half the day over hill and meadow like a fox-hunter, and then study law-books half the night like a jurist. When she was busy at her embroidery or water-colors, her father, who had a poor opinion of such accomplishments, would bring to her the "Revised Statutes," and say, "My daughter, here is a book which, if you read it, will give you something sensible to say to Mr. Spencer and Mr. Williams when they next make us a visit." Mr. Spencer and Mr. Williams were legal magnates who made Judge Cady's dinner-table a frequent arena for the discussion of nice points of law. So Elizabeth, with a fine determination to make herself the peer of the whole table, diligently began and pursued that study of the laws of her country which has since armed and equipped her, as from an arsenal of weapons, for her struggle against the legislation which oppresses her country-women. As to her horse-riding, she has of late years discontinued it, for the reason (if I may be so ungallant as to hint it) that a lady of very elegant but also very solid proportions is more at her ease in a carriage than in a saddle.

In 1839, in her twenty-fourth year, while on a visit to her distinguished cousin, Gerrit Smith, at Peterboro', in the central part of New York State, she made the acquaintance of Mr. Henry B. Stanton, then a young and fervid orator, who had won distinction in the anti-slavery movement. The acquaintances speedily became friends; the friends grew into lovers; the lovers after a short courtship married, and immediately set sail for Europe.

This voyage was undertaken, not merely for pleasure and sight-seeing, but that her husband might fulfil the mission of a delegate to the "World's Anti-Slavery Convention," to be held in London in 1840. Many well-known American women were delegates; but, on presenting their credentials, were denied membership on account of their sex. Lucretia Mott, Sarah Pugh, Emily Winslow, Abby Kimber, Mary Grew, and Ann Green Phillips—women who could meet no superiors in all England for moral worth—found to their astonishment that after having devoted their whole lives to the anti-slavery cause, they were repulsed from an anti-slavery convention which they had travelled three thousand miles to attend. Wendell Phillips argued manfully for their admission, but in vain. William Lloyd Garrison, who, having crossed in a tardy ship, did not arrive till after the question had been decided, and decided unjustly, refused to present his credentials, took no part in the proceedings, and sat a silent spectator in the gallery—one of the most chivalrous acts of his life. Beaten in the committee, the ladies transferred the question to the social circles. Every dinner-table at which they were present grew lively with the theme. At a dinner-table in Queen Street, Mrs. Lucretia Mott—then in the prime of her intellectual powers, and with a head which Combe, the phrenologist, pronounced the finest he had ever seen on a woman—replied so skilfully to the arguments of a dozen friendly opponents, chiefly clergymen, that she was acknowledged the victor in the debate. It was then and there that Mrs. Stanton for the first time saw, heard, and loved Lucretia Mott. Many a time during her maidenly years Elizabeth Cady had pondered the many-sided question of woman's relation to society, to the state, to the industrial arts, and to the laws of property. But in thinking these thoughts, she had hitherto supposed herself to be alone in the world. Now, however, during a six weeks' constant and familiar companionship with Mrs. Mott, she wonderingly heard the whole cyclopedia of her own hidden but sweetly-cherished convictions openly confessed by another's lips.

All the women with whom Mrs. Stanton had ever associated in America had without exception belonged to the circle of conservative opinion. Mrs. Mott was the first liberal thinker on womanhood whom she had ever encountered. Elizabeth's delight at thus finding a woman who had thought farther than herself on some of the most vital questions affecting the human soul, was as glowing and enchanting as if she had suddenly discovered a cavern of hidden jewels. It is not too much to say that the influence of the elder of these women on the younger was greater than the combined influence of everything else which that younger saw and heard during her foreign tour. This is not an exaggerated statement. I once asked her the question, "What most impressed you in Europe;" and she instantly replied, "Lucretia Mott!" One day, as a party of a dozen or more friends were visiting the British Museum, Mrs. Mott and Mrs. Stanton, who were of the company, had hardly entered the building when they sat down and began to talk to each other. The rest went forward, made the circuit of the curiosities, and came back to the entrance, to find that the two talkers still sat with their heads together, never having stirred from their places. The sympathetic twain had found in each other more than either cared to look for in the whole British Museum! Mrs. Stanton's enthusiasm for Mrs. Mott is as fresh and warm now as then. And no wonder; for in the same sense in which the greatest man ever produced in this country was Benjamin Franklin, so the greatest woman ever produced in this country is Lucretia Mott. They were cousins. Blood tells!

On returning to America, Mr. Stanton began the practice of law in Boston, where, with his wife and family, he resided for five years. The east winds, growing unfriendly to his throat, then drove him to take shelter in the greater kindliness of an inland climate, and he transferred his household and business to Seneca Falls, in the State of New York.

The first "Woman's Rights Convention" (known to history by that name) was held July 19th and 20th, 1848, in the Wesleyan Chapel at Seneca Falls. Copies of the official report of the proceedings (I mean the original edition) are now rare, and will one day be hunted for by antiquarians—a petite pamphlet, about the size of a man's hand, resembling in letter (though not in spirit) a tract by the American Tract Society. My own copy has become yellow-tinted by time. I look back with a reverential interest on this modest chronicle of a great event. That convention little thought it would be historic. But it was the first of a chain of similar conventions which, like the links round a Leyden jar, have since girdled the whole world with the brightness of a new idea. The chief agent in calling the convention was Mrs. Stanton; it met in the town of her residence; its resolutions and declarations of sentiment were the offspring of her pen; its one great leading idea—the elective franchise—was a suggestion of her brain. I do not know of any public demand for woman's suffrage, made by any organized convention, previous to Mrs. Stanton's demand for it in the following resolution: "Resolved, that it is the duty of the women of this country to secure to themselves their sacred right to the elective franchise." I am aware that women long before had voted (for a short time) in New Jersey. But woman's political rights had been slumbering for years, when Mrs. Stanton suddenly jarred them into a wide-awake activity. This she did to the consternation of her best friends. The convention at Seneca Falls was called, as the advertisement ran, "to discuss the social, civil, and religious condition of women." Nothing was said of their political condition, except so far as that might be ambiguously included in their civil. Probably very few of the delegates, on going to the meeting, carried to it any such idea as woman's suffrage. When Mrs. Stanton privately proposed to introduce the resolution which I have quoted, even Mrs. Mott—who (as the report mentions) was "the ruling spirit of the occasion"—attempted to dissuade the bold innovator. But the bold innovator would not be dissuaded. She offered her resolution, and in its support made for the first time in her life a public speech. Not a natural orator, she at first shrank from taking the floor. But a sense of duty impelling her to utter her thoughts, she conquered her bewilderment, stated her views, answered the convention's objections, fought a courageous battle, and carried her proposition. No American woman ever rendered a more signal service to her country than was on that day bashfully, yet gracefully, and triumphantly performed by Mrs. Stanton.

The convention, and especially its demand for woman's suffrage, excited the laughter of the whole nation. Wonder-stricken people asked each other "What sort of creatures could those women at Seneca Falls have been?" It was never suspected by the general public that they were among the finest ladies in the land. Even their own relatives and friends, who knew their personal virtues, lamented their public eccentricities, and joined the general outcry of critics and satirists. Judge Cady, on hearing of what his daughter had done, fancied her crazy, and immediately journeyed from Johnstown to Seneca Falls to learn for himself whether or not her brilliant brain had been turned. "After my father's arrival," she said, "he talked with me a whole evening till one o'clock in the morning, trying to reason me out of my position. At length, kissing me good night, he said, 'My child, I wish you had waited till I was under the sod, before you had done this foolish thing!' But I replied, laughing, 'Ah, sir, don't you remember how you used to give me law-books to read in order that I might have something sensible to say to your friends Mr. Spencer and Mr. Williams when they came to dine with us? It was by reading those law-books that I found out the injustice of the laws toward woman. I never would have known anything on the subject except for yourself." Never till his death (which occurred several years afterward), did the good man relax his opposition to his daughter's views, but he came to cherish a secret pride at the skill, vigor, and eloquence with which she maintained them against all antagonists.

From the day of the Seneca Falls Convention till now, Mrs. Stanton has been one of the representative women of America. At a similar convention held at Cleveland, Ohio, in 1853, Mrs. Mott proposed the adoption of the declaration of sentiments put forth at Seneca Falls in 1848. "She thought," says the official report, "that this would be but a fitting honor to her who initiated these movements in behalf of the women of our country—Elizabeth Cady Stanton."

I have seen the old and tattered manuscript of the first "set speech" which Mrs. Stanton ever delivered. It was a lyceum-lecture, ably and elaborately written; and was repeated at several places in the interior of the State of New York, during the first months that followed the first convention. The manuscript, after unaccountably slipping out of the author's hands, passed from friend to friend, from town to town, and from state to state, until she not only lost sight of it for a time, but gave up all hope of ever seeing it again. Eighteen years afterward it was returned to her, somewhat the worse for wear. It had meanwhile travelled I know not how many hundreds of miles, and been read by I know not how many hundreds of persons. On recovering the lost scroll, she penned on its margin this inscription, addressed to her daughters:

"DEAR MAGGIE AND HATTIE: This is my first speech. It was delivered several times immediately after the first Woman's Rights Convention. It contains all I knew at that time. I did not speak again for several years. The manuscript has ever since been a wanderer through the land. Now, after a separation of nearly eighteen years, I press my first-born to my heart once more. As I recall my younger days, I weep over the apathy and indifference of women concerning their own degradation. I give this manuscript to my precious daughters, in the hope that they will finish the work which I have begun."

Miss Susan B. Anthony—a well-known, indefatigable, and life-long advocate of Temperance, Anti-slavery, and Woman's Rights—has been since 1850 Mrs. Stanton's intimate associate in reformatory labors. These celebrated women are of about equal ages, but of the most opposite characteristics, and illustrate the theory of counterparts in affection by entertaining for each other an attachment of extraordinary strength. Mrs. Stanton is a fine writer, but poor executant; Miss Anthony is no writer at all, but a thorough manager. Both have large brains and great hearts; neither has any selfish ambition for celebrity; and each vies with the other in enthusiasm for the cause to which they unitedly devote their lives. Nevertheless, to describe them critically, I ought to say that, opposites though they be, each does not so much supplement the other's deficiencies as augment the other's eccentricities. They often stimulate each other's aggressiveness, and at the same time diminish each other's discretion. But whatever may be the imprudent utterances of the one, or the impolitic methods of the other, I know that the animating motives of both, judged by the highest moral standards, are evermore white as the light. The good which they do is by design; the harm, by accident. These two women, sitting together in their parlor, have for the last fifteen years been diligent forgers of all manner of projectiles, from fireworks to thunderbolts, and have hurled them with unexpected explosion into the midst of all manner of educational, reformatory, and religious conventions—sometimes to the pleasant surprise and half-welcome of the members; more often to the bewilderment and prostration of numerous victims; and, in a few signal instances, to the gnashing of angry men's teeth. I know of no two more pertinacious and agreeable incendiaries in the whole country! Nor will they themselves deny my good-humored indictment. In fact, this noise-making pair are the two sticks of a drum for keeping up what Daniel Webster called "the rub-a-dub of agitation."

The practice of going before a legislature to present the claims of an unpopular cause has been more common in many other States than in New York; most common, perhaps, in Massachusetts. With the single exception of Mrs. Lucy Stone—a noble and gifted woman to whom all other women owe gratitude, not merely for an eloquence that has charmed thousands of ears, but for practical efforts in abolishing laws tyrannous to their sex—I believe that Mrs. Stanton has appeared oftener before a

State legislature than can be said of any of her co-laborers. She has repeatedly addressed the Legislature of New York at Albany, and on these occasions has always been honored by the presence of a brilliant audience, and has always spoken with dignity and ability. Her chief topics have been the needful changes in the laws relating to intemperance, education, divorce, slavery, and suffrage. "Yes, gentlemen," said she in her address of 1854, "we, the daughters of the revolutionary heroes of '76, demand at your hands the redress of our grievances—a revision of your State constitution—a new code of laws."

At the close of that grand and glowing argument, a lawyer who had listened to it, and who knew and revered Mrs. Stanton's father, shook hands with the orator and said, "Madam, it was as fine a production as if it had been written and pronounced by Judge Cady himself." This, to the daughter's cars, was sufficiently high praise.

I have carefully read several of Mrs. Stanton's other addresses before the New York legislature, and have felt in reading them that so able a woman ought long ago to have been eligible to membership in a body whom she thus so admirably addressed. But there will come a day —and heaven speed it!—when no legislature or congress will be considered as representing the whole people of a state or a nation, until women as well as men shall sit as its duly chosen members—until women as well as men shall be as much expected to make, as they are to obey, the laws of the land—until women as well as men shall be held politically responsible for the Christian government of the republic. "Ye are members one of another," says the wise Book; and the saying is no more true of the family than of society—no more true of the church than of the state. It has taken a terrific contest (not yet ended) to achieve the political rights of American citizens without distinction of color. But from this point onward, without an appeal to arms, and without a testimony of blood, a more peaceful but not less glorious struggle is to achieve the political rights of American citizens without distinction of sex.

In a cabinet of curiosities, I have laid away as an interesting relic a little white ballot, two inches square, and inscribed:

For Representative in Congress,
ELIZABETH CADY STANTON.

Mrs. Stanton is the only woman in the United States who as yet has been a candidate for Congress. In conformity with a practice prevalent in some parts of this country, and very prevalent in England, she nominated herself. The public letter in which she proclaimed her candidacy was as follows:—

"TO THE ELECTORS OF THE EIGHTH CONGRESSIONAL DISTRICT.

"Although by the Constitution of the State of New York woman is denied the elective franchise, yet she is eligible to office; therefore I present myself to you as a candidate for Representative to Congress. Belonging to a disfranchised class, I have no political antecedents to recommend me to your support, but my creed is *free speech*, *free press*, *free men*, and *free trade*—the cardinal points of Democracy. Viewing all questions from the standpoint of principle rather than expediency, there is a fixed uniform law, as yet unrecognized by either of the leading parties, governing alike the social and political life of men and nations. The Republican party has occasionally a clear vision of personal rights, while in its protective policy it seems wholly blind to the rights of property and interests of commerce. While it recognizes the duty of benevolence between man and man, it teaches the narrowest selfishness in trade between nations. The Democrats, on the contrary, while holding sound and liberal principles in trade and commerce, have ever in their political affiliations maintained the idea of class and caste among men—an idea wholly at variance with the genius of our free institutions and fatal to a high civilization. One party fails at one point, and one at another. In asking your suffrages—believing alike in free men and free trade—I could not represent either party as now constituted.

"Nevertheless, as an independent candidate, I desire an election at this time as a rebuke to the dominant party for its retrogressive legislation in so amending the constitution as to make invidious distinctions on the ground of sex.

"That instrument recognizes as persons all citizens who obey the laws and support the State, and if the constitutions of the several States were brought into harmony with the broad principles of the Federal Constitution, the women of the nation would no longer be taxed without representation, or governed without their consent. One word should not be added to that great charter of rights to the insult or injury of the humblest of our citizens. I would gladly have a voice and vote in the fortieth Congress to demand universal suffrage, that thus a republican form of government might be secured to every State in the Union.

"If the party now in the ascendancy makes its demand for 'negro suffrage' in good faith, on the ground of natural right, and because the highest good of the state demands that the republican idea be vindicated, on no principle of justice or safety can the women of the nation be ignored.

"In view of the fact that the freedmen of the South and the millions of foreigners now crowding our Western shores, most of whom represent neither property, education, nor civilization, are all, in the progress of events, to be enfranchised, the best interests of the nation demand that we outweigh this incoming pauperism, ignorance, and degradation, with the wealth, education, and refinement of the women of the republic. On the high ground of safety to the nation and justice to its citizens, I ask your support in the coming election.

"ELIZABETH CADY STANTON.

"NEW YORK, October 10, 1866."

The New York Herald, though of course with no sincerity, since that journal is never sincere in anything, warmly advocated Mrs. Stanton's election. "A lady of fine presence and accomplishments in the House of Representatives," it said (and said truly), "would wield a wholesome influence over the rough and disorderly elements of that body." *The Anti-slavery Standard* with genuine commendation said, "The electors of the eighth district would honor themselves and do well by the country in giving her a triumphant election." The other candidates in the same district were Mr. James Brooks, democrat, and Mr. LeGrand B. Cannon, republican. The result of the election was as follows: Mr. Brooks received 13,216 votes, Mr. Cannon 8,210, and Mrs. Stanton 24. It will be seen that the number of sensible people in the district was limited. The excellent lady, in looking back on her successful defeat, regrets that she did not, before it became too late, procure the photographs of her two dozen unknown friends.

In the summer of 1867 the people of Kansas were to debate, and in the autumn to decide, the most novel, noble, and beautiful question ever put to a popular vote in the United States—the question of adopting a new constitution extending the elective franchise not merely to "white male citizens," but to those of what Frederick Douglass calls "the less fashionable color," and to those also of what Horace Greeley calls "the less muscular sex." Mrs. Lucy Stone and Miss Olympia Brown—helped by other ladies less famous, and by several earnest men, including the Hon. Samuel C. Pomeroy, Senator of the United States—made public speeches at prominent places in that State, urging the people to give the new idea a hospitable welcome at the polls. This canvass was as chivalrous as a tournament, and abounded with romantic incidents. To hear from the lips of Mrs. Stone (in that delightful eloquence of conversation which she has never surpassed on the platform) a recital of the most serious or the most comical of these, is as pleasant an entertainment as a tea-table talk can well afford. Toward the close of that memorable campaign, Mrs. Stanton and Miss Anthony, like a reserved force, joined themselves to the general battle. Accidentally associated with them (first with Miss Anthony and afterward with Mrs. Stanton) was Mr. George Francis Train—soldier of fortune, hero of Fenianism, martyr to creditors, guest of jails, and candidate for the presidency. *The Tribune* has admiringly called Mr. Train "a charlatan and blatherskite." Ampler justice compels me to add that he is of all mountebanks the most amiable, and of all clowns the most innocent. These women of substance and this man of froth formed in Kansas a coalition which provoked their opponents to smiles, and their friends to regrets. Anxious watchers of the progress of the good cause were apprehensive that the flightiness of Mr. Train's speeches would bring the new question into disrepute. But the history of reforms in all countries, and especially in this, has shown that neither the wildest friends nor the fiercest foes of a great idea can any more trample it under their feet than if they had trodden on a sunbeam. The result of the vote on the new constitution was flattering beyond the most sanguine expectation. No wise observer of the signs of the times had looked for the adoption of that radical instrument, but only for a generous minority in its support. The figures stood 9,000 for, and 19,000 against the change. I have never met any student of American politics who was not greatly surprised thus to find that one-third of the voters in any State of the Union were sufficiently advanced in opinion to demand at the ballot-box the political equality of the sexes. If the Anti-slavery party in Massachusetts, like the woman's suffrage party in Kansas, had received on a first trial at the polls one-third of the votes cast, the early abolitionists would have shouted for joy and rung the church-bells for a jubilee. Whether the vote in Kansas was increased or diminished by Mr. Train's harangues, I am unable to say. But it is proper to say that the Anti-slavery movement, gathering, as it did, to its annual platforms, many of the greatest as well as some of the shallowest of human brains; and the woman's suffrage movemant, constantly repeating, as it does, these same phenomena; thereby furnish a magnificent proof of the universality of those great ideas which thus make known their power upon all classes of human beings, great and small, wise and simple, sane and mad. God has ordained that the noble army of reformers, headed by the choicest spirits of the age, should give honorable rank also to Tag, Rag, and Bobtail. I can see no reason why the gifted leaders of great movements should decline to make common cause with all who work for the common end.

After the election in Kansas, Mrs. Stanton, Miss Anthony, and Mr. Train, made a slow progress eastward, stopping at the chief cities, and addressing public meetings on woman's rights. These meetings provoked merited criticism on account of the performances of Mr. Train, who amused his audiences with the capers of a harlequin. The previous substantial reputation of the two ladies as earnest reformers was on this account greatly shaken. And yet their own speeches, on all these occasions, were grave, earnest, and impressive—always worthy of their authors and of the cause. By the time the three travellers had reached New York, they had projected a weekly journal, which made its appearance at the beginning of 1868, under the topsy-turvying title of *The Revolution*, edited by Elizabeth Cady Stanton and Parker Pillsbury, and published by Susan B. Anthony. Like Jupiter Tonans in the rainy season, this sheet always thunders. It is the stormiest of journals. Its pages, as one turns them over, seem to crinkle, flutter, and snap with electric heats. Examine almost any number of *The Revolution*, and it will be found the strangest mixture of sense and nonsense known anywhere in American journalism—a rag-bag of the most incongruous topics. The articles signed "E. C. S." and "P. P." are full of force and fire—never common-place nor tame. Mr.

Pillsbury has a gorgeous and sombre imagination which, when it plays about any subject that can bear its strong colors, makes some of his best essays truly magnificent. Mrs. Stanton, who is always in high animal spirits, and who, like a ripe grape, carries a whole summer's sunshine in her blood, fills her most serious articles with fun, frolic, and satire, and even in her most humorous escapades shows a rare vein of tenderness, pathos, and eloquence. She so abounds in metaphors and pithy phrases that a characteristic article from her pen is like a Chinese jar of chow-chow—filled with little lumps of citron, apricot, and ginger, all swimming in a sweet and biting syrup. The political disquisitions of this co-working yet non-assimilating pair are sometimes grand and just, sometimes visionary and absurd. During the first year of *The Revolution*, Mr. Train and his money-writers danced up and down through one-third of each week's space in the paper, and held a high carnival of balderdash. One particular contribution, kept up every week, so coruscated with outlandish notions, comments, and criticisms, as to remind one of a barn-door in a dark night, scrawled over in phosphorus with "gorgons, hydras, and chimeras dire." In the spring of 1869 Mr. Train rendered to *The Revolution* a generous service by retiring from it; since which time the great public have discovered that the unique little sheet is no longer to be laughed at, but listened to —no longer a vain voice, but a solid power. In spite of all the criticism justly urged against its contents, I am bound to say that some of the noblest thoughts and utterances pertinent to this day and generation—ringing words for liberty, justice, and womanhood—glowing rebukes of false customs, social tyrannies, and degrading conventionalities—eloquent appeals for a more liberal civil polity, and a more equitable social order—fervid aspirations toward whatever dignifies human nature and purifies the immortal soul—these, too, "thoughts that breathe, and words that burn," are spread week by week upon the pages of *The Revolution*, and from no brain oftener than from the fiery, wayward, sympathetic, and Christian soul of Elizabeth Cady Stanton.

I may now paint her features and sum up her character.

Mrs. Stanton's face is thought to resemble Martha Washington's, but is less regular and more animated; her hair—which was early gray, and is now frosty white—falls about her head in thick clusters of curls; her eyes twinkle with amiable mischief; her voice, though hardly musical, is mellow and agreeable; her figure is of the middle height, and just stout enough to suggest a preference for short walks and long rides. In reality, however, she can walk like an English-woman—though if, during a stroll in the street, some jest sets her to laughing, she is forced to halt, cover her countenance with her veil, and shake contagiously till the spasm be past. The costume that most becomes her (and in which her historic portrait ought to be garmented) is a blue silk dress and a red India shawl—an array which, topped with her magnificent white hair, makes her a patriotic embodiment of "red, white, and blue."

Her gift of gifts is conversation. Her throne of queenship is not the official chair of the Woman's Rights Convention (though she always presides with dignity and ease), but is rather a seat at the social board where the company are elderly conservative gentlemen who combine to argue her down. I think she was never argued down in her life. Go into a fruit-orchard, jar the ripe and laden trees one after another, and not a greater shower of plums, cherries, and pomegranates will fall about your head, than the witticisms, anecdotes, and repartees which this bounteous woman sheds down in her table-talk. House-keeping and babies, free trade and temperance, woman's suffrage and the "white male citizen:"—these are her favorite themes. Many a person, on spending a delightful evening in her society, has gone away, saying, "Well, that is Madame de Staël alive again."

Never had a human being a kindlier nature than Mrs. Stanton's. Pity is her chief vice; charity, her besetting sin. She has not the heart to see a chicken killed, or a child punished. If robbed of all her property, she could not endure to have sentence passed on the thief. When a wretch does wrong, she is apt to think his act not so much his own fault as the fault of the law under which he lives. A judge punishes the offender, and lets the law go uncondemned; but this judge of judges lets the offender go free, and condemns the law instead. On the one hand her sense of justice is so sensitive, and on the other her tender-heartedness is so excessive, that she compounds for pardoning the criminal by attacking all those usages of society which have lured him to his crime. Seeing a man drunken in the streets, she does not chide the culprit, but straightway denounces the sale of liquor; seeing a seamstress underpaid, she does not arraign the employer, but rails at the narrow range of women's employments; seeing a widow cheated out of her inheritance, she would not so eagerly attempt to punish the scoundrel as to secure woman's suffrage for woman's self-protection.

"It is a settled maxim with me," she says, "that the existing public sentiment on any subject is wrong."

Accordingly, as against the customary laws of divorce, she holds to the doctrine of John Milton ; as against the prevailing tariffs, she argues vehemently for free trade ; as against old-fashioned religious opinions, she inclines to an unchecked free-thinking ; as against the common notion of what constitutes woman's sphere, she holds that woman's sphere is to be widened unto equal greatness with man's.

If it be supposed that in all this she aims to make woman unwomanly, such a supposition is unjust. It is because, under the present canons of society, woman's nature is denied its true growth, defrauded of its true liberty, and diverted from its true end, that Mrs. Stanton, being herself a true woman, so earnestly tries to take woman's feet out of the Chinese shoes of dwarfing custom, to rescue her from her present constraint in a restrictive social order, to restore her to her own truer self, and to present her back once more to God.

Mrs. Stanton's knowledge of human life, in its various experiences, has been as rich, varied, and profound as often falls to the lot of a human being. The sacred lore of motherhood is to her a familiar study. Five sons and two daughters sit around her table, all as proud of their mother as if she were a queen of Fairyland, and they her pages in waiting. Drinking not seldom at the fountain of sorrow, she has found in its bitter waters strength for her soul. Religious and worshipful by nature, she has cast off in her later life the superstitions of her earlier, but has never lost her childhood's faith in God. Society (as she looks at it) being full of hollowness and falsity, she often yearns for its reformation as if her heart would break. The cause of woman's elevation being with her not merely a passion but a religion, she would willingly give her body to be burned, for the sake of seeing her sex enfranchised. But over all this aching and restless earnestness of her inward life, nature has kindly drawn a countenance of sunny smiles, a perpetual good-humor, and an irresistible flow of spirits; so that as she faces the world, she is one of the most fascinating, exhaustless, and perennial of companions; and as she turns away from it, and faces God alone, she offers to him a soul whose very sorrows, disappointments, and hopes deferred have long ago wrought within her a solemn, cheerful, and immortal peace. Nothing in her outward career—nothing in her gayety and wit—nothing in the whole cluster of those fine faculties that make her one of the ablest women of our day—nothing in any part of her mind, character, or life is so truly admirable as her central trait of moral energy, which, like an ember hidden within her brain, kindles her to a fiery indignation against all forms of oppression, to a holy love of liberty and justice, and to a perpetual appeal from the falseness of society to the justice of God.

MAY 1, 1869.

SUPPRESSIO VERI.

THE noblest of man's attributes is the ability to know the truth; and the manliest of his virtues is the courage to speak it.

Take an instance: the custom of writing letters and signing papers at the request of applicants for public office. Not ten in a hundred such recommendations express what their writers actually believe concerning the persons of whom they write. "I cordially approve the above application," says a signer who, in the very act of signing, knows that the appointment, if made, will fasten on the Government a commonplace, inefficient, and unsuitable man. And yet such papers are signed by the bushel—signed, too, by men who are secretly ashamed of their act, and who, if they were a little more frank and firm, would peremptorily refuse, or at least politely withhold, the use of their names. Nine out of every ten applications for public office are made by men who, although goodish and clever in many respects, are nevertheless unsuccessful in earning their living at any private employment, and who ask to be supported at the public expense. This practice ought to receive its death-blow by a Civil Service bill. Meanwhile, a few words of protest by persons to whom such papers are presented for signature would drive back in dismay and totally rout whole armies of those office-beggars who now systematically take the Government's best posts by storm. If the President's appointments are ever to prove judicious, every man who signs a candidate's application should thereby express a well-grounded opinion, and not a mere conventional compliment. To gloss over the truth is to impose upon the Government.

Take another instance: the adroit deceptions, the ingenious equivocations, the dextrous mental reservations by which business men avoid manly straight-forwardness of speech. "What are the prospects of the Dilwater stock?" asks a man of his neighbor interested in it. "It can never pay a dividend," replies the other; who, at the same time, is secretly securing all the purchasable shares, in the expectation that the dividends will be great. Sincere answers to such questions are seldom given even by persons of unblemished commercial reputation. The evasion is considered justifiable; yet, in nine cases out of ten, even where it appears harmless, the man who allows himself to practice it must suffer damage to his moral nature.

Take another instance: the lack of an unpartisan criticism of current politics, literature, society, and religion. We do not mean a carping verdict by opponents, but a just judgment by friends. Early in our civil history the satirizing of public men and measures was carried to a blameworthy extreme. The newspaper lampoons on Martha Washington were more bitter and spiteful than any diatribes on Mrs. Lincoln. In respect of partisan rancor we have no wish to see a return of those "good old times," which, good as they were, nevertheless were worse than our own. Thirty years ago the strifes between representative journals of different religious sects were violent to a degree which would no longer be tolerable. But our existing religious journals are gentle, courteous, and high-minded; heralds of a mellowing age. There was a time (on both sides of the sea) when anybody who wrote a book, or published a pamphlet, or fabricated a sonnet, expected to be satirized without mercy. Witness the early numbers of *The Edinburgh Review*, and (chief among the victims) John Keats, whose soul, although a "very fiery particle," was nevertheless "extinguished by an article." Those days of arrows and stings, of wounds and death, have passed away. A milder season now reigns. An era of better feeling spreads a more genial glow through men's tempers. It is the happy fortune of this generation to bask in the sunshine of a day more golden than our fathers experienced in their storm-clouded sky. But, in acknowledging all this, we cannot help acknowledging also a too general lack of frank utterance concerning public men, current opinions, dominant creeds, established churches, and everything that needs just criticism. "The price of liberty," says the proverb, "is eternal vigilance." Mr. Stuart Mill has strikingly pointed out the need of perpetually examining and re-examining the grounds of our belief on all subjects. We cannot too constantly, too patiently, too devotedly challenge the popular opinion on any and every current question, and compel it to justify itself afresh to reason and good sense. In no country in the world is free discussion carried so far as in this; yet every third man in the streets is impatient at hearing his neighbor express an opinion antagonistic to his own. Let *The Tribune* speak with just censure of some of its political associates, and a dozen angry Republicans will shout by the next mail, "Stop my paper." Or let some *Atlantic* writer, whom Boston is accustomed to praise, suddenly hear a fresh foreign critic, to whom Boston is not a sacred city, put forth an honest protest against that superfine Cambridge style which, like bolted flour, loses its wholesome bran; and such criticism is superbly rejected by those whom it would chiefly benefit, and is appreciated most by those who need it least. Or let some distinguished clergyman be good-humoredly satirized for certain faults of pulpit oratory—faults which his best friends mention to each other, but not to him —and straightway some pure-hearted and shallow-minded deacon inquires of the critic, "Why do you injure the practical usefulness of that excellent man?" But a just criticism injures no man's proper influence. Free speech—such as neither fears one's enemies nor favors one's friends—is the crowning virtue of a free press, and ought to be the dearest aim of an independent journal. Let every man be courageous to speak the truth of others, and be patient to hear the truth spoken of himself. This ought to be, but is not, the fashion of the hour. The opposite rule prevails instead. "Hide his blemishes," exclaims some over-eager politician concerning his candidate's many-spotted character. "Shield his conduct," say the friends of the bank president who has squandered the securities of the bank in private speculations; "Blink his faults," pleads some doting sheep, in simpering sympathy with the grandiloquent pastor of the flock. How much more manly than all this was truth-loving Cromwell, who took off his hat, laid aside his gauntlets, sat in the artist's chair for his portrait, and exclaimed, "Paint the wrinkles."

Take still another instance: a species of "confession" which is exceedingly "good for the soul," yet which few souls make haste to profit by—the making known, by friend to friend, of one's most advanced convictions on topics on which one's mind is at war with received standards of opinion in church and state. To compare notes with some judicious person concerning the very foundation principles of society, of civil government, of moral obligation, of religious faith; not fearing, in such interchange, to plunge toward the bottom of the deepest problems that surge through our mortal and our immortal life; such communings, if they could be more frequent among thinkers, would help forward the whole world's thought. How few persons do we meet to whom we are willing to unveil our secret souls! How many a man goes about burdened with some new thought, or opinion, or conviction, which he aches to unfold to some confidant, but finds among the whole circle of his associates not one to whom he is willing to make the revelation. Do you think you know what are your neighbor's religious views? Not because you sit in the pew next to his in church! Perhaps you fancy him unchanged and old-fashioned in his orthodoxy. No; he is one of that great army of undetected heretics who prefer to sit in the shadow, rather than expose themselves to the sun. The church is full of such to-day—men and women who, if they should express themselves frankly, would deny many of their once cherished dogmas, and espouse views which would have made our forefathers apprehensive for such men's souls. And of all such thinkers, the most cowardly are the professedly radical—the very class who seem the boldest. They who think furthest shrink most from expressing their advanced thought. A witness in the box makes oath to tell "the truth, the whole truth, and nothing but the truth;" but, if every writer or speaker were compelled to make full and unreserved disclosure of his supremest thoughts, he would make his confessions with fear and trembling. We who edit newspapers, we who preach sermons, we who teach classes, we who mould public opinion—oh! dear brethren, what a pack of time-servers we all are! How few among us give half so much reverence to the new conviction born within us as to the old tradition dying around us! How constantly we are forced to acknowledge, with Milton, that the greatest of tyrants is Custom, to whom we perpetually render a meek obeisance, and from whom we outwardly accept opinions which we inwardly reject! How many clergymen harbor in the cloister a theological formula which they do not venture to utter in the pulpit! How many politicians acknowledge in the cloak-room what they deny in the senate-chamber! What becomes of our solemn prating about "the truth, the whole truth, and nothing but the truth?" Only the Hebrew poet's sad answer: "All men are liars." We know not a few aggressive and defiant writers whose unwritten views so far outreach the circumscribed statements which they commit to the world as to cause an inward groaning in their minds at the conscious weight of a yoke which, in the present state of society, even the freest must wear. Of course, there is a time to speak, and a time to be silent. Care is to be taken not to shock too violently at the beginning prejudices which we hope to overcome in the end. "I have many things to say unto you," said the Great Teacher, "but ye cannot bear them now." The genius of Common-sense is the good and guardian angel of all useful agitation. Nevertheless, we do not say, "Happy is he who never thinks further than he dares express;" but we say rather, "Thrice happy is he who dares express his utmost thought." Many a sweet, pure, and gifted thinker whose mind sweeps far ahead of his day and generation; whose conclusions are at holy variance with the existing order of things; whose wholesome philosophy would be shuddered at by the multitude as unsettling and chaotic; many such a one, on account of the hardness of men's hearts which he attempts not to soften, and of the blindness of a generation among whom he ought to stand as a light in the world—suppresses the truth which God has given him to utter, and buries in his solitary bosom what ought to be kept at vital heat in the common heart of all mankind.

These, and many more instances which might be given, all go to show that, next to the inestimable value of the truth itself, is the almost equal preciousness of openly uttering it. If a man is ashamed to give his thoughts expression, it is time to ask himself if he ought not to be ashamed of the thoughts themselves. But the great hindrance to "the truth, the whole truth, and nothing but the truth," is not so much a repugnance to speak it as an unwillingness to hear it. Many men would be only too glad to speak their minds except for fear of their neighbors. How fiercely we pounce upon our best friends when their opinions are the opposites of our own! How little we tolerate liberty of thought in others though claiming it passionately for ourselves! How ostentatiously we write down in our "supreme law of the land" a solemn guaranty of "freedom of speech and of the press;" and yet how restive we all are under that public criticism which follows as the best boon of that very freedom! Every day our nerveless newspapers continue to praise men at whom they secretly smile, and to stigmatize men whom they inwardly revere; and all this for a partisan, or sectarian, or personal purpose which perishes with the hour. Frankness of speech is generally chidden, seldom welcomed. The party-leader says, "Fling no criticism at me." The pulpit orator says, "Aim no satire at me."

Every other gentle culprit says, "Point no finger at me." And so, as a precaution against the hubbub which is sure to be caused by speaking the honest truth, the whole world is complacently given to conventional lies. "O my soul, come not thou into their secret; unto their assembly, mine honor, be not thou united!"

HENRY JARVIS RAYMOND.

N saying peace to the ashes of our late editorial neighbor, our uppermost thought of him is rather as of a private friend than of a public leader. We knew him well—as well as one comes to know another in the companionship of travel, or in the late-at-night converse which pours itself out in self-revelations. Not to know him thus intimately was not to know him at all. On a mere superficial acquaintance, he appeared reserved and undemonstrative. Indeed many of his political associates who knew him only on the outside, and had never entered into the chambers of his soul, commonly spoke of him as polite but cold, as agreeable but self-absorbed. When however he chose to impart himself to one or more companions, he became a flowing fountain of anecdote, reminiscence, and gentle satire. He did not wear his heart on his sleeve. Outwardly placid and passionless, strangers little suspected that under the surface he was profoundly restless and unhappy. His cheery spirit was shaded with an unmistakable tinge of something like misanthropy—not the result of nature, but of circumstances—we need not say how or why. To his friends he sometimes confessed that there was a worm in his soul gradually gnawing away the fine aspirations of his earlier years. It is useless to draw his intellectual portraiture without recognizing this dominant fact. There are certain frosts of the human heart which, when they blight it once, make it sere for

ever. Not that he grew weary of the world—he was too patient and cheerful for that; but he gradually ripened into Solomon's desolate conviction that all things are vanity. Many of his critics, not knowing this to be the standpoint from which he judged, misconstrued his judgments. Thus, though eminently a man of the world, he did not cling to the world with any eagerness. Called an aspirant for political office, we thoroughly know how lightly he valued even the most shining prizes of life. Supposed by some to be a money lover, he was on the contrary almost a spendthrift, and in his secret benefactions was profuse to prodigality. Though an incessant toiler, yet his industry was more for the work's sake than for the reward. To have nothing to do was with him to be miserable. His muscular intellect craved perpetual activity. His gift of gifts was debate. Nature conferred on him her university degree of "senior wrangler." She made him a gymnast of logic. Accordingly, in spite of the fact that he rose to be one of the less than half-dozen great journalists of the United States, we believe he might have made a still better choice of a profession than the editorial chair. In spite of the fact that his career in Congress was a conspicuous failure, we believe that he would have made a wiser use than he did of his forensic abilities had he devoted his life to jurisprudence and legislation. Knowing himself well, he always regretted that he had not been a lawyer, and frequently confessed that the intensest pleasure of his life was in participating in deliberative assemblies. As a presiding officer, he was a peer with the best. Not an orator (since he seldom touched the moral, or the emotional, but chiefly the intellectual chords of his audience), yet he was one of the most fluent, forceful, logical, and instructive of all our political speakers. His political integrity was often called in question, but it was accused unjustly, and remained unblemished. The reason why he was on one side one day, and on another the next, was not because he played fast and loose with his convictions, but because his convictions played fast and loose with himself. Generally speaking, when any proposition was presented to his mind, he saw an equal number of reasons for and against it. This duality of vision was sometimes a torment to him. "If those of my friends," said he, "who call me a waverer could only know how impossible it is for me to see but one aspect of a question, or to espouse but one side of a cause, they would pity rather than condemn me ; and, however much I may wish myself differently constituted, yet I cannot unmake the original structure of my mind." During his congressional career he saw clearly that this intellectual peculiarity, rather than any other cause, was the shipwreck of his congressional success. But when his whole mind *did* go into any special advocacy—when his consenting judicial faculties (which rarely all consented) reported a unanimous judgment to his will — he then proved himself a man of uncommon strength, nerve, and courage, holding the talisman of leadership. This was shown by his brave and patriotic course at the outbreak of the war, and also by his conspicuous heroism during the New York riot. Not a great character, he possessed great characteristics. He was capable of sublime enthusiasms, but he rose to them only under sublime provocation. Urbanity, suavity, kindliness, charity—these traits were pre-eminent in his disposition. A tale of distress would make him weep like a child. Right royally could he forgive an injury. Vindictiveness had no seat among the governing motives of his mind. Had his nature been more highly religious and poetic, he would, with the same intellectual faculties, have ranked as a man of genius. On the whole, his general career will be called by some a success, and by others a failure. To us it always seemed that what he built up with his right hand he pulled down with his left. But whatever were his errors in policy (and to our thinking they were often grievous and fatal), yet his motives throughout his public course were as white and fair as the funeral flowers which on Monday last were strewn on his bier. His fame, while he lived, was as wide as the nation; but he belonged to a profession which sends its best men to graves over which the unvarying epitaph always says, "Here lies one whose name was writ in water."

JUNE 24, 1869.

THE ASSUMPTION OF THE VIRGIN.

T is reported from Rome that the forthcoming Œcumenical Council is to decree as one of its dogmas the coporeal assumption of the Virgin Mary. Some English journals throw discredit on the report, though we see no reason for disputing its authenticity. The worship of Mary yearly increases throughout that great church which does homage to her as the Mother of God and Queen of Heaven. We are quite prepared to find devout Romanists seeking now to lavish upon her some new idolatry.

The biography of Mary is one of the most charming fictions among the legends of the Saints. As the story runs, Joachim, a rich Jew, married Anna, a beautiful Jewess. The married pair dwelt near Mt. Carmel. Their lives were ornamented with every beauty of wedded love, except one. There was no offspring. Among the Jews, to be without children was to be without honor. On one occasion, Joachim, in carrying his offerings to the temple, was repulsed by the high priest, who declined to accept such a tribute from one whom God had long disfavored by denying him issue of his bone and flesh. The childless husband turned away in sorrow, sought his garden, and with prayer and tears called upon the Lord to purge away his servant's shame in Israel. At the same hour, the pious Anna, sitting under a laurel-tree, observed a goldfinch feeding her young. The motherly bird awakened in the childless wife a pitiful sense of her barrenness, and inspired her to utter a like prayer with her husband's.

The Lord heard her entreaties, and sent two swift angels to the garden—one to Joachim, the other to Anna—with mutual promise to the married pair that a daughter should be born to them, and that she should grow to be the most illustrious of her sex. Each of the future parents then rose to seek the other and communicate the wondrous intelligence, when behold at the garden-gate they unexpectedly met, the husband fervently kissed his wife, and, according to one of the legends, at that moment the babe Mary was suddenly laid in her mother's arms — born as the supernatural fruition of Joachim's kiss; a gentler fable than its stern prototype—Minerva's armed emergence from the brain of Jove.

So much for the fable of Mary's birth. An equal fiction hangs like an aureole round her death. Good Catholics believe that, after surviving her husband Joseph for many years, she was at last (some say at sixty, others at seventy-five) forewarned of the hour of her translation, and in view of that solemn event, she prayed to her long-ascended Son to give her a convoy of angels; that a palm-branch was brought by one of them and lodged in her hands; that as she desired to bequeath her blessing on the apostles who were then scattered over the face of the earth, suddenly John who was at Ephesus, and Peter who was at Antioch, and all the rest of the glorious army, from whatsoever city they tarried in, were transported through the air at midnight and set down in bodily presence round her bed; and that, to crown the scene, the Lord himself then appeared among them in splendor, received His mother's expiring soul, and bore it to heaven.

This is the first or spiritual assumption of the Virgin.

Her lifeless body, which remained behind, was tenderly caressed by pious women, who, as they were about to disrobe it and wash the flesh, suddenly beheld it caught away in a cloud out of their sight—in order (as some say) that her comely and immortal limbs might never be seen of sinful and mortal eyes. Or, according to another version, her body (like her Son's) was laid three days in a sepulchre, and at the end of that time, at her Son's command, was uplifted from earth to heaven, while the abandoned sepulchre was strewn with lilies and roses by angelic hands.

This is the second or corporeal assumption of the Virgin.

For twelve centuries it has been a Romish custom to celebrate the spiritual assumption by a solemn feast, held annually on the 15th of August—the traditional day of her death. The corporeal assumption has never yet been made an article of faith; but the Œcumenical Council (if report be true) propose now to make her corporeal like her spiritual assumption a dogma of the Romish creed.

The Romish Church has long been dextrously taught to give a flesh-and-blood reality to this pleasing fable through the bewitching handicraft of her great painters, with most of whom it was an adored theme. Without exception (so far as we now recall) these great interpreters all unite in portraying an assumption which includes the body as well as the soul. Nor was this an artistic necessity, but merely an esthetic choice. For in the well-known modern picture of the death of St. Catharine, by Muckë (engravings of which have been multitudinously scattered among American private dwellings), the figure of the dead or sleeping saint is borne through the air by four angels, two supporting her head and two her feet; a composition in which, though the artist was reduced to the necessity of portraying St. Catharine's body, yet the spectator instantly recognizes that the body in this instance means not the body at all, but the soul disembodied. If, however, the artist had given to the passive figure a living instead of a deathly look, and waking eyes instead of closed lids, the spectator would just as readily have understood that the idea to be conveyed was, not the resurrection of a disembodied soul, but of a body containing its soul. Titian, if he had chosen, could just as well have represented the Assumption of the Virgin by expressing her soul only, as by expressing both soul and body. But Titian, and Andrea del Sarto, and Murillo, and all the other great masters of this never-mastered subject, preferred to paint the body with the soul immortally united to it, rather than the soul with the body mortally divided from it. Titian's picture will take a new glory from the Œcumenical Council. His matchless rendering of the majestic spectacle will more or less give shape to the fancies of the learned prelates who are to unite in the dogmatic decree. Even had he foreseen the assembling of the Council, he could not have composed a work more commensurate in dignity with the event which is to be celebrated by it. Not a few critics regard Titian's Assumption of the Virgin as the most impressive picture in all Europe. He has painted Mary's upturned face, her outspread arms, her flying mantle, her bare feet on the cloud—all in such a way as to render her, for one immortal moment, the central object of the whole universe—adored by the Father from above and by the Church from below. It will be impossible for any rescript of any council to add anything to the divine humanity thus portrayed by a painter who with his brush, as Dante with his pen, paid the highest possible tribute of human genius to a woman whom both equally saluted, saying:

"Hail, Virgin Mother, daughter of thy Son."

It is a tendency of human nature to invest sacred, heroic, and legendary personages with a supernatural birth, life, and death. Greek warriors fought, conquered, died, and afterward took a lodgement in the world's esteem as gods. Christian martyrs endured faggot, pincer, and rack, and thereby became enshrined in the calendar as powerful and protecting saints. This beautiful tendency of our human nature works a passing harm, but also a permanent good, to the human race. Its harm consists in elevating a few choice and worthy souls to an elevation where they stand as objects of the idolatry of mankind. On the other hand, its good consists in proving the ineradicable divinity of our common humanity. The fact that mortal beings attain divine honors proves something more than that the human race has a proneness to superstition; it proves also that in all manhood there is some element of godhood; it is another way of saying (as against the dismal notion of total depravity) that we are all creatures of a glorious immortality; it is a restatement of the sublime truth that within the frail temple of the human breast abides the veiled majesty of the kingdom of God.

Of course, to our Protestant cast of mind, the Assumption of the Virgin is a cunningly devised fable, and any dogma based upon it is an idle breath; but while we reject both the fact and the doctrine, we cannot refrain from paying to the winsome fiction a tender reverence for the triple reason: first, because of its intrinsic poetic beauty; second, because of its precious artistic associations; and third, because of its triune deification of Woman, Maternity, and Human Nature.

JULY 15, 1869.

WILLIAM PITT FESSENDEN.

T seems to us that, in the comments which Mr. Fessenden's death has elicited from our metropolitan press, justice has not been done to his memory.

"A man capable, but not great," says a political opponent; and yet Mr. Fessenden was certainly a great man; not a parliamentary conqueror like either the elder or the younger Pitt, from both of whom he was named, but neither of whom he resembled; not a miracle-worker in finance like Hamilton, of whom Webster said that he "touched the dead body of the public credit and it sprang to its feet;" not a prophetic seer like Jefferson, wise to discern the signs of coming times; but, take him for all in all, he was so acute a lawyer, so sound a financier, so masterly a debater, and so influential a senator, that, if we cannot give to this one man the rank of greatness, we must give to all his compeers the rank of mediocrity.

"He has left," says another critic, "a reputation for tearing down more than for building up;" a remark which for that very reputation's sake we could wish more true than it is, since iconoclasm was the American statesman's chief duty during the long anti-slavery struggle which occupied Mr. Fessenden's lifetime, but not his life. To prove the remark *not* true, we have only to cite his unwillingness to change the existing order of things, his fondness for antiquated precedents, his dislike of a forward movement in public opinion, and his faith in Macaulay's doctrine that "the essence of politics is compromise." Instead of a disposition to tear down, Mr. Fessenden had too great a disposition to let stand. Mend, not rend, seemed to be his maxim. Even when his countrymen demanded new wine, he would still urge them to keep it in the old bottles; and when they adopted new cloth, he would still beg them to sew it on the old garments.

"Better at the thrust and parry of sharp debate," says a friendly pen, "than at the less exciting details of solid legislative work;" which is true so far as implying that his chief ability was in argument, but far from true as implying that he was not also signally industrious, fastidious, and painstaking in the committee-room.

"He never, as a lawyer," says another, "made a figure in a celebrated case;" which must have been penned by a writer who forgot (though most other writers remembered) that he once took an adverse decision of Judge Story's, carried it up to the Supreme Court of the United States, and procured its reversal amid the general plaudits of the whole bar for his triumph.

"He was never moved himself," says a critic of his oratory, "and never moved others;" whereas, though he generally spoke in cold blood, he was sometimes moved with a stormy passion, particularly with that which is styled "a short madness." Nor was he incapable of more generous eloquence; for we recall a memorable occasion when, alluding to the death of one of his sons in the war, and to the honorable wounds of another, he melted half the senate and all the gallery to tears.

But it must be acknowledged, in parrying these criticisms on Mr. Fessenden, that there is a point of truthfulness in each. Except in a supreme hour of debate, he rarely seemed in possession of his whole powers. Born like the eagle to the highest flights, Nature seems afterward to have slightly clipped each feather of his wings. Thus, almost a genius in his aptitude for affairs, he rarely took a responsibility equal to his opportunity, and accordingly made but few master-strokes of policy; almost an orator through his power to convince, he lacked the coal of fire which the imagination touches to the lips, and so has left no monumental speeches; almost a judge for fairness and impartiality, he could nevertheless be as one-sided as a bigot, and became often a very Samson of judicial blindness; almost a reformer by inherited instinct, he nevertheless had a counter-impulse of hostility to reform, and generally his worst invectives were against radicals; almost a king in dignity of demeanor, he was never safe against loss of temper, and there was scarcely a senator whom sooner or later he did not sting; almost a model legislator in his adaptability to the senatorial office, his fifteen years of service show how ably a man may fill a great station, and at the same time how few memorable results he may accomplish in it.

Like all the leading statesmen of his day, Mr. Fessenden's public services must be ranked by their influence for or against the overthrow of American slavery. His father was pelted with stones as an abolitionist; the son escaped such missiles as a conservative. True, Mr. Fessenden was in early years once or twice a candidate of the Liberty party. But Daniel Webster, who had stood godfather at his baptism, seems to have anointed the young politician to a lifetime of compromise. Like the fabled trees of the Hellespont, whose tops withered as fast as they grew high enough to overlook the walls of Troy, Mr. Fessenden generally suffered himself to grow only to the height of the Whig party's platform, and then stopped. In this way he became one of those favored and unfortunate New England statesmen whom the Boston conservatives liked to dine and wine. Robert C. Winthrop's blindness crept into William P. Fessenden's eyes. During a long period while all the South and half the North were howling at Mr. Garrison and *The Liberator*, Mr. Fessenden was one of those harmless enemies of slavery who frowned at it with a fierce face but stroked it with a soft hand. Afterward came rebellion, emancipation, and reconstruction. A nation's crisis is a statesman's opportunity. Mr. Fessenden's opportunity was partly improved, partly wasted. He showed a brave zeal for quelling the rebellion; he lent a noble support to the edict of emancipation; but he was a mechanic of patchwork in the architecture of reconstruction. He was perfectly willing to leave the negro in the slough of the Fourteenth Amendment. Had Mr. Fessenden's famous plan been adopted, the South would in five years have been regent of the Union, and the North the loser of its victory—a calamity from which we have not yet wholly escaped. But it is just to Mr. Fessenden to say that not many months before his death, in a speech at home, he informed his neighbors that at the time when he publicly proposed the Fourteenth Amendment, he privately preferred the Fifteenth. Had he never consented to the Fourteenth, which enabled the South to disfranchise the negro, he would long ago have seen the passage of the Fifteenth, which gives the negro his ballot. But its passage looks more doubtful now than at any time since the amendment was first proposed.

The controlling elements in Mr. Fessenden's destiny were two: one, the inadequacy of his physical to support his intellectual constitution; the other, the absence of an ambition which could not sleep at the trophies of Miltiades. Possibly the first deficiency gave rise to the second, for a weak body is the assassin of a strong mind. Both these causes, acting in him together, kept him from reaching that full height of civil fame to which his abilities would have elevated, and at which they could have sustained, such a man. Nor even would the world have known as much as it now does of this small, sick gentleman except for the masterful will with which as with a whip he lashed himself to his daily duty against the half-unheeded murmurs of his suffering flesh. His slender frame—enfeebled by long violation of the laws of health, until finally he became a constant victim of dyspepsia and headache—necessarily failed him in such a position as the Treasury Department; where, notwithstanding his vigor of brain, his Evarts-like fragility of skeleton was unequal to burdens which then needed

> "Atlantean shoulders fit to bear
> The weight of mightiest monarchy;"

and where afterward Mr. McCullough had sufficient shoulders but not sufficient head. If it seem surprising that Mr. Fessenden was not greatly ambitious, we have only to add that few men were ever more careless of personal reputation; few men ever sought less to make a public impression; few men (except of the Coriolanus order) ever set less value on popular applause. In fact, and almost without knowing it himself, he half-disdained his fellow-countrymen and their opinions, and harbored a partial contempt for all men save "the judicious few."

A strong conscience governs a good man just as imperiously whether its dictates be from unreasonable prejudice or from righteous conviction. Mr. Fessenden always had a conscience, and generally had a prejudice. Often when he thought he was acting from conscience, he was simply acting from prejudice. It is a moral certainty (to our thinking) that if Mr. Grimes, whom he liked, instead of Mr. Wade, whom he disliked, had been the prospective successor of President Johnson deposed, Mr. Fessenden would have had the same conscience for the traitor's conviction which he otherwise had for his acquittal. Nor, in saying this (which we believe to be psychologically the exact truth), do we discredit Mr. Fessenden's motives. We never discredited these. Not a more self-consciously honest man ever sat in the Senate. But he was a rare victim to personal antipathies; and these entered, though without his suspecting it, into many of his intellectual judgments and moral convictions. When the Impeachment trial was waiting for its verdict, Mr. Fessenden, by a course of conduct which to himself seemed candid but to others crafty, beguiled his friends into a belief that he would vote for conviction; asking the Senate to postpone the vote for a day or two, in order (as he said) to allow him an opportunity, by a calm review of the proceedings, to bring himself if possible into complete accord with the majority of his senatorial brethren; and then, at the expiration of the brief time, he unexpectedly unrolled in the Senate a labored argument, which he was supposed to have been a fortnight in writing, taking the opposite view from the one he had foreshadowed at the very moment when that voluminous argument must have been well-nigh written. The indignation of the Senate was great—not because of Mr. Fessenden's opinion on impeachment, but because of his tactics toward his peers. He afterward asseverated that he had never intended to mislead his associates; and his word is to be taken.

Nevertheless, his associates *were* misled, all except the accomplices of the impeached culprit. The circumstance affords an illustration of Mr. Fessenden's aptness to judge a wrong act to be right, and to crown his perverted judgment with the white aureole of an approving conscience. This tendency was lodged in him incurably. It was a moral dyspepsia.

As a parliamentarian he moulded himself after the traditions of a former day. He ought to have lived anterior to Congressional *Globes*. His only solicitude about a speech was as to its effect on the Senate, not as to its success in print. In preparing his speeches, he was a contemner of manuscripts. He wrote too little to write well; not that he wrote awkwardly, but only without comeliness of style. We happened in upon him while he was composing his funeral tribute to Senator Foote of Vermont, and he greatly complained of the irksomeness of literary work. His famous Report on the Reconstruction of the Union—the ablest state paper of his life—was logical and cogent, simple and earnest; but even had it been something more than the half-way, time-serving measure which it was; even had it been as right and ringing as the Declaration of Independence, which it ought to have been; nevertheless it could never have caught from his pen the chaste lustre which Jefferson, Madison, and Hamilton gave to their papers by the fine gold of a pure English style.

In manners (and manners are tell-tales of men) he always appeared to us as an aristocrat—a character unseemly in our eyes. Even to his friends, during the first few moments of every renewed interview, he exhibited something forbidding in his demeanor. His countenance, even in its lightest mood, never wholly lost its severity.

His merriest laugh did not altogether unwrinkle those lines of his face which showed him to be a good hater. His graven image on our fractional currency is flabbily devoid of all his Roman dignity. Self-respect sat upon him like a supreme virtue. It is a mistake to suppose (as some have asserted) that he suffered a perpetual pang at the remembrance of his illegitimate birth. No civil tie can constitute, nor the absence of it nullify, the natural and unshamed allegiance which a manly son must ever bear to his mother. Not till man's estate did Mr. Fessenden come to the knowledge of his shadowed origin; but when he suddenly discovered that there was living in New England a lady of whose existence he had been utterly ignorant, but who had brought him into the world, he made haste to see her face, to fall upon her neck, and to mingle his tears of joy and sorrow with her own. Nothing in all his career was nobler than the filial affection and respect which he never ceased to render to this superior woman during her remaining years on earth.

It will be a satisfaction to the friends of Mr. Fessenden and Mr. Sumner to know that the long estrangement between these gentlemen was happily concluded several months ago. Their restored friendship increased in heartiness to the last. A day or two before Mr. Fessenden's death, a visitor to his bedside reported that a telegram had just come from Boston to the bulletins in Portland, in these words: "The Hon. Charles Sumner is dying." Mr. Fessenden suddenly raised his head and exclaimed: "Is it possible? I had a paper from Mr. Sumner only yesterday. How transitory is human life. What a loss to the country!" And, paying his friend the loftiest of tributes, he spoke of their reconciliation in the most grateful of terms.

The brief encomiums with which the leading journals accompanied their announcements of Mr. Fessenden's death show how far less was his hold on the country than on the senate. These notices show too that their writers and the people generally have not fully known how grand were his powers, how rich his feelings, and how just his aims. We ourselves may be writing of him without judgment, but not without knowledge. We have sat with him in his chamber in Washington, and walked with him in his garden in Portland. We knew him well. Proud, bitter, and indifferent in his outer life—pure, gentle, and sorrowful in his inner—he presented to us the spectacle of a strong nature in a seeming triumph over the world, but in a losing struggle against itself. The portrait of the younger Pitt that hung on his library-wall fitly shed down on its namesake the reflection of a tempest-tossed soul. Domestic bereavement—of which he had a more than common share—pierced his heart of hearts with a succession of many wounds. They who love deeply, and for love's sake suffer strongly, make no common claim on the world's sympathy. A man who would go to a vine which had been planted by dear, dead hands, and would caress its blossoms till his eyes grew dewy with remembrance, deserves over his own clay a memorial tear.

"Set him down gently at the iron door."

Probably the next generation will neither totally forget nor vividly remember William Pitt Fessenden; but those of his cotemporaries who understood his character, and particularly those who by criticism of his public actions have earned a right to praise his private virtues, may tenderly contribute the chaplet with which sincere mourners honor the urn of a lamented friend.

SEPTEMBER 16, 1869.

GOLDEN-HAIRED GERTRUDE.

A STORY FOR CHILDREN.

CRACK went a stone through a pane of glass!

"Who threw that?" exclaimed Gertrude, sitting at the broken window, and looking up from her book astonished. It was the second story front-window of Dame Stockel's house, and stood open because of the fine spring weather. Gertrude, shutting her book and leaning out her head, her golden hair falling like sunshine on her shoulders, looked up and down the quiet street.

"I see nobody," she said, "and yet stones never throw themselves."

Any one then looking at beautiful Gertrude would have called her neither too old for a girl nor too young for a woman: so guess her age if you can!

Stooping to the floor, she picked up the broken pieces of glass and laid them on her work-table.

"The stone must be somewhere in the room," she said.

But on searching, she could not find it. Then, leaning back in her old rocking-chair, she fell to thinking. A penny for your thoughts, Gertrude! Her thoughts were in her mother's grave. Two long years had her mother been dead. Gertrude was an orphan, living with her aunt, who was called Dame Stockel. "My aunt," said the maiden, "is good, but cross; she does not love me; nobody loves me. Can anybody love like a mother? I wonder how a bridegroom loves his bride? Will *I* ever be a bride? Who then will be the bridegroom?" Such were Gertrude's thoughts.

Just then, happening to cast her eyes at the ceiling, she spied an arrow sticking slantwise in a rafter.

"Heigh-ho!" she cried; "so not a stone, but an arrow broke the glass! Now, my pretty Jenny,"—meaning her canary, whose cage hung in the window—"I am thankful that whoever was wicked enough to take aim at your little body, had not the skill to kill you!"

Standing tiptoe on her chair, Gertrude reached up her beautiful bare arm, and plucked the arrow down. It was a strange-looking shaft, neither ash, nor yew, nor hornbeam (such as arrows are commonly made of), but jointed like bamboo, and feathered.

"It is a hollow reed," said she; "I can bend it double."

Then, as she bent it, snap it went, breaking in twain; and from the inside fell a wisp of paper, on which Gertrude, who unrolled it, found written in beautiful letters these singular words:

Fly straight, O arrow! through the air,
And tell the maid with golden hair,
The poorest man in all the land
Shall come to seek her heart and hand!

Great was Gertrude's astonishment. She read the pretty writing over and over again. The oftener she read it, the more she was charmed. "Some one loves me," she whispered to herself, and her eyes sparkled. "Who can it be? The poorest man in all the land! What of that? Poverty is no wrong. Let him be poor or rich, if only he love me truly."

Suddenly Gertrude went to the looking-glass to see the maiden that this poor man had fallen in love with!

Smoothing her hair—that kept always fringing out, like ravelled gold-lace—she asked herself, "Where did he ever see me? Maybe at the window. Then I will never sit at the window again. Yes, I will," she said—changing her mind, as girls do—"I will sit there all the time!"

Knowing how her aunt would scold about the broken window, Gertrude resolved to tell her of the accident before the crabbed old lady should find it out herself. So in great fear the girl went to her aunt, and said, "A pane of my window is broken."

"Then, you young minx!" exclaimed her aunt, "go back and shut yourself in your room for the rest of the day!"

Dame Stockel's mouth had a knife-blade in it instead of a tongue!

"But—" said the girl.

"Hush!" screamed the Dame.

Gertrude was going to say that she was not to blame for the accident; that somebody in the street had thrown something against the window. But glad that Dame Stockel was too cross to ask troublesome questions, the golden-haired innocent culprit went tripping back to her room in tears.

"Nance!" cried Dame Stockel to the kitchen-maid. "Nance! I say. You huzzy! Must I call you a hundred times? Now listen! If you see a glazier passing by, call him in. Do you hear that, you minx?"

Dame Stockel thought every young woman a minx.

Nance blushed like a red apple. And why? Was it because she was scolded? No: she was used to that. It was because she happened to be in love with a glazier! Sometimes, of an evening, this glazier would lean his elbows on the wicket-gate in the rear of Dame Stockel's house, and wait till Nance could slip out for a chat. So this is the reason why Nance blushed at the mention of a glazier. Presently she heard a cry in the street,

"Glass put in! Glass put in!"

"Well!" shouted Nance, running to the window, "Come here, lazybones! and earn butter for your bread!"

Nance was short and fat, and always kept her mouth wide open like a pea-blossom. She opened it wider yet, when she saw that the glazier was not her sweetheart but a stranger. But this strange glazier wore the other's clothes, for Nance recognized on one elbow a gray patch, and on the other a brown; and if the truth were told, these same patches had been taken by Nance from Dame Stockel's rag-bag, without asking. Nance wondered how the right man had slipped out of those clothes, and the wrong had slipped in! The next minute she turned on her heels, and trotted back to her kitchen in disgust.

Dame Stockel went to the front door.

The glazier set down his box of glass under Gertrude's window.

"Now, young man!" said the knife-blade in the Dame's mouth, "pay attention, sir! What is the price for putting in a small pane of glass which a good-for-nothing girl broke out, and she ought to have her ears pinched! But, fudge! You are in rags. What a shame to be a beggar!"

Dame Stockel would rather scold than eat cherries.

"Madame," said the glazier, "look at *me;* I am poor. Look at yourself; *you* are rich."

The Dame was pleased at being called rich, for she was poor.

"*I* live in the streets," said he, "*you* live in a fine house."

The Dame was delighted at hearing her house called fine, for it was plain.

"*I* am in rags," said he; "*you* are in silks."

The Dame was charmed at hearing her dress called silk, for it was bombazine.

"You are a mannerly young man," she said. "Now follow me up stairs." So the Dame and the mannerly young man entered Gertrude's room.

The next moment the glazier, who had a ball of putty in his hand, threw it out of the window.

"Ting-a-ling-ling!" tinkled the door-bell, just afterward.

"Somebody to see Dame Stockel," cried Nance.

The Dame with great dignity went down stairs. Now who was the visitor that rang the bell? A black-eyed, merry-faced lad, dressed in green silk as a king's page.

"Is this Dame Stockel?" he inquired politely.

"Yes," answered the old lady—taking off her spectacles, rubbing them, and putting them on again.

"I have a letter for you," he said, holding out his right hand empty.

"Then where is it?" she inquired, "for it is not in your hand."

The boy, looking astonished, replied, "I am certain I brought the letter."

"Then you have lost it on the way," she angrily exclaimed.

"Maybe it's in my pocket," said he; but feeling in his pocket, it was not there.

"You are a young rascal!" she cried.

"Maybe it's in my cap," said he; but taking off his cap, it was not there.

"You shall go to jail!" she screamed.

"Maybe it's in one of my shoes," said he; but taking off his right shoe, it was not there.

"Your hair shall be pulled!" she threatened, getting into a rage.

"Ha-ha-ha! here's the letter!" he exclaimed, shaking it from his jacket-sleeve, and running away.

If Aunt Stockel had caught the rogue, she would have boxed his ears. But the old lady was too lame to hobble after such nimble legs. So after fretting awhile, she went into the house, and sat down to enjoy her letter. Now what said the letter? Nothing but these words:

Dame Stockel is fidgety, cross, and old,
And never does anything now but scold!

Dame Stockel flew into a passion! Behind her spectacles, her eyes sparkled like a pussy-cat's. "Whose trick is this?" she cried. "If I knew, I would throw the tongs at his head! Dear me, what shall I do? I will scold Nance! No, I will whip Gertrude! No, I will go smooth my hair, and be polite to the mannerly young man.

Now, as the letter called Dame Stockel old, she thought of pulling out her gray hairs, to make herself young. What a foolish dame!

Meanwhile, what of Gertrude and the glazier? Gertrude sat reading the history of Peter the Great's Dwarfs. The glazier stood cutting the glass with his diamond, fastening it into the sash with putty, and scouring it clean with chamois-leather. In a few minutes his work was done, but he seemed in no hurry to go. On Gertrude's work-table he arranged the pieces of the broken pane into the shape of the pane before it was broken. Presently, without looking up, he said,

"It was not a stone that cracked this glass."

Gertrude raised her eyes.

"Nor was it anybody's elbow," said he.

Gertrude shut her book.

"Nor a broomstick," he added.

Gertrude rose from her chair.

"Nor a pistol-ball," he continued.

"What then?" inquired Gertrude, wondering if the glazier knew.

"Do you see," said he, "a white speck on the edge of this broken piece?"

"Yes; but what of that?"

"Well," said he, "it looks like a bit of white feather."

Gertrude, remembering that the arrow was feathered, said to herself, "This young man is good at guessing!"

"It was a white goose," said he, "that feathered the arrow that broke this pane."

Gertrude, who had been looking down at the glass, now looked up at the glazier. A strange thought stole into her head. Who was this fellow? His clothes were torn, his shoes begrimed, his hands stained, yet his face was comely, and his voice kind. Could this be the unknown writer of the love-letter? Certainly this glazier was ragged enough to be the poorest man in the land!

"Since you guessed the arrow," she said, "can you guess the archer?"

"Try me," said he.

"Then who was it?"

"It was your friend."

"No, I have no friend."

"Yes, you have better than a friend."

"What?"

"A lover."

"Who?"

"I."

Gertrude's cheeks burned! She was ashamed, bewildered, and delighted—all in the same moment! Yes, this glazier must be the self-same lover who shot the arrow that pricked her heart! But though he be a true lover, thought she, he has a strange way of making love.

"What is your name?" the glazier inquired.

"You may guess," answered Gertrude, who hardly knew whether to be pleased or displeased.

"A beautiful maid," said he, "ought to have a beautiful name: so your name is—"

But, instead of speaking it, he cut with his diamond on the new pane the word

Gertrude.

The letters looked like spiders' threads on the glass.

"Now what is *your* name?" asked Gertrude.

"You may guess!" said he, answering in her own words.

"Is it Christopher?" she asked.

"No."

"Is it Rudolph?"

"No."

"Is it Constantine?"

"No."

"Then I cannot guess it."

"Well," said he, laughing, "It begins with R, and ends with X."

"I never heard such a name," she exclaimed.

"You have heard it a hundred times," he replied.

"No, I never heard it in my life," returned the baffled

girl, whose curiosity and eagerness now made her face more beautiful than ever.

The glazier stood silently gazing at the floor. Then taking his glass-cutter, he twirled it between his fingers, hardly knowing what he did. Soon, in a low and tender voice, he said,

"Gertrude, listen to me. I have seen you at your window many times. I love you! Dear Gertrude, with an honest heart I love you purely. I have poor clothes, but I can earn better. Now, if I work hard, and make myself a gentleman, will you love me? Tell me, Gertrude!" And looking at his raggedness, he blushed.

Gertrude's heart beat quick. She saw none of the rags. Why? Was it for the tears in her eyes? Not exactly. But the glazier's kind words made him so beautiful in her sight, that she did not notice his grotesque garments. Never since her mother's death had any one spoken to the orphan so tenderly as this young and manly stranger. Happiness filled her heart like a fountain. And she had so much to say that she said nothing.

"Gertrude," he whispered, "you give me no answer."

Now why did the foolish fellow say that? It only made Gertrude fall to weeping. Many times had she wept for sorrow, but now she wept for joy.

"Gertrude," said he, laying his hand courteously on her shoulder, "my father and mother sleep in their graves, and I am an orphan."

"I too am an orphan," sobbed the maiden, who was hardly able to speak.

"Then," said he, still more tenderly, "since we have no one else to love us, let us love one another."

Now just as this scene grew interesting, Dame Stockel's footsteps came creaking up stairs, and put an end to the love-talk. Hastily Gertrude brushed away her tears, seized her book, and looked studious. Just as hastily the glazier turned his face to the window, whistled a tune, and pretended to be puttying.

"Young man!" said Dame Stockel amiably.

"Your ladyship!" responded the glazier humbly.

The Dame was captivated at being called her ladyship.

"How much is to pay?" she inquired, taking out a purse with no money in it.

"Nothing at all," was the generous reply, "except that your ladyship will speak well of me at court."

The Dame was enchanted at being esteemed a lady of the court.

"Young gentleman!" said she.

"Your highness!" said he.

Whereupon Gertrude, although she had been weeping, was now laughing.

"Will your grace," asked the glazier, "have the great goodness to present me to the king?"

Now Dame Stockel had never been near enough to his Majesty to tread on his shadow. But she answered, "Yes, young gentleman; you shall see the king, you shall see the king."

The glazier made a bow, like a Turk's salaam. This compliment tickled the Dame like snuff, and she sneezed. But how could she present the glazier to the king? This was a puzzle! "I have it!" she cried, catching a bright thought. "Young gentleman, you want to see his Majesty. Very well. His Majesty rides on a horse to-morrow in a procession through the great square. All people who stand in the great square will see his Majesty on a horse. Now if you stand in the great square on a horse, you will see his Majesty."

Saying which, Dame Stockel immediately marched in a respectable and rheumatic manner down stairs.

Up spoke the glazier the moment she was gone, saying,

"Gertrude, when my father was dying, he left me a beautiful ring. But a beggar in rags ought not to wear a jewel. So keep it for my sake, dear Gertrude!"

Then out of his pocket he drew a diamond ring, the like of which for brilliancy she never saw before—sparkling like a rain-drop in the sun.

"Sometimes," said he, "I wear it on my little finger. See, it just fits your forefinger! Every maiden engaged to be married wears a ring on her forefinger."

Gertrude was startled at these words. Was *she* engaged to be married? Any one may guess she was delighted. What maiden would not be delighted with such a ring on her forefinger?

"But you have not told me your name," she complained.

"Then," said he, with a mischievous smile, "for one lock of your golden hair, I will tell you my name."

"I will not give that," said Gertrude, resolutely.

"Then for one kiss of your sweet lips."

"I will not give that," she answered, not so resolutely.

"Well," said he, "my name is Ferdinand."

"That," said she, "neither begins with R nor ends with X."

"Yes it does, if you spell it right," cried he, in great glee.

Now, just as the glazier was about to give Gertrude a kiss, Dame Stockel came into the room, ready for more talk with the mannerly young man. But all in vain! Instantly the mannerly young man took up his box of glass, and said "Good afternoon."

That night, after Gertrude went to bed, the diamond twinkled like a fire-fly on her hand. She kept her arm outside the coverlet in the cool moonlight. Many hours she lay awake, thinking. A penny for your thoughts, Gertrude! Her thoughts were of her sweetheart. "How delightful to be loved," thought she. "But what a strange lover! I hope he is good and true. Is he the poorest man in all the land? How can a poor man possess such a diamond? That is enough to make him rich. Did he get it honestly? What if he stole it! No, it was his father's gift. O Ferdinand! I love you!" And with this happy thought, Gertrude wept herself to sleep. Then in a dream she saw a beautiful vision. A company of angels came about her bed, one of whom kissed her forehead at the parting of her hair, and the kiss remained a few moments like a star at the edge of a cloud. "My lovely child," whispered the angel, "pleasant be thy pathway through life, for thou art loved both on earth and in heaven!" And the angel who said this was Gertrude's mother. This was the good child's dream.

The next day the young king rode on a milk-white horse at the head of his cavalry through the great square, taking off his hat and bowing to the shouting people.

"He is the best king we ever had," remarked one.

"Yes, he is a good king," answered another, "but he is not married, and we have no queen."

Now, neither Dame Stockel, nor Gertrude, nor Nance, went to see the procession. "For young folks should stay at home," said the Dame, "so none of us can go out."

But the glazier was there, and saw whatever the king saw!

Gertrude spent the afternoon in finishing the History

of the Dwarfs; Aunt Stockel, in taking a long nap; and Nance, in watching if anybody was leaning his elbows on the wicket-gate. Sure enough, by and by the glazier came—not the one who mended Gertrude's window, but the one who looked with sheep's eyes at Nance. Now Nance opened her mouth wide, because her affectionate young friend was so gayly dressed she hardly knew him. Not a gray nor a blue patch to be seen!

"Pigeon," said he, "I have good news."

"Pigeon," said she, "how strange you look!"

They called themselves pigeons, because like those birds they were constantly loving and quarrelling.

"Yesterday," said he, "as I was coming here to lean on the gate, I saw a gilt-buttoned young nobleman, attended by a page. The young lord stopped me and said, 'Are you an honest lad?' 'Yes,' said I. 'Then,' said he, 'you deserve better than rags. I will give you *my* clothes for *yours*; is it a bargain?' 'Heigh-ho, yes,' said I. 'But I want your glazier's box too,' said he. 'Then what will you give for it?' said I. 'All the money in my pocket,' said he. 'A bargain,' said I. Now, Pigeon, what do you think? Then the young buck said, 'Let us go into this stable and change clothes.' So in we went, he a gentleman and I a beggar; and out we came, he a beggar and I a gentleman! Pigeon, I found a purse in the pocket big enough to make us rich for life!"

The pea-blossom opened wider and wider, until she exclaimed, "Lawks! me! Then we shall be married, and I shall live like a lady, and ride in a coach. Heigh-ho! fiddle-de-dee!"

"Ting-a-ling-ling!" tinkled the bell. The female Pigeon flew to open the door. The male Pigeon quitted his perch on the gate, and hopped away. For if Dame

Stockel had caught the two pigeons together, that would have been the end of their billing and cooing.

Heavy footsteps now sounded at the front door. Gertrude, peeping over her window-sill, saw three officers on the steps.

"This is the house," said they.

Dame Stockel opened the door and snapped her tongue at them, exclaiming,

"What do you want?"

"We are the king's officers," replied the spokesman.

"Well, the king don't live here," cried the Dame, "and if he did, he is not at home this afternoon. So go about your business."

"We *are* about our business," they rejoined, "for the king has missed his diamond ring, and has sent us here to look for it."

"What!" shouted Dame Stockel, who could hardly get the idea into her head.

Gertrude, who overheard every word, was thunderstruck. "Was it the king's ring?" she wondered. "Did Ferdinand steal it to make himself rich?" And the dear, frightened maiden clasped her hands as in prayer.

"A great reward," continued the officer, "will be given to anybody who will restore the ring; and there will be no punishment; for the king has set his heart on getting back his treasure; it was his father's gift."

"Well," screamed the Dame, "*I* am not the king, and *I* have not the king's ring!"

The officer continued,

"A beggar in rags gave information that the ring was in this house, and yonder he comes!" pointing to Ferdinand, who at this moment ran up the steps.

"Your ladyship!" said the glazier, waving his hand.

"You scoundrel!" cried Aunt Stockel, shaking her finger.

"Dame!" said he, "did you think when I mended your glass for nothing yesterday, I was to gain nothing by it to-day? Aha! I found out that the king's ring was in this house, and his Majesty now knows that fact. The pretty maiden up stairs has the ring! Officers, follow me!"

Up stairs went the glazier, the officers, the Dame, and Nance.

Gertrude, rising to meet her accusers, looked very pale, but soon gained a good courage, for she had done no wrong.

"Have you the king's ring?" asked the chief officer, admiring Gertrude's lovely face and hair.

"I have a diamond ring," she replied, "but I know not whether it be the king's; here it is."

"Now, since I am a glazier," exclaimed Ferdinand, "I can tell whether it be the true ring."

So, taking it in his hand, he went to the window, and over Gertrude's name he cut the word

Ferdinand.

"Yes," cried he, "it is a true diamond; it cuts glass; it is the king's."

The Pigeon's mouth of course was wide open.

Dame Stockel's, for a wonder, was shut.

Gertrude sat on the side of her bed, covering her face with her hands.

"What a pity," exclaimed the chief officer, "that so fair a damsel should be a thief!"

"Indeed, I am no thief," responded Gertrude, indignantly; "this young man gave me the ring yesterday; he can tell you all about it; he will tell the truth."

"Yes, I will tell the truth," said the glazier, "she *is* a thief, for she has stolen my heart!"

Whereupon he suddenly threw off his rags and stood in a splendid array of silk and pearls!

The poor man grew rich in a single minute!

"Gertrude!" said he, to the astonished maiden, "can you tell who I am?"

"You are a nobleman," she modestly replied.

"My name begins with R and ends with X," said he; "I will engrave it on the glass." And going to the window, after Ferdinand he wrote

which means the King.

"Now, dear Gertrude, will you be my golden-haired wife?"

Gertrude stammered out a few broken words, which nobody could understand, and which she never afterward could remember.

"Now," exclaimed Ferdinand, "I am the happiest man in the kingdom." And going once more to the window, after Gertrude's name he wrote

which means the Queen.

"Gertrude, you shall be crowned the queen," he said, proudly.

Never was a maiden more bewildered and happy than golden-haired Gertrude at that moment!

"But why?" she asked, after a little while, half smiling, half weeping, "why did you call yourself a poor man?"

"Every man is poor," he replied, "till he gets a sweet wife; then he is rich."

"But why did you come like a beggar, and not like a king?"

"Because," said he, "a maiden might marry a king for a crown, but would marry a beggar only for love; and I, though a king, wished to be married only for love."

The bride blushed and softly replied,

"And that is all I will marry you for."

Now, who can guess where the wedding was held? Neither in Gertrude's house, nor in Ferdinand's palace, nor in a great church, but in the royal garden. It was the first day of summer. Roses bloomed and birds sang. The happy spot was a bank of moss, shaded by orange-trees. Ferdinand was dressed in black velvet, and Gertrude in white satin. A great company came from near and far. Of course Dame Stockel and the two Pigeons were there. But no beggar in rags was seen. The ceremony was solemn and beautiful. Ferdinand kissed Gertrude's forehead on the same spot where the angel left the star. The festivities lasted three days. On the fourth, which was Sunday, Nance and the real glazier were quietly married in a chapel, and afterward received many house-keeping gifts from the king and queen. But nobody in the kingdom would marry Dame Stockel, for nobody was willing to be cut to pieces by her tongue. Gertrude's bird Jenny no longer was kept in a small cage, but in a green-house of plants and flowers, where the happy creature hopped from bough to bough, carolling from morning till night. "Never," said Gertrude, "will Jenny and I forget the arrow and the broken pane!"

But the children who have just read this story will soon forget all about it!

Waiting for the Verdict. By Mrs. Rebecca Harding Davis, author of "Margaret Howth," "Life Among the Iron Mills," &c., &c. One vol., octavo, illustrated, bound in cloth. Price, $2.00.

This is a story of unusual power and thrilling interest.

"It is not only the most elaborate work of its author, but it is one of the most powerful works of fiction by any American writer."—*New York Times.*

The Life and Letters of Rev. Geo. W. Bethune, D.D. By Rev. Abraham R. Van Nest, D.D. One vol., large 12mo., illustrated by an elegant steel-plate Likeness of Dr. Bethune. Price, $2.00.

This is one of the most charming biographies ever written. As a genial and jovial friend, as an enthusiastic sportsman, as a thorough theologian, as one of the most eloquent and gifted divines of his day, Dr. Bethune took a firm hold of the hearts of all with whom he came in contact.

Dr. Bethune's Theology, or Expository Lectures on the Heidelberg Catechism. By Geo. W. Bethune, D.D. Two vols., crown octavo (Riverside edition), on tinted paper. Price, cloth, $4.50; half calf, or morocco, extra, $8.50.

This was the great life work of the late Dr. Bethune, and will remain a monument of his thorough scholarship, the classical purity and beauty of his style, and above all, his deep and abiding piety.

"When the Rev. Dr. Bethune, whose memory is yet green and fragrant in the Church, was about to leave this country, he committed his manuscripts to a few friends, giving them discretionary power with regard to their publication. Among them was the great work of his life; in his opinion *the* work, and that from which he hoped the most usefulness while he lived, and after he was dead, if it should then be given to the press. This work was his course of lectures on the Catechism of the Church in which he was a burning and shining light.—*New York Observer.*

The Life and Labors of Francis Wayland, D.D., L.L.D. Late President of Brown University; by his sons, Hon. Francis Wayland, and Rev. H. L. Wayland. Two vols., 12mo., illustrated by two steel-plate Likenesses of Dr. Wayland Price, $4.00.

This is a most interesting memoir of one of those noble specimens of a man, who now and then appear and direct, and give tone to the thoughts of their generation. The volumes are enriched by Dr. Wayland's correspondence with most of the leading men of his day.

DR. WAYLAND'S WORKS.

Principles and Practices of Baptists. By Francis Wayland, D.D. 1 vol., 12mo., cloth. Price, $1.50.

"We hope the book will find its way into every family in every Baptist church in the land, and should be glad to know it was generally circulated in the families of other churches."
Christian Chronicle.

A Memoir of the Life and Labors of the Rev. Adoniram Judson, D.D. By Francis Wayland, D.D. Illustrated with a fine Portrait of Dr. Judson. Two vols. in one, 12mo. Price, $2.50.

The Elements of Intellectual Philosophy. By Francis Wayland, D.D. One vol., 12mo. Price, $1.75.

Sermons to the Churches. By Francis Wayland, D.D. One vol., 12mo. Price, $1.00.

"Dr. Wayland is a clear thinker, and a strong and elegant writer. His Sermons are models worthy of study."—*Christian Intelligencer.*

The Life and Letters of Mrs. Emily C. Judson (Fanny Forrester), third wife of the Rev. Adoniram Judson, D.D., Missionary to Burmah. By A. C. Kendrick, Professor of Greek in the University of Rochester. With a steel-plate Portrait of Mrs. Judson. One vol., 12mo. Price, $1.75.

The Sexton's Tale, and other Poems. By Theodore Tilton, Editor of the New York Independent. Illustrated by an ornamental title-page and elegant tail-pieces for each Poem, printed on tinted paper, and bound with beveled boards and fancy cloth. One vol., 16mo. Price, $1.50.

This is the first collected edition of Mr. Tilton's poems, many of them as sweet as any thing in our language.

The Autobiography of Elder Jacob Knapp, the great Revivalist. One vol., large 12mo., with steel-plate Likeness of the Author. Price, $2.00

In this book the author gives an account of the many won derful scenes through which he has passed, more interesting and remarkable than any tales of fiction.

A new Enlarged Edition of Mrs. Putnam's Receipt Book, and Young Housekeeper's Assistant. A chapter on Carving has been added, and a very large number of new receipts, with special reference to economy in cooking. One vol., 12mo. Price, $1.50.

A Complete Manual of English Literature. By Thomas B. Shaw, Author of "Shaw's Outlines of English Literature." Edited, with Notes and Illustrations, by William Smith, LL.D., author of "Smith's Bible and Classical Dictionaries," with a Sketch of American Literature, by Henry T. Tuckerman. One vol., large 12mo. Price, $2.00.

Life of George Washington. By EDWARD EVERETT, LL.D. With a steel-plate Likeness of Mr. Everett, from the celebrated bust by Hiram Powers. One vol., 12mo., pp. 348. Price, cloth, $1.50.

"The biography is a model of condensation, and, by its rapid narrative and attractive style, must commend itself to the mass of readers as the standard popular Life of Washington."—*Correspondence of the Boston Post.*

The Science of Government, in connection with American Institutions. By JOSEPH ALDEN, D.D., LL.D., President of State Normal School, Albany. One vol., 12mo. Price, $1.50. Adapted to the wants of High Schools and Colleges.

Alden's Citizen's Manual. A Text-Book on Government in connection with American Institutions, adapted to the wants of Common Schools. It is in the form of questions and answers. By JOSEPH ALDEN, D.D., LL.D., President of State Normal School, Albany. In one vol., 16mo. Price, 50 cts.

"There is no more important secular study than the study of the institutions of our own country; and there is no book on the subject so clear, comprehensive, and complete in itself as the volume before us."—*New York Independent.*

Macaulay's Essays. The Critical, Historical, and Miscellaneous Essays of the Right Hon. THOMAS BABINGTON MACAULAY, with an Introduction and Biographical Sketch of the Author, by E. P. WHIPPLE, and containing a new steel-plate Likeness of Macaulay, and a complete index. Six vols., crown octavo. Price, on tinted paper, extra cloth, $13.50; on tinted paper, half calf or morocco, $27.00.

Sherman's March through the South. With Sketches and Incidents of the Campaign. By Capt. DAVID P. CONYNGHAM. 12mo., cloth. Price, $1.75.

"It is the only one that is entitled to credit for real ability, truth, and fairness."—*J. W. Geary, Maj.-Gen. U. S. A.*

Lieutenant-General Winfield Scott's Autobiography. Two vols., 12mo., illustrated with two steel-plate Likenesses of the General. Price, per set, in cloth, $4.00; half calf, $8.00. An elegant "large paper" edition of this valuable book, on tinted paper, price $10.00; half calf, or morocco, $12.50.

Milman's Latin Christianity. History of Latin Christianity, including that of the Popes to the pontificate of Nicolas V. By HENRY HART MILMAN, D.D., Dean of St. Paul's. Eight vols., crown octavo. Price, extra cloth, $20.00.

"In beauty and brilliancy of style he excels Hallam, approaches Gibbon, and is only surpassed by the unrivaled Macaulay."—*Mercersburg Review.*

Fleming's Vocabulary of Philosophy. With Additions by CHARLES P. KRAUTH, D.D. Small 8vo. Price, $2.50.

"To students of mental science this book is invaluable Dr. K. has done good service by the additions to the work of Dr. Fleming, and the whole volume is one which will be eagerly sought and cordially appreciated."—*Evangelical Quarterly.*

Long's Classical Atlas. Constructed by WM. HUGHES and edited by GEORGE LONG, with a Sketch of Classical Geography. With fifty-two Maps, and an Index of Places.

This Atlas will be an invaluable aid to the student of Ancient History, as well as the Bible student. One vol., quarto. Price, $4.50.

"Now that we are so well supplied with classical dictionaries, it is highly desirable that we should have an atlas worthy to accompany them. In the volume before us is to be found all that can be desired."—*London Athenæun.*

Baird's Classical Manual. By James S. S. Baird, F.C.D. One vol., 16mo. Price, cloth, 90 cts.

It is an epitome of Ancient Geography, Greek and Roman Mythology, Antiquities, and Chronology.

Croquet as played by "The Newport Croquet Club." By One of the Members. 16mo. Price, paper, 25 cts.; cloth, 50 cts.

"This manual is the only one which really grapples with a difficult case, and deals with it as if heaven and earth depended on the adjudication."—*Atlantic Monthly.*

Helps to the Pulpit. Sketches and Skeletons of Sermons. One vol., large 12mo. Price, $2.00.

"Here is a work that may be a help by its proper use, or a hindrance by its abuse."—*Christian Messenger.*

Pulpit Themes and Preacher's Assistant. By the author of "Helps to the Pulpit." One vol., large 12mo. Price, $2.00.

"We have no doubt but that it will be a welcome book to every candidate for the ministry, and also to pastors in almost every congregation."—*Lutheran Herald.*

A Text-Book of the History of Christian Doctrines. By K. R. Hagenbach, Professor of Theology in the University of Basle. The Edinburgh translation of C. W. Buch, revised, with large Additions from the fourth German Edition, and other sources, by Henry B. Smith, D.D., Professor in the Union Theological Seminary of the City of New York. Two vols., octavo. Price, cloth, $6.00.

"It exceeds, in point of completeness, every other treatise, English as well as German, and we have, therefore, no hesitation in calling it the most perfect manual of the History of Christian Doctrines which Protestant literature has as yet produced."—*Methodist, N. Y.*

Biblical Commentary on the New Testament. By Dr. HERMANN OLSHAUSEN. Continued after his death by Ebrard and Wiesinger. Carefully revised, after the last German Edition, by A. C. KENDRICK, D.D., Greek Professor in the University of Rochester. Six vols., large octavo. Price, cloth, $18.00.

"I regard the Commentary as the most valuable of those on the New Testament in the English language, happily combining the religious spirit of the English expositors with the critical learning of the German. The American editor has evidently performed his task well, as might be expected from his eminent qualifications."—*President Sears, of Brown University.*

The Annotated Paragraph Bible. According to the authorized version, arranged in Paragraphs and Parallelisms, with Explanatory Notes, Prefaces to the several Books, and an entirely new Selection of References to Parallel and Illustrative Passages. An issue of the London Religious Tract Society,—republished. Complete in one royal octavo volume, with Maps, &c. Price, library sheep, $8.00.

The Annotated Paragraph New Testament. In one octavo volume, uniform style. Price, muslin, $2.50.

"I have carefully examined a considerable portion of the work, and consider it eminently adapted to increase and diffuse a knowledge of the Word of God. I heartily recommend it to Christians of every denomination, and especially to teachers of Bible Classes and Sabbath Schools, to whom it will prove an invaluable aid."—*Rev. Dr. Wayland.*

Tholuck on the Gospel of John. Translated by CHARLES J. KRAUTH, D.D. One vol., octavo. Price, $3.00.

"We hail with much pleasure the appearance of Krauth's translation of 'Tholuck on the Gospel of John.' We trust the work, in this its English dress, will find a wide circulation."—*Bibliotheca Sacra.*

Neander's Planting and Training of the Christian Church by the Apostles. Translated from the German by J. E. Ryland. Translation revised and corrected according to the fourth German edition. By E. G. Robinson, D.D., Professor in the Rochester Theological Seminary. One vol., octavo, cloth. Price, $4.00.

"The patient scholarship, the critical sagacity, and the simple and unaffected piety of the author, are manifest throughout. Such a history should find a place in the library of every one who seeks a familiar knowledge of the early shaping of the Christian Churches. An excellent index adds to its value."—*Evangelist.*

Bible Illustrations. Being a Store-house of Similies, Allegories, and Anecdotes—with an introduction by Richard Newton, D.D. One vol., 12mo. Price, $1.50. Every Sabbath School teacher should have this book.

"It is impossible not to commend a book like this."—*Editor of Encyc. of Religious Knowledge.*

"We think that Sabbath School teachers especially would be profited by reading it; and many of the anecdotes will help to point the arrow of the preacher."—*Christian Herald.*

SPURGEON'S WORKS.

Sermons of the Rev. C. H. Spurgeon, of London, in uniform styles of binding.

First Series. With an Introduction and Sketch of his Life, by the Rev. E. L. Magoon, D.D. With a fine steel-plate Portrait. One vol., 12mo., pp. 400. Price, $1.50.

Second Series. Revised by the Author, and published with his sanction. Containing a new steel-plate Portrait, engraved expressly for the volume. Price, $1.50.

Third Series. Revised by the Author, and published with his sanction. Containing a steel-plate view of Surrey Music Hall, London, engraved expressly for the volume. Price, $1.50.

SPURGEON'S WORKS.--Continued.

Fourth Series. Revised by the Author, and published with his sanction. Containing twenty-six Sermons. pp. 450, Price, $1.50.

Fifth Series. Revised by the Author, and published with his sanction. Illustrated with a fine steel plate representing the Rev. C. H. Spurgeon preaching in Surrey Music Hall. One vol., 12mo. Price, $1.50.

Sixth Series. Revised by the Author, and published with his sanction. Illustrated with a fine steel plate of Mr. Spurgeon's new Tabernacle. One vol., 12mo. Price, $1.50.

Seventh Series. Containing some of Mr. Spurgeon's later and more brilliant Sermons. One vol., 12mo. Price, $1.50.

Eighth Series. Containing Spurgeon's celebrated Doctrinal Discourses, which made a most profound impression throughout England. One vol., 12mo., cloth. Price, $1.50.

Morning by Morning, or Daily Bible Readings. By Rev. C. H. Spurgeon. One vol., 12mo. Price, $1.75.

"Though no printed sermon can give a perfect representation of the same thing spoken by an eloquent and impassioned orator, yet the reader of these will not wonder at their author's popularity. Though he may not sympathize with Mr. Spurgeon's theological opinions, he can not fail to see that the preacher is really in earnest, that he heartily believes what he says, and knows how to say it in a way to arouse and keep alive the attention of his hearers."—*Boston Advertiser.*

The Saint and His Saviour. By the Rev. C. H. Spurgeon. One vol., 12mo. Price, $1.50.

This is the first extended religious work by this distinguished preacher, and one which in its fervid devotional spirit, the richness of its sentiments, and the beauty of its imagery, fully sustains his high reputation..

Spurgeon's Gems. Being Brilliant Passages from the Sermons of the Rev. C. H. Spurgeon, of London. One vol., 12mo. Price, $1.50.

"The Publishers present this book as a specimen of Mr. Spurgeon's happiest thoughts,—gems from his discourses,—which will glow in the mind of the reader, and quicken in him a desire to read and hear more of this remarkable youthful preacher.

www.ingramcontent.com/pod-product-compliance
Lightning Source LLC
LaVergne TN
LVHW020212110826
845151LV00003B/686

* 9 7 8 1 4 2 5 5 3 4 1 9 6 *

www.ingramcontent.com/pod-product-compliance
Lightning Source LLC
LaVergne TN
LVHW020212110826
845151LV00003B/684

* 9 7 8 1 4 2 5 5 3 4 2 5 7 *